WHEN MARCH WENT MAD

A Celebration of NC State's 1982-83 National Championship

TIM PEELER

FOREWORD BY
DICK VITALE

SPORTS
PUBLISHING
L.L.C.

SportsPublishingLLC.com

ISBN 13: 978-1-59670-188-5

Publishers: Peter L. Bannon and Joseph J. Bannon Sr.
Senior managing editor: Susan M. Moyer
Developmental editor: Laura Podeschi
Art director: Dustin J. Hubbart
Cover design: Joseph Brumleve
Interior design: Dustin J. Hubbart
Photo editor: Jessica Martinich

Sports Publishing L.L.C.
804 North Neil Street
Champaign, IL 61820
Phone: 1-877-424-2665
Fax: 1-217-363-2073
SportsPublishingLLC.com

Printed in the United States of America

CIP data available upon request.

TO MY BEST FRIEND, ELIZABETH,
WHOM I WOULD NEVER GIVE UP

CONTENTS

FOREWORD
BY DICK VITALE

THIS MAGIC MOMENT

"March Madness" has become a unique time of the year for sports fans across America. To me, it is the greatest sporting event of them all. There is nothing like the passion and the love and the incredible spirit that is generated by the student body, by the alumni, and by the people who just come out of the woodwork to follow college hoops.

Obviously, I am a little biased, but when I think about "March Madness," I think about my old buddy, the late Jimmy V, and the unbelievably dramatic moment he gave us in 1983. Here were a bunch of kids at North Carolina State who weren't given much of a chance to even make the NCAA Tournament unless they came alive in the ACC Tournament down in Atlanta. All they had to do there was face the likes of North Carolina, with Michael Jordan, and Virginia, with Ralph Sampson, two of the best teams in the ACC and two of the best teams in the nation.

Somehow, Jimmy Valvano, with his magical touch, his spirit, and his incredible motivational and inspirational ability, was able to bring his players—Sidney Lowe, Dereck Whittenburg, Thurl Bailey, Lorenzo Charles, Cozell McQueen, Terry Gannon, and the whole gang—together in a difficult season. That March, they captivated America, winning one dramatic game after another until they ultimately faced Phi Slama Jama Houston and future Hall of Famers Hakeem Olajuwon and Clyde Drexler. Coach Guy V. Lewis' team, which had been to the Final Four in 1982, was the prohibitive favorite.

You couldn't convince the irrepressible Jimmy V and his bunch of kids, who realized they were able to respond during those 40 minutes of play. After 39 minutes and 16 seconds, the game was tied and Jimmy V had all he ever wanted in any game: to be in a position to win at the end. With 44 seconds remaining, he and his team were very near to fulfilling his lifelong and often repeated dream.

It wasn't a perfectly executed possession, and Jimmy was thrown a little off-guard by Houston's defense, but the result, Dereck Whittenburg's airball and Lorenzo Charles' dunk, will be shown in the highlights as long as the NCAA Tournament is played. It truly is one of the most unbelievable stories in the history of college basketball.

Who could ever forget Coach V running around, looking for someone to love and to share his dream and enthusiasm with? It was one of the most captivating moments in the history of the Final Four, and perhaps the seminal moment in what we now call "March Madness." There is no question that North Carolina State's victory made an impact across the nation, because it showed that the little guy always has a chance.

College basketball, I believe, is light-years ahead of college football. We put 65 teams out on the court and send them on an unbelievable journey to try to win six in a row, and an entire nation of hoops fans get caught up in every step of the way. We see so many magical moments, like in 2005, when we watched George Mason beat the likes of North Carolina, Connecticut, and Michigan State and march on to the Final Four. Who would have ever believed that?

That dream started in 1983, when Jimmy V and his sixth-seeded Cardiac Pack went on a roll and won the whole thing on one of the greatest spontaneous plays in the history of the tournament. "Survive and advance," Jimmy used to say. That's what "March Madness" is all about. It's about "chasing the dream," as Jimmy V would say, and putting the team together to play with emotion, to play with enthusiasm, to play with energy, and to play for the moment.

That, my friends, usually leads to magical moments.

PREFACE

THEY HAVE NEVER GIVEN UP

Sidney Lowe was cornered by the media in a small dressing room in the lower hallways of the St. Pete Times Forum in Tampa, Florida, on a sunny afternoon in March of 2007. In his first year as NC State's 18th head basketball coach, Lowe had directed his team to consecutive upsets over Duke, Virginia, and Virginia Tech to earn a spot in the Atlantic Coast Conference Tournament championship game against—of all teams—archrival North Carolina.

It was a remarkable accomplishment for a team that was the overwhelming choice to finish last in the league. Neither the players nor the coach believed that would happen. Lowe never let his team grow despondent, despite a string of bad fortune throughout December, January, and February. By the time the postseason arrived, the Wolfpack believed it was capable of beating any team in the country.

Lowe could not help but think his mentor, the late Jim Valvano, would respect how this squad had put itself in position to win another championship for a school so rich in basketball tradition. Lowe, hired just 10 months earlier, was eager to add his name to the list of coaches who had won ACC championships at NC State: Everett Case, Press Maravich, Norman Sloan, and Valvano.

"He would be proud of their passion," Lowe said. "He would be proud that they have never given up."

Lowe was an integral part of the team that defined this spirit for all of college basketball. They picked up several nicknames along the way—the Cardiac Pack, Destiny's Darlings, and Phi Pack Attacka—but in reality they were a collection of capable players, led by three uniquely talented seniors, who happened to find the right mix of motivation and execution to play their best basketball at the end of the season.

"They were the perfect team," Valvano once said.

On that muggy afternoon in Tampa, Lowe went out on a limb to suggest that his 2007 Wolfpack was on the verge of exceeding that

Valvano-led group, who gained come-from-behind victories over Wake Forest, North Carolina, and Virginia to win the 1983 ACC Tournament. But it did not happen—Lowe's inaugural team lost to North Carolina in the title game.

In a quarter century of college basketball surprises, no one has surpassed what the Cardiac Pack accomplished in 1983, when it captivated the world of college basketball with a 10-game tear that ended in one of the game's biggest upsets. Lowe is one of the few coaches who could ever invoke a claim to top what Valvano and his teammates did back then. He knew firsthand that anything could happen in the postseason: miraculous comebacks, improbable victories, and an airball that turned, Cinderella-like, into a game-winning dunk.

He was there the first time, when March went mad.

1 "IF FIRE HYDRANTS COULD JUMP . . ."

Squid and Tweetie Bird met at summer camp. They were a couple of basketball junkies from the hard streets of Washington, D.C., whose idea of the great outdoors was playing ball with a couple hundred other playground stars on St. John's High School's exposed asphalt courts. In the summer of 1976, the rest of the country may have been celebrating the Bicentennial, but Squid and Tweetie Bird were interested only in catching the eye of the summer camp's director, legendary high school basketball coach Morgan Wootten.

The two had just finished their freshman years at different public high schools. They knew if they could impress Wootten, they might get the chance to play for his nationally recognized basketball program at DeMatha Catholic, a private school run by Trinitarian monks in suburban Hyattsville, Maryland. Squid, one of nine children, was the best player in Washington, D.C. The point guard had learned the fundamentals of the game at the age of seven while playing for Fletcher Tinsley at Ludlow-Taylor Elementary School and in the city's Police Boys' Club league. Tweetie Bird, from Prince Georges County, Maryland, was an unabashed scorer who grew up with his toes on the three-point line of the Beltway.

They had never met until that first afternoon of camp, but they had heard of each other. Both were products of the Metro area's fertile playgrounds that had produced such basketball superstars as Elgin Baylor, Austin Carr, Dave Bing, and Adrian Dantley. Like everyone else that day, Squid and Tweetie Bird were hoping that Wootten, the man who had won so many championships at DeMatha and was perhaps the country's most successful and decorated basketball coach, would notice them. Few other players on the courts had the guile and ability of these two look-alike 15-year-olds, but they were not prototypical guards. They were stocky, quick, comparatively short, and athletic—exactly the kind of basketball players you might get if fire hydrants could jump.

In either a fantastic stroke of destiny or because a legendary coach was looking for his next starting backcourt, Squid and Tweetie Bird were paired on the same team that first day at camp. They ran that day against older and more experienced players without breaking stride. Their roles on the court were never in doubt. Squid, who grew up in the roughest part of the city, liked taking control of the offense and had already developed an uncanny knowledge of the game. Tweetie Bird, a distant cousin of high-flying basketball superstar David Thompson, had a 39-inch vertical leap and a high-arching jumper that easily cleared the game's tallest players. The two clicked from the moment they were paired together, while playing, while watching, while resting.

A championship backcourt was born.

"I knew that day we were going to be good," said Sidney Lowe, who received the nickname "Squid" after he arrived at NC State.

"What we did that day was put on a show," said Dereck Whittenburg, who left the name "Tweetie Bird" behind when he arrived in Raleigh. "We were running up and down the court, stealing the ball. Sid had about 1,000 assists and I scored about 40 points. That trial game really showed us to be two guards who would make people say, 'Where did those guys come from?'"

Put off by the idea of wearing a blue blazer, gray slacks, and a necktie to school every day, Lowe wanted no part of DeMatha at first. This resistance was actually surprising for a player whose game was based on structure and control. But his mother, Carrie Lowe, insisted that he give it a try, even though she had to work overtime as a maid in the apartment building where her family lived to afford the $1,000-per-year tuition. Headstrong Sidney agreed to give DeMatha a few weeks, given the option that he could return to public school if he didn't like it. "After a week and a half, I told my mother, 'There is no way I would transfer from this school,'" Lowe said.

Whittenburg loved DeMatha from the start, showing up everyday with a briefcase full of notes and books. He was eager to participate in the school's disciplined approach to education and Wootten's well-rounded basketball program, which included pregame poetry readings.

Both athletes played sparingly as sophomores at DeMatha, but made the trip when Wootten took his team on a 21-day summer tour of Brazil. As juniors, they were reserves on a squad that went 12 deep in all-stars, Lowe playing behind point guard Dutch Morley and Whittenburg playing behind prep All-American Joe Washington. But they were spectacular when they were on the court together, whether at DeMatha, on a summer league team at the Jelleff Branch Boys and Girls Club, or on the Maryland AAU All-Stars. DeMatha went undefeated their junior season and was declared the nation's top team, and the two guards won their first national championship together.

Though neither of them knew it at the time, one of the most significant incidents of their partnership occurred in the summer of 1978. They had just pulled off a triple-overtime upset of the New York AAU All-Stars, which featured brothers Scooter and Rodney McCray, in the prestigious Boston Shootout, one of the few national AAU tournaments at the time. The two guards were standing on the court when one of the many college recruiters broke away from the pack and rushed up to them. He embraced them from behind, putting them in dual choke holds. "I love you two guys," the coach said in his raspy, mile-a-minute voice. "Why don't you come play for me? We can do something special."

He left after the long embrace, leaving quizzical looks on the two players' faces. They wouldn't see him for another two and a half years.

"What the hell was that?" Lowe asked.

"I don't know," Whittenburg answered, "but he said he owned a school."

His name was Jim Valvano, head coach at Iona College.

Not far away, in the Maryland suburb of Seat Pleasant, lived a skinny trombone player named Thurl Bailey. Basketball was not his first passion, but he took up the game after winning a raffle to attend a summer basketball camp. What else was a 6-foot-7 seventh grader to do? He was awfully slim, all arms and legs, with little coordination and few basketball skills. Maybe that was why he was twice cut from his junior high basketball team. He vowed to get better. By the time he was ready for high school, he had improved enough to earn a little playing time, thanks to a trip to NC State coach Norman Sloan's basketball camp. But he also had to adjust to a different atmosphere. He wasn't heading to a private school that doubled as a basketball factory—he was heading to the suburbs of Bladensburg, Maryland, some 20 minutes from his home, as part of a federally mandated busing program to integrate area schools. Bladensburg was certainly no match for the DeMatha dynasty. Bailey's team played against Lowe and Whittenburg just once: DeMatha humiliated Bladensburg by nearly 60 points.

"They were way out of our league," Bailey said. "And afterwards, they had to run suicides because their coach thought they played so poorly. That was kind of mind-blowing to me."

The three ran into each other off the court on several occasions, as their basketball careers followed parallel tracks. As seniors, they all went to Maryland for a weekend recruiting visit to see Lefty Driesell's program. It was the first time the trio ever spent any meaningful time together. By then, Lowe was considered one of the nation's top point guards, while Whittenburg and Bailey were still developing. None of them had thought about the possibility that they might attend the same college.

Lowe was heading for the big time. He couldn't wait to show off his skills when he arrived at his school of choice, Notre Dame. But that marriage never worked out: Fighting Irish coach Digger Phelps signed All-American John Paxson as his point guard, leaving Lowe uncertain of his future.

Recruiters also loved Whittenburg because of his athletic ability, his vertical leap, and his jump shot. They were willing to overlook his diminutive stature until the defining moment of his senior year at DeMatha. Early in a game against Houston's Phyllis Wheatley High School in Lake Charles, Louisiana, Whittenburg landed funny on an opponent's foot and had to leave the game. DeMatha eventually won the contest in five overtimes, thanks to Lowe's triple-double of 18 points, 12 rebounds, and 11 assists. When the team returned to Washington, X-rays showed that Whittenburg had suffered a broken fifth metatarsal in his right foot, a painful injury that would keep him out of the Stags' lineup for eight games. During Whittenburg's 35-day absence, Lowe upped his scoring to nearly 23 points a game to keep the Stags in the running for the city championship. Whittenburg learned to hobble around campus on crutches, another skill he would later need in his college career. But he also returned too soon. He scored 22 points in his first game back in late January, but re-injured the same foot within 10 days in one of the Stags' two losses that season. He didn't rejoin the lineup until the team squared off against Dunbar in the 1979 City Championship game at Maryland's Cole Field House. He scored 16 points in that game, which DeMatha won on a jump shot by John Carroll with 13 seconds to play. Dunbar could have stolen the championship in the final seconds, but a long-launched ball went in and out of the basket and an offensive rebound rolled off the rim as the buzzer sounded. It was a setup identical to what Lowe and Whittenburg would see in their final college game four years later, but with opposite results. Dunbar's two missed shots gave DeMatha its second consecutive city championship.

Their high school season over, Lowe and Whittenburg tried to decide which college they would attend. They briefly talked about going to the same school, but the possibility seemed remote. Lowe started looking at NC State after Notre Dame fell through. Sloan, the NC State coach, had recently hired one of Wootten's longtime DeMatha assistants, Marty Fletcher, for his staff. Sloan had already tapped into the DeMatha pipeline twice, signing Stag legends Kenny Carr and Hawkeye Whitney to play for his Wolfpack. By Lowe's senior year at DeMatha, Carr had already gone to the NBA and Whitney was a high-flying power forward finishing up his junior season. Sloan desperately wanted Lowe to round out what might have been his best recruiting class since he lured the core of the 1974 NCAA championship team to his program in the spring of 1971. Sloan was expecting verbal commitments from Sidney Green of Brooklyn, New York, and one of the nation's most talked about high school players, Dominique Wilkins. Sloan was confident both would sign following their appearances in high school all-star games.

Lowe was anxious to spend his career with such talented players and to play one year with Whitney, the high-scoring forward who graduated from DeMatha a year before Lowe arrived. Whittenburg was still considering his options, though Rutgers seemed to be the front-runner for his services. He did take several other recruiting visits, including a couple with Lowe.

On the weekend the two headed to Raleigh to visit NC State, they nearly turned around to go back home before ever meeting with the coaching staff. Whitney, the powerful forward who still ranks fifth on the school's career-scoring list with 1,964 points, was responsible for hosting the two DeMatha seniors during their recruiting visit. They had been picked up at the airport and dropped off in a vacant room at the College Inn on the corner of Avent Ferry Road and Western Boulevard. But Whitney showed up too late to take them partying on fraternity row. Lowe and Whittenburg sat seething in their poolside room, watching television with one eye and keeping the other on the door.

When Whitney finally showed up around one o'clock in the morning, the hungry and anxious recruits were so angry they jumped Whitney. Not a smart move against the street-tough forward. "I think he threw Dereck on the bed and hit me on the forehead, and that was the end of that," Lowe said. "But if anyone ever had a worse official visit than we did, I'd like to hear about it." Yet the bad visit did not prevent Lowe from signing his letter of intent soon afterwards, giving Sloan the point guard he desperately needed.

Despite what people have come to believe over the years, Whittenburg and Lowe were not a package deal. In his previous 23 years at DeMatha, Wootten had never sent two players to the same school in the same recruiting class. Whittenburg, a leaping guard who averaged three dunks per game in high school, was behind the likes of Wilkins and Quintin Dailey on the list of shooting guards Sloan was pursuing. Whittenburg was being recruited by a number of schools, but it wasn't until Wilkins made a ballyhooed (and highly suspicious) switch to Georgia that Whittenburg was offered a scholarship to play for the Wolfpack.

Bailey—still considered a project by many even though he averaged 19 points, 20 rebounds, and six blocked shots as a high school senior—received some attention from Maryland, Georgetown, and Davidson, which had just hired former NC State assistant Eddie Biedenbach as its head coach. Biedenbach had been in charge of recruiting the Washington area for State, and had landed both Carr and Whitney for Sloan's program before accepting his first head coaching job. Bailey signed early with the Wolfpack, which believed it had uncovered an unpolished gem in the Maryland suburbs.

Like Wilkins, Green pulled a late switch on Sloan, opting to play for Jerry Tarkanian at Nevada-Las Vegas. Before their college careers ended, Lowe, Whittenburg, and Bailey made sure that UNLV and Georgia received their proper "thank yous" for making it possible for the trio to play for the same program.

But it was never their intention to end up in the same place. Lowe signed his letter of intent first. Whittenburg signed more than a week later. They didn't even know they would be college teammates until Wootten called them into his office one day and said, "Guess what? You two get to spend the next four years together."

"It was sheer coincidence that we all ended up going to NC State," Lowe said. "Sheer coincidence."

The first time the trio ever played together was March 29, 1979, at the Capital Centre in Washington, D.C., as members of the Metro All-Stars in the Capital Classic, an all-star game between the best players from the D.C. area and the best players from the rest of the country. It was a bellwether group: the senior class of 1979 is the greatest collection of basketball talent in history, the benchmark to which all other recruiting classes are compared. Every school in the country wanted the nation's tallest player, 7-foot-3 center Ralph Sampson of Harrisonburg, Virginia. Just as many wanted Wilkins, who was known even then as "The Human Highlight Film." And James Worthy of Gastonia, North Carolina, was the absolute prize North Carolina coach Dean Smith needed to win his first NCAA championship. Green, Dailey, and Paxson, along with Sam Bowie, Clark Kellogg, Dirk Minniefield, Antoine Carr, and Byron Scott, all went on to have spectacular college and NBA careers.

On March 23, 1979, many of them—including Lowe and Whittenburg—had gathered in Charlotte, North Carolina, for the second-annual McDonald's All-America game. (Bailey did not make the team.) A crowd of 11,219 spectators saw the best players from the East go against the best players from the West in a game that was deep in talent, size, and future NBA All-Stars. But Whittenburg, the smallest player on either roster, made the biggest difference: not only did he sink two free throws to send the high-scoring, star-studded affair into overtime, he drained a game-winning shot with just seconds to play, giving the East a 106-105 victory.

Less than a week later, most of the same players assembled in Washington for the Capital Classic. This time, Bailey joined Lowe and Whittenburg on the Metro team to play in front of 19,035 spectators, which was believed to be the biggest crowd ever for a game involving high school players. The future teammates were an afterthought in the pregame buzz, as everyone awaited the "Battle of the Giants" between Sampson and Bowie. But wouldn't you know it? Whittenburg stole the show again. His team trailing by one point and needing a basket to win the game, Whittenburg found himself alone for a wide-open jump shot with eight seconds to play. He saw no reason to hesitate. His 18-footer went down smoothly to give the Metro All-Stars an 86-85 victory. Those two jumpers sent Whittenburg to college confident that no matter how much time was left, no matter how big the stage was, and no matter how many eyes were on him, he could make game-winning shots to win championships.

"Dereck had always had that confidence—in elementary school, in junior high, in high school, whatever," Lowe said. "He had done it so many times. And then he did it in the McDonald's game and the Capital Classic."

Not until four years later did Whittenburg have the chance to take another game-winning, buzzer-beating shot. And then, on the biggest stage of all, against the biggest opponent he ever faced, Whittenburg launched the most famous airball in college basketball history.

SIDNEY LOWE

Sidney Lowe always wanted to be a virtuoso. His mother, Carrie, thought the youngest of her nine children might be talented enough to elevate his fortunes from the family's humble inner-city background to perform on the grandest of stages. She gave him a violin when he was little more than a toddler, and he loved playing the instrument.

But at the age of seven, an elementary school teacher and youth league coach named Fletcher Tinsley took the bow out of Lowe's hands and replaced it with a basketball. He's been a court maestro ever since.

Lowe found his grand stage as a point guard and as a coach. To be honest, those two roles are the same. Morgan Wootten, who benefited from Lowe's playground-sharpened skills for three years as the head coach at DeMatha, said he never had a player with Lowe's intuition and court sense.

"He understood the game so thoroughly," Wootten explained.

"He made everybody else better. He made everybody else believe in themselves. He wanted to be part of something greater than himself. He left his ego at the door. When Sidney had the ball in his hands, you knew everything was going to be all right."

That's how Jim Valvano felt when he became NC State's head coach in 1980, inheriting the DeMatha-bred backcourt of Lowe and Dereck Whittenburg. The day he got the job, Valvano called his younger brother, Bob. The first insight he had about his new team was not the depth of its talent, the grand scale of the program, or the passion of people who followed the Wolfpack. It was a simple observation: "This is going to be fun because I've got the best point guard I've ever had," Valvano said. For the next three years, Valvano called the plucky player "Coach Lowe." When the ball was in play, Valvano gave Lowe full rein of the team. The guard had permission to call any play he thought would work and to overrule the coach on any possession. The only thing Lowe wasn't allowed to do? Come out of the game. Whenever he asked to take a breather, Valvano either ignored him or repeated the line he first told Lowe as a sophomore: "You are not coming out of the game until your eligibility is up."

Lowe never complained. He wanted to be in the game, not to score, but to conduct the symphony that played out every night on the basketball court. His unselfish attitude made him a coach's delight. "I'm not going to score if it'll take points away from somebody else," he once told Tom Harris of Raleigh's News & Observer. "My job is to keep everybody—the players, the coaches—happy. If I score, it helps one person—me. If I pass off to someone and he scores, I'm helping three times as many or more ... because I get an assist, the player gets the points, and that helps the team. If I pass to somebody and he goes in for a dunk, that helps even more because it fires up the crowd and makes the team play harder."

Valvano and Wootten—as well as other coaches such as Bill Musselman, Mike Fratello, and Flip Saunders—wanted Lowe by their sides for a reason: he had a winning intuition. At DeMatha, he had to wait his turn in one of the nation's most accomplished high school basketball programs—he wasn't a regular starter until his senior season. Still, under Lowe's baton, DeMatha won back-to-back city and state championships in 1978 and '79, the same years he wore an upperclassman's red jacket instead of one of the blue blazers that identified the school's underclassmen. He made an immediate impact at NC State, replacing three-year starter Clyde Austin as the Wolfpack's starting point guard and finishing second to Virginia's Ralph Sampson in the ACC Rookie of the Year race. Lowe went on his only international tour in 1981, leading Team USA to a gold medal in the World University Games in Bucharest, Romania, with a hero's symphony in two parts. First, he made a 70-foot jumper from the top of his own key at the end of the first half of what turned out to be a double-overtime classic against the Soviet Union. Days later, in the final moments of the gold-medal game, the fearless 6-foot guard drove past 7-foot-5 center Vladimir Tkachenko for a game-sealing three-point play.

At NC State, Lowe quickly elevated himself among the school's great conductors, Lou Pucillo and Monte Towe. The Wolfpack appeared in three NCAA Tournaments in his four years and won both the 1983 ACC Tournament and NCAA Tournament championships. His ACC-record 762 career assists was eventually surpassed, but in the 25 years since he played, no guard has come close to his career 2.94 assist-to-turnover ratio. He twice led the ACC in assists, was twice named all-conference, and won the Everett Case Award as the 1983 ACC Tournament's most outstanding player. As a professional player, he won three Continental Basketball Association championships as Musselman's floor leader.

Lowe never found the same kind of success in the NBA, bouncing through five different organizations as a player. But the stocky guard did work his way back from the brink of retirement to become a productive role player for the Minnesota Timberwolves, a comeback that led Lowe to the coaching box. The Chicago Bulls took Lowe in the second round of the 1983 NBA Draft as the 25th overall selection, then immediately traded him to the Indiana Pacers. He spent one season there and bounced from Atlanta to Detroit in the NBA before finding a permanent home with the CBA's Tampa Bay Thrillers in 1984-85. After winning back-to-back CBA championships with the Thrillers, he gave up his dream of returning to the NBA in the summer of 1986. He took the only job he's ever had outside of basketball, managing The Magic Moment, an upscale Sarasota, Florida, restaurant owned by his Thrillers boss, Jeff Rosenberg. Lowe enjoyed running the 275-seat restaurant, handling inventory, checking in food supplies, and closing the place down at night. He went an entire year without touching a basketball, spending his free time playing golf and tennis. But Lowe was a conductor, not a chef. He needed to return to basketball. Besides, what restaurant lets the maître d' wear a red sports coat?

In the summer of 1987, Lowe bumped into former Wolfpack teammate Thurl Bailey at a basketball camp in Utah. After he watched Lowe play a few games, Bailey convinced his friend to give basketball another try. Lowe rejoined Musselman with the Albany, New York, Patroons, which set a modern-day record for winning percentage with a 48-6 mark in the regular-season and won another CBA title. By the next year, however, Lowe returned to the Thrillers' franchise, which had moved to Rapid City, South Dakota. It was a crossroads in Lowe's career: Rapid City was far from his family, which had long been settled in Raleigh while Lowe was off chasing his hoop dreams, and far from the bright lights of the NBA or even the lowered lights of the restaurant lounge. Would Leonard Bernstein go to the Black Hills to lead a high school band in Sousa marches?

Just as Lowe prepared for another trip to the CBA playoffs, he received a call from the Charlotte Hornets. The second-year NBA franchise signed him to a 10-day contract, offering him a chance to return to the highest level of professional basketball and to his family in North Carolina. (Lowe married his college sweetheart, Melonie Moultry of Winston-Salem, North Carolina, soon after she graduated from NC State in the summer of 1984; she has maintained his family's permanent residence in Raleigh since 1985.) The next season, he signed a $500,000 contract to play for the expansion Minnesota Timberwolves and Musselman, his longtime professional mentor. It was the beginning of a long-standing relationship with the franchise that included a post-playing career as a television analyst and an assistant coach for both Musselman and Jimmy Rodgers.

On January 11, 1993, Rodgers was fired and Lowe was elevated to lead the struggling Timberwolves. At 34, he was easily the youngest head coach in the NBA. Valvano, for one, could barely contain his excitement. "Sidney Lowe was the brightest player I ever coached in 23 years," said Valvano, who had just begun his public battle with cancer. "He was the epitome of the cliché 'coach on the floor.' I have already updated my resume and applied for an assistant's position with him."

It was an unusual and difficult year for Lowe—one of the players on the Timberwolves roster was Bailey, the former NC State teammate who had convinced Lowe to give the NBA another shot. "Beyond weird," Bailey said when describing what it was like to play for Lowe. The franchise had little chance to succeed in those pre-Kevin Garnett days in Minneapolis, and the losses took their toll on a coach who had won national championships in high school and college and three professional titles as a player. Lowe thought that he could make his young players work as hard as he would have, that he could force them to make the right decisions, and that they would care about every game as much as he did. It was a time of great personal reflection for the young coach. "I missed my exit several times, going home late at night," Lowe said. "I drove past it by 20 miles sometimes."

During one road trip to Phoenix, legendary Suns coach Cotton Fitzsimmons asked Lowe to drop by for a little free advice. "He took me in a room and said, 'Listen, the only thing you can do is make sure your kids play hard and that they are organized. The reality right now is that you are not going to win many games.' I didn't want to accept that," Lowe said. "But what he was telling me was that I had a very young team, and I needed to make sure we did all the small things." Lowe learned that he didn't have to conduct with a mallet.

Like his two predecessors in Minnesota, however, Lowe didn't last long as the head coach of the Timberwolves. The franchise fired Lowe after just a year and a half. He spent the next five years as an assistant coach with Mike Fratello and the Cleveland Cavaliers, positioning himself for another opportunity as an NBA head coach. That chance came on June 1, 2000, when he was hired as the head coach of the Vancouver Grizzlies. He shepherded the team's relocation to Memphis, but resigned from the job after the Grizzlies lost their first eight games in 2002, ending his NBA head coaching career with a 79-228 record. Lowe once again returned to Minnesota, this time as an assistant for Timberwolves head coach Flip Saunders. He stayed there until 2005, when Saunders and his entire staff moved to the Detroit Pistons.

It was near the end of Lowe's first season with the Pistons— which had amassed the best regular-season record in the NBA—that he began working with NC State athletic director Lee Fowler to select candidates for the university's head coaching position. At first, Lowe simply gave Fowler his thoughts about high-profile candidates whom Fowler was courting. "We need to get someone who really ... understands the competition, that understands the ACC, that understands that you can walk out of your house and your next-door neighbor may be in blue," Lowe said. Eventually, it dawned on

Lowe exactly who he was talking about—himself. "I think I'm going to go for this job, because everything I told Lee, that's me," Lowe told his wife. He was eager to bring his coaching knowledge and his NBA experience back to the school that he loved, even though he had never coached or recruited on the collegiate level. Fowler jumped at the chance to reunite NC State with one of its most decorated alums and was willing to wait for the Pistons to finish their season.

But there was a problem: through all of Lowe's travels while chasing his NBA dream, he never completed his business management degree, despite his many promises to his mother, Carrie Lowe, that he would one day become the first member of his family to graduate from college. He was well short of that degree when he left school in 1983. He spent the next two decades chasing other dreams. "When I went to the NBA, I had a family," Lowe said. "At the time, my priorities were God first, my family second. I had to support them. That meant working camps in the summer and concentrating on taking care of them as opposed to worrying about myself."

Lowe had always wanted to buy his parents a new house and move them out of the inner-city Washington apartment for which his mother was a maid. During his final season at NC State, Lowe told a group of junior high students, "I have a dream ... to someday put my mama in a big house and let her have a maid to bring her cookies." When he signed his biggest contract with the Timberwolves, Lowe purchased a house for his parents and moved them, along with three of his sisters, to Raleigh. He considered it just a small part of his repayment for the sacrifices his mother made to support nine children and a disabled husband.

But Carrie Lowe was looking for a different kind of reward. "I always asked him, 'What's going on with your degree? OK, get to it,'" she said. "I constantly reminded him that he needed that degree." He also got an earful from his frequent golfing buddy, Dwayne

Green, a former NC State football player who waved his degree in front of his friend's face every time Lowe won on the golf course.

Over two decades, Lowe gradually reduced the number of hours he needed to obtain the degree, and by the time Fowler came calling, he was only two classes short. Fowler made the degree a requirement for employment, and Lowe made a commitment to finish his remaining hours at St. Paul's College in Virginia.

In an emotional press conference on NC State's campus on May 6, 2006, Lowe was introduced as the 18th head coach in Wolfpack basketball history, a position Valvano once predicted he would have. In his first meeting with his new team, Lowe made a simple promise to the players: "I told them I don't have a lot of rules, just a few. To play hard, to play smart, to play together, and the most important thing of all—the biggest rule I have—is to have fun." After perfunctory questions from the media, Lowe walked along the floor of the Dail Basketball Practice Center, the site of his introduction, through the woods, and down the hill to the Paul Derr Track, where nearly a thousand Wolfpack fans were eagerly waiting to welcome him home.

Wearing red and white, they shouted his name and cheered his arrival. For the next 45 minutes, Lowe talked and mingled. He introduced his family to faces he hadn't seen in many years. Before he left, Lowe raised both arms to flash the traditional wolf sign, and the crowd cheered wildly. The maestro was on his home stage once again.

Weeks later, with tears in his eyes, Lowe knocked on the door of the home he bought his parents and handed his mother the diploma he had just received in the mail. "Through all of the athletic accomplishments and all the things I have done in coaching, she is more proud of me getting that degree than anything else I have done," Lowe said. "To be able to show her that diploma, basically at the same time I was named the head coach at NC State, is a dream I never thought would come true in a million years. I think there was some kind of divine help here that made everything possible for me. It worked out perfectly."

At times, the Wolfpack struggled during Lowe's first season. He had a short bench, a thin roster, a long learning curve, and a rash of untimely injuries: many of the hurdles that new coaches face during a transitional season. Lowe was not deterred. "I am the head coach at NC State University," he said. "How can I not be excited?" He showed his enthusiasm by ordering a tailor-made red jacket to wear to big games, just as Valvano used to do. He unveiled the good-luck charm on a January afternoon, when the Wolfpack beat second-ranked North Carolina in Raleigh. By the end of the season, Lowe had a dry cleaner on call to keep his jacket clean during a four-day charge to the ACC Tournament title game in Tampa, Florida. The Wolfpack came up short against the heavily favored Tar Heels in the final game, but Lowe's first-year message was clear to anyone who might have doubted that he could put the Wolfpack in position to win, as he did during his playing days.

He's ready to conduct the encore.

2 "WE HAD NO CHOICE BUT TO BELIEVE HIM"

Norman Sloan loved NC State University, but February 1980 was the winter of his discontent. He was nearing the end of his 14th season as the head basketball coach of his alma mater, where he had been a three-sport letter winner and an Indiana-bred protégé of NC State legendary basketball coach Everett Case. A fiery sideline coach and an explosive off-court general—he was called "Stormin' Norman" by a snickering press—Sloan had been successful during his tenure, taking the Wolfpack to heights that Case never reached. He won the first of his three ACC championships just four years after he arrived from the University of Florida in 1966, which allowed him to lure 7-foot-4 center Tommy Burleson from the North Carolina mountains down to Raleigh for his first big recruiting coup. He used that success to get Burleson's friend, high-flying David Thompson, a year later. More than three decades after Thompson played his last collegiate game, he is still inarguably the greatest player in ACC basketball history. With Burleson, Thompson, and a tiny point guard named Monte Towe, Sloan compiled a 57-1 record in back-to-back seasons from 1972 to '74, a two-year mark that is unmatched in ACC annals. They won consecutive ACC titles and ended UCLA's stronghold on the NCAA Tournament by upsetting the Bill Walton-led Bruins in the semifinals of the 1974 tournament and then beating Marquette in the championship game.

The team was so full of talent that Sloan mostly stayed out of the way as a coach and let the players work their magic on the court. His primary job was to model the spiffy plaid jackets that were his trademark on the sidelines and to spat with members of the "worm brigade," Sloan's loving nickname for the press corps that covered his team.

Six years after winning the NCAA title, Sloan was having a hard time keeping up with some of his counterparts in the ACC, including North Carolina's Dean Smith, Maryland's Lefty Driesell, and Virginia's up-and-comer Terry Holland. The Wolfpack had not been back to the NCAA Tournament since winning in 1974; the runner-up finish in the 1978 National Invitation Tournament did not have the same appeal. Sloan was also the lowest paid coach in the ACC, bringing in some $75,000 a year from his university salary, his independent television show, and his summer basketball camps. In the fall of 1979, he had asked both athletic director Willis Casey and the board that oversaw the department for a raise, not only for himself, but also for his assistant coaches. Towe, who had joined Sloan as an assistant coach, had a university salary of $15,000 in his final year at NC State. The salary increase requests were denied.

Sloan began to feel that he could not take the program any higher. After a chance meeting with a longtime friend, Fred Montsdeoca, while the Wolfpack was playing a game at Maryland on January 23, 1980, Sloan became intrigued about the possibility of returning to Florida, where he had been the head basketball coach before he arrived at NC State in 1966. Montsdeoca, who had been on staff with

Sloan at The Citadel back in the 1950s, was on the search committee to find Florida a new basketball coach. Having just finished off a 12,000-seat arena, the Gators were making a new commitment to basketball. Sloan knew that the state of Florida was an untapped hotbed of basketball talent and believed he could build a national power there, a prediction that eventually came true at Florida three decades later.

Sloan and Casey had a rocky history dating back to 1969, when longtime athletics director Roy Clogston retired. Casey was NC State's swimming coach at the time, having won 11 ACC championships and coached 33 All-Americans. He was also Clogston's second-in-command in the athletic department. For years, he had handled the department's finances with a tight fist. Sloan was in his third year of building the foundation for his championship program, but was eager to begin a career in athletic administration. Surprisingly, Sloan received the first call to replace Clogston. But when he found out that he would be forced to give up his head coaching job to become athletic director, Sloan balked and Casey was named the department's director. The two got along fine publicly, but Sloan never called Casey "boss." Casey had a difficult job—the resources for NC State's athletics programs had always been extremely limited, even during the school's unprecedented athletics success of the early 1970s. Casey had to do things on the cheap, which he did brilliantly. He found it hard to keep his best coaches, but he had a knack for identifying good ones. He hired a football coach from William & Mary who had a career losing record: Lou Holtz. In the days just after Title IX was passed, he hired a coach who had never played college sports to lead his women's program: Kay Yow. And when Holtz got mad and left NC State for the NFL's New York Jets, he handed the reins over to Holtz's top assistant: Bo Rein. His last hire was another football coach that dozens of schools had tried to lure away from tiny Furman University: Dick Sheridan.

By the winter of 1980, Sloan was at a crossroads in his career. Like Duke's Bill Foster, he was having a hard time winning in-state recruiting battles with North Carolina. He was trying to take care of his family and his assistant coaches. Although things weren't optimal for Sloan, the Wolfpack wasn't in bad shape on the court. His 1979-80 team finished tied for second in the ACC, thanks to a spectacular performance by Hawkeye Whitney against North Carolina in his final game at Reynolds Coliseum. The burly forward capped off his amazing career hitting 11 of his 12 field goals and scoring 26 points in a 63-50 win over the Tar Heels. The freshman trio of Lowe, Whittenburg, and Bailey was developing nicely. Lowe had supplanted senior Clyde "The Glide" Austin as the starting point guard during the season. They were joined by sophomore Max Perry, who became eligible midway through the season after transferring to NC State from Oklahoma the year before. Whittenburg was splitting time with Kenny Matthews and Austin at the shooting guard position. And Bailey was honing the skills that he had lacked when he arrived at NC State. A handful of competent frontcourt players—Art Jones, Craig Watts, Scott Parzych, and 7-foot-5 giant Chuck Nevitt—aided the program, and the Wolfpack was on course to return to the NCAA Tournament for the first time in six years.

But off the court, Sloan was making the necessary—and extremely private—connections to move on. He asked one of NC State's sports information assistants, Mike Finn, to help him put together a resume for the Florida job. Finn, a Florida graduate, knew many of the people in the Gators athletic department, but was a little wary of Sloan's request. "Coach, are you sure you really want to do this?" Finn asked. "I really think you have the foundation to win a national championship here."

Finn, now an associate commissioner in the Atlantic Coast Conference office, was certain that Sloan didn't agree. "He looked at me in a way that only Norm could," Finn said in a 2006 interview. "I know he was thinking, 'You are out of your damned mind.'" Sometimes, it takes a different sort of dreamer to believe in that sort of thing.

Sloan announced the Monday before the 1980 ACC Tournament that he would be returning to Florida as the Gators' head coach. Casey knew exactly who he wanted to hire as Sloan's replacement— DeMatha's Morgan Wootten. No one outside of Sloan's staff had more to do with NC State's success following the 1974 NCAA championship than Wootten, a Durham, North Carolina, native who had coached Wolfpack players Kenny Carr, Whitney, Lowe, and Whittenburg in high school. After the two met in Greensboro at the ACC Tournament— where the Wolfpack lost to Duke in the first round—Casey offered Wootten a five-year contract worth a reported $700,000 to lead the Wolfpack, no small potatoes for a guy with zero college coaching experience. Lowe, Whittenburg, and Whitney all called Wootten, asking him to consider the job. In the end, however, Wootten decided not to mess with a good thing: his family wanted to stay in Washington. He had already won 649 games at DeMatha and would go on to win another 625 more over the next 22 seasons before he retired in 2002. He won more games than any prep coach in history and in 2000 became the first—and so far only—high school coach to earn a spot in the Naismith Memorial Basketball Hall of Fame.

It took Casey another two weeks to hire Sloan's replacement, a relative unknown in the basketball-crazy South: Iona's Jim Valvano.

When Whittenburg heard who the Wolfpack's new coach would be, he said to a distraught Lowe, "Do you know who our new coach is? That crazy guy who about choked us in Boston."

Lowe wasn't listening. He was too busy figuring out if he could go with Sloan to Florida. He went to Sloan's office in tears, vowing that he was going to Gainesville, too. But Sloan wouldn't let him. "No, this is the best situation for you," Sloan said. "I told you that when I recruited you." Bailey was also upset that Sloan was leaving and decided to consider his options. Whittenburg, the most stubborn of the three, gave no thought to transferring. "NC State was the place I wanted to be," he said. "It's where my cousin played and won a national championship. I wanted to do the same thing. I wasn't going anywhere."

After wowing Casey, Chancellor Joab Thomas, and other top administrators in a raucous lunch interview at the Capital City Club in downtown Raleigh, Valvano was introduced on March 21, 1980. The press conference was exactly one week after another relatively obscure coach—Army's Mike Krzyzewski—was hired at Duke. Valvano, the Italian would-be comedian, knew how to work a crowd, whether it was the media, fans, or his players, and he had no trouble convincing his three rising sophomores and the rest of the remaining players to stay. While others were distracted by Valvano's raspy standup routine, his animated sideline antics, and his vivacious personality, the players were impressed by Valvano's singular devotion to his life-long obsession: to win a national championship. In their very first meeting, the coach made it clear that he left Iona—which had won 14 more games and suffered nine fewer defeats than the Wolfpack the previous two years—because he thought he had a better chance of winning a national championship in Raleigh than in New Rochelle, New York.

"When we met him that first day, he told us about this dream he had to win a national championship," Bailey said. "We are all sitting there, all pissed off that Coach Sloan has left, and here is this little Italian guy who is telling us that he is going to win a national championship. He told us flat out if we could visualize the dream, we could do it. He said he was going to do it, and if we wanted to be there when it happened, it was up to us. And he kept talking about it, and talking about it, until eventually we had no choice but to believe him.

"From that day on, whether we lost a game or had a bad practice or whatever, everything we did was geared toward that dream of his. Guys came and went, but that dream was the thing he kept talking about."

Whittenburg said, "It was brought up every year."

But to realize that championship, Valvano needed more talent than what he had on hand. Valvano essentially missed an entire recruiting season after he was hired. He brought in only one player his first year, forward Harold Thompson of Raeford, North Carolina, who had committed to the program when Sloan was still the coach. Thompson's Hoke County High School coach had advised the lifelong NC State fan not to attend the university. Orlando "Tubby" Smith did not think Thompson would fit in well with Valvano's transition offense. Thompson went to Raleigh anyway. Valvano knew he would have to make up for that year with a big splash during the next recruiting season.

"My next goal is to have the greatest recruiting class in the nation next year," Valvano told Mark Donovan of the *Raleigh Times* during the spring of 1980. "I'm going to go after the greatest players and do what I do best: sell. If this doesn't work out, I can always do what I thought I should be doing to begin with: selling shoes."

Of course, Valvano ended up doing a great deal of both over the next few years, but that is a different story.

For his first season with the Wolfpack, Valvano had a solid core of sophomores in Lowe, Whittenburg, and Bailey. But the rest of the roster was hardly stocked with championship-caliber talent. Senior forward Art Jones, 7-foot-5 center Chuck Nevitt, forward Scott Parzych, and Craig Watts joined Bailey in the frontcourt, but the backcourt was thin, with Lowe at the point and Whittenburg and junior Kenny Matthews on the wings. His only other backcourt options were Max Perry, the Oklahoma transfer, and walk-on Emmett Lay. The Wolfpack struggled to a 14-13 season overall and finished next-to-last in the Atlantic Coast Conference, winning just four of 14 league games.

The coach built his second recruiting class on the player everybody identified as one of the best in the nation: Walter "Dinky" Proctor, a 6-foot-9 point guard from Somerset, New Jersey, who college recruiters were calling the next Magic Johnson. Valvano kept no secrets about his affection for the Rutgers Prep star: "If we get this kid, we will win a national championship while he is here." Proctor was clearly the centerpiece of a class that was stocked with a couple of projects. Center Cozell McQueen, a high school All-American from Bennettsville, South Carolina, was the next to enlist with the Wolfpack, shunning offers from Clemson, Dayton, and, ironically enough, Houston to sign a scholarship in mid-December of 1980.

Valvano then brought in his first local recruit, 6-foot-7 forward, Mike Warren, who played at Broughton, the same Raleigh high school as basketball legend Pete Maravich, the son of one-time NC State coach Press Maravich.

A small shooting guard with a big scoring average named Terry Gannon from Joliet, Illinois, signed on after Valvano impressed Gannon's dad, Jim, a longtime high school basketball coach in Joliet. Gannon had wanted to go to Notre Dame, but Fighting Irish coach Digger Phelps thought Gannon was too small to be a regular contributor, despite his obvious shooting skills. Gannon, a two-sport star at Joliet Catholic who hoped to play both basketball and baseball in college, came to Raleigh primarily because one of his closest friends, Mike Pesavento, was already a pitcher on the Wolfpack baseball team. The final piece of Valvano's first true recruiting class was burly forward Lorenzo Charles, a Brooklyn, New York, native few coaches— including Valvano—were overly impressed with as a high school senior. The Wolfpack staff recruited Charles early, but turned their attention to other players in the winter of 1981. When Valvano determined he needed one more frontcourt player, he sent assistant coach Ray Martin after Charles, who was on the verge of signing with Massachusetts, one more time. "Lorenzo was not that highly thought of by the recruiting experts and the various other recruiting services," Valvano once told Jim Pomeranz. "We were involved with a lot of other players. All reports on Lorenzo said that he was strong, but not the caliber of player in the [ACC]."

On paper, it wasn't the greatest recruiting class Valvano had ever signed. But it didn't have to be: with the maturing backcourt of Lowe and Whittenburg, the Wolfpack went into Valvano's second year in Raleigh greatly improved. Bailey had led the team in scoring and rebounding as a sophomore and was developing into an offensive and defensive star. Lowe was the best point guard in a league dominated by stars, and Whittenburg was finally ready to step into the starting lineup. None of the freshman players were big contributors: McQueen was the only one in the group who played in all 32 games in 1981-82, but he barely averaged two points per game. But they all saw some action, with Gannon finishing second behind McQueen for freshman playing time.

Valvano put together another large, four-player recruiting class heading into the 1982-83 season, headlined by McDonald's All-American Ernie Myers, one of the nation's top three recruits that year. Just about every school in the country was looking to sign the perimeter star from New York's Tolentine High School, but Valvano thought he had the inside track for two reasons. First, Valvano's father, Rocco, used to be the head coach at St. Nicholas of Tolentine High School, and one of Rocco Valvano's former players, Bobby Austin, was currently the school's head coach. Secondly, while the younger Valvano was at Iona, he saw Myers play and promised to come back in two years to recruit him—a promise Valvano kept even though he had switched employers. In the end, neither of those things made a big difference. NC State can thank a rival recruiter—and one of the best basketball players in Wolfpack history—for sealing Myers' decision to play at NC State.

Myers was on his recruiting trip to Raleigh in the fall of 1981. He and Sidney Lowe, who was showing him around town, were getting ready to go into Carter-Finley Stadium when they ran into Georgia assistant coach Eddie Biedenbach, who had been recruiting Myers to play at the University of Georgia. Myers had no idea that Biedenbach was an All-ACC player at NC State under Everett Case, Press Maravich, and Norm Sloan during the mid-1960s. In the middle of a brief conversation, a Wolfpack fan came up to Biedenbach and asked, "What's the best school in the world?" Biedenbach turned Wolfpack red, looked Myers right in the eye, and said, "Ernie, I cannot tell a lie. This is the best place to be." Myers, who had narrowed his choices to NC State, Georgia, and Georgia Tech, decided then that he was headed to NC State. He signed with the Wolfpack days later.

Valvano brought in two more frontcourt players, Rocky Mount, North Carolina, native Alvin Battle and Tuscaloosa, Alabama, native Walt Densmore, hoping to add some offensive pop in a lineup already equipped with Charles and McQueen. Battle had spent two years at Merced Junior College in California and was named the national junior college player of the year after his sophomore season. He wanted to return to the East Coast and committed to play at Virginia Tech after being recruited by passionate Hokies assistant Tom Abatemarco. But when Wolfpack assistant Marty Fletcher was named head coach at Virginia Military Institute, Abatemarco joined Valvano's staff for the second time in his career. Valvano had given Abatemarco his first full-time job as an assistant while at Iona in 1975. Battle immediately became intrigued enough to look into playing for the Wolfpack. "I am not sure if that violates NCAA rules or not, but I ended up going to NC State after Abatemarco went there," Battle said.

The final member of the recruiting class was high-scoring point guard George McClain, also from Rocky Mount. He was a basketball prodigy who attended the same high school as ACC stars Phil Ford and Buck Williams. His job was to spend one year learning from Lowe so he could take over as the Wolfpack's next point guard.

Two former roommates at Louisburg (North Carolina) Junior College who both won roster spots at open tryouts on campus filled out the 1982-83 team. Quinton Leonard, a Louisburg native who longed to play at NC State, earned his spot for the next two years, becoming the final addition to Valvano's largest collection of newcomers. Tommy DiNardo, the son of Everett Case-era forward Phil DiNardo, joined the team in 1982-83 after sitting out an entire season to catch up on his mechanical engineering curriculum.

While history remembers the 1982-83 Wolfpack as an unexpected champion, it was a talented, experienced, and deep team whose roster was filled with just the right number of role players to maintain good chemistry. But it also took a little dose of Valvano magic and a devastating injury that turned out to be a blessing in disguise to turn this varied collection into a squad that would change college basketball forever.

"There is no other coach—I say this in hindsight of having covered college basketball for the last 20 years—no other coach I know of who could have won a national championship with that team," Gannon said in a 2006 interview. "He created a belief, an aura, and environment for that team to do things that even we did not know we were capable of doing without him."

THURL BAILEY

Thurl Bailey came to NC State as more of a trombone player than a power forward. Some would say he was a better actor and student leader than a rebounder and shot blocker. Few who saw him on the day he arrived in Raleigh as a lanky, somewhat green basketball player would have believed that Bailey would play longer professionally than anyone in NC State basketball history.

By the time Bailey was a college senior, however, no one doubted that his leadership and unique athletic abilities on the court made him the heart of the Cardiac Pack.

No NC State fan will ever forget Bailey weeping openly at midcourt the afternoon he helped the Wolfpack beat defending national champion North Carolina in Reynolds Coliseum, the game that jumpstarted the team's run to the national championship. That outpouring would repeat continuously throughout the next six weeks as Bailey unabashedly let his emotions stream down his face while his college basketball career came to an end.

The simple fact is that Bailey spent most of his early years proving that he could play basketball at the highest level.

Bailey had to prove it to his parents, especially his headstrong mom, Retha, who was reluctant to let him play pickup basketball games on the dangerous playgrounds near their home in Seat Pleasant, Maryland, a Washington, D.C., suburb that was anything but pleasant.

Bailey had to prove it to Herb Gray, the junior high basketball coach who *twice* cut the future star after open tryouts, even though Bailey, at nearly 6-foot-5, was the tallest student in the school. Today, Bailey considers Gray—a guy who told him to give up the game and stop wasting his time because he didn't have what it takes to be a basketball player—one of the biggest influences on his life. "He helped me more than I could ever imagine," Bailey said. "He helped me realize who I was and what I wanted."

Bailey had to prove it to former NC State coach Norm Sloan, who wasn't convinced that the athlete, despite his athletic 6-foot-11 frame, would ever become a significant college basketball player. "Norm wasn't sold on him at all," said Eddie Biedenbach, the ex-Wolfpack player and assistant coach who landed talents like David Thompson, Kenny Carr, and Charles "Hawkeye" Whitney for Sloan's program. Instead, Sloan was heavily recruiting Washington, North Carolina, superstar Dominique Wilkins and Brooklyn's Sidney Green.

And finally, Bailey had to prove it to Green himself, who chose Nevada-Las Vegas over NC State and made the fateful comment, "[Bailey] hasn't shown me much" before the two faced off in the second round of the 1983 NCAA Tournament. That became Bailey's inspiration in one of the many miracle wins during the Wolfpack's improbable journey to the championship. Bailey's tip-in on a missed free throw over the top of Green at the buzzer allowed the Wolfpack to beat UNLV in the team's fifth consecutive last-second, postseason victory.

Today, after a professional basketball career that spanned 16 years and three countries, Thurl Bailey is still living an unexpected and, to some, unusual life, proving to everyone that he can thrive and inspire others in a Christian faith that is less than one percent African-American. Bailey grew up singing in the choir and attending weekly Sunday school at a Baptist Church, but converted to the Church of Latter Day Saints on December 31, 1995, a little over a year and a half after he was married to the former Sindi Southwick, a former Utah Valley State basketball player he had met when she worked his basketball camp in 1989.

They quickly became one of the highest profile interracial couples in the 175-year history of the Mormon faith, as Thurl traveled far and wide to conduct dozens of "fireside talks" for the church. Bailey's retired from basketball, living a bucolic life with Sindi and their three children, but he's busier than ever.

In addition to his charity work—he's held the same non-profit youth basketball camp for nearly two decades—Bailey is an accomplished businessman. In the summer of 2006, he made an exploratory two-week trip to China to pursue business opportunities. He does postgame television commentary for the Utah Jazz and radio color commentary for University of Utah basketball. He has his own clothing line, has released three inspirational music CDs, and, like his former college basketball coach Jim Valvano once was, is an extremely popular corporate motivational speaker whose $10,000 appearance fee is always negotiable for worthy causes.

Bailey's path to this life was hardly as smooth and silky as his baritone singing voice.

Life was not simple for Bailey as a youth. His parents struggled to stay together, and the future star was witness to domestic violence. Bailey's father, Carl, had been briefly paralyzed in a construction accident not long after Thurl was born. Money was tight. Tempers were always on edge.

Twice, Bailey's mom shot at his father. On a couple of occasions, Bailey's brothers and sisters had to call the cops to calm their parents down. When Bailey took Sindi on her first visit to his family's home, he showed her the bullet hole that remains in the dresser in his now-divorced parents' bedroom.

"I would see them fight—a lot—and not just with words," he said. "My mom got mad when she read a story one time when I talked about the bullet holes, but I just told her, 'Hey, Mom, that's how you and Dad were.' The best thing that could have happened to them was to split up. It was a tough environment."

Millions of kids grow up in broken homes, and some of them never get over that trauma. Bailey wasn't going to be one of them. "I knew I could be a product of my environment or I could be different," said Bailey. That's why he first learned to play the trombone, along with the baritone and tuba. That's why he learned to act.

"All of my activities were an escape," Bailey said. "My parents, especially my mom, did a very good job of keeping us sheltered from some of the stuff that was going on in our neighborhood, even though we lived right in the middle of all of it. Some of the guys I grew up with, by the time we were in high school, were in jail or dead. I think she did a really good job of keeping us busy enough that we weren't involved in a lot of bad stuff.'"

Because his parents did not want him to hang around the rough element frequently on the courts near their home, Bailey never really developed the same kind of passion that either his father or brothers had for the sport. One day, however, a Washington, D.C.-area AAU coach named Sterling Parker saw Bailey carrying groceries home from the store. "Do you play basketball?" Parker asked the 6-foot-5, 13-year-old boy. "Nope," Bailey said. "How about giving it a try?" Parker replied.

"He basically talked me into giving it a shot," Bailey said.

Bailey had already learned to play the trombone, the baritone, and the tuba. He could act and he could sing. Why not?

"Basketball . . . was something I gradually fell in love with as I gradually improved and got better and learned from my brother and my dad," Bailey said. "The nice thing is, when I decided I wanted to do it, I always had really good teachers and coaches."

After being cut by Gray, Bailey found inspiration, arriving an hour early at school to work on the game's fundamentals. He spent two years playing junior varsity at Bladensburg (Maryland) High School, becoming more and more coordinated and more skilled. But he wasn't good enough to make the varsity team, and he didn't have much self-confidence.

He changed that when he became more involved in school activities. He still remembers the day during his junior year when he excitedly told his mom that he was going to run for student body vice president.

"Why not president?" she asked.

"I didn't think I could win," he answered.

But he did. He gained more confidence playing in the school band and performing in school plays. As a member of the high school band, he performed at Walt Disney World. As a senior in the drama club, he played a king in a Shakespearean play and a pregnant woman in another performance. At some point during his high school days, he was the president of nine different clubs, including the obscure flag-raising club, which consisted of just Bailey and a younger student.

"That was a great club, man," Bailey said. "There were only two of us in it. We were responsible for raising and lowering the flag every morning and afternoon. The other guy was a little fellow. I told him, 'Welcome to the flag-raising club. I am the president and you are the vice president.' It was as simple as that."

By the time Bailey was a junior, he had also become a talented basketball player under respected head coach Ernie Welch. NC State was one of the first colleges to contact him. He came to Raleigh for basketball camp after his junior year in high school and Biedenbach, the assistant in charge of recruiting the D.C. area, kept a constant eye on his growth spurts.

"You could tell he was going to be a good player," Biedenbach said. "He grew a couple of inches and just got better and better."

Bailey, however, was hardly a hot commodity. When Biedenbach left NC State for his first head coaching job at Davidson after the 1978 season, Bailey almost decided to follow, mainly because Maryland coach Lefty Driesell didn't seem to be all that interested and Sloan wasn't convinced that Bailey, who was tall but extremely skinny, would be an impact player on the collegiate level.

But just as in the spring of 1983, a bit of destiny stepped in. Bailey received a last-minute spot in the Capital Classic, a national high school all-star game played at the Capital Centre in Washington. It was a game filled with marquee athletes from what might have been the best senior class in the history of high school basketball. Bailey's team was seemingly outmanned, even though it had the nation's top-rated high school player, a fellow by the name of Ralph Sampson, along with Quintin Dailey and future NC State teammates Dereck Whittenburg and Sidney Lowe. On the opposing team were Green and Wilkins—both of who had decided to go elsewhere—as well as Sam Bowie, James Worthy, Clark Kellogg, John Paxson, and Dirk Minniefield.

In 21 minutes, Bailey scored six points and had three rebounds in a game billed as the ultimate matchup between Sampson and Bowie. But Whittenburg hit the game-winning shot, just as he had a week earlier in the third annual McDonald's All-Star Game in Charlotte, North Carolina. Those two baskets were precursors to the most famous airball in NCAA Tournament history.

Bailey went to NC State, not knowing that his neighbors, Lowe and Whittenburg, would be attending as well.

"When Thurl came to NC State, he was a skinny kid—not much more than a musician who played basketball," said Lowe, laughing at the memory of the long and lanky Bailey trying to push Lowe's fire-plug frame into the lane. "He had trouble posting me up. He could shoot over me, but he had trouble backing me down. It wasn't long until that changed. He worked on his game while he was here. He always approached the game like a pro. He was very serious about improving his game. He has always been like that."

Lorenzo Charles, two years behind Bailey at NC State, quietly watched Bailey and emulated his game.

"Thurl led by example," Charles said. "He worked hard in practice every day. What he did in practice led to production. He was our quiet leader. He just went out there and laid it on the line every night and everyone else just tried to follow. You could tell playing basketball meant a lot to Thurl. He was a little on the emotional side. That's what basketball should be for a player. You can't just throw on your sneakers and go out there and play. The game has to mean something. It's got to be one of the most important things in the world to you. And it was for Thurl."

Bailey remained involved in other activities while at the university. Following his sophomore year, he served as a congressional page for North Carolina congressman Walter B. Jones. As a junior at NC State, he played Crooks in a campus production of John Steinbeck's *Of Mice and Men*. On the basketball court, he led the Wolfpack in scoring and rebounding three consecutive seasons.

NC State's magical run in the NCAA Tournament was a huge economic boon for Bailey. When the season ended, Valvano implored Utah Jazz president Frank Layden to take Bailey early in the 1983 NBA draft. "This kid is one of the best-kept secrets in the country," Valvano said midway through Bailey's senior season. "Speed, quickness, he's got all that. But he also has character. He works hard, he goes to class, he listens, he's coachable. He might fill out to be a monster."

Valvano told Layden, "Don't think of Thurl as just a player. As a person he will be good for your team and the community."

Layden took Valvano's advice, and the Jazz made him the No. 7 pick in the 1983 NBA draft. He spent 10 years with the team, became the fifth-leading scorer in franchise history and was quietly the team captain on a squad that included perennial NBA All-Stars John Stockton and Karl Malone. The athlete also played for a short time with the Minnesota Timberwolves and in Italy and Greece with the European professional leagues.

Bailey has lived a life that he never expected and has done more than what was expected of him. Even though he has a different faith than he had in college, Bailey still believes that something was born from that 1983 championship that continues to bless him now.

"I just always believed in a higher power, especially during the year of the championship," Bailey said. "There is no way that anybody could ever tell me that there wasn't divine intervention involved. We had to do our parts and use our God-given talents, but it wasn't just luck. I think we were instruments. I think we transcended normal basketball."

And Bailey, all heart still, continues to transcend what people believe to be a normal basketball player.

"WE WERE JUST
3 STANDING AROUND
OUT THERE"

This is how mature NC State's Sidney Lowe and Dereck Whittenburg were during their junior season: the experienced backcourt made a solemn vow with senior Max Perry to do everything in its power to turn freshmen Cozell McQueen and Lorenzo Charles into better college basketball players.

They did not sit the two players down for long, heartfelt discussions. They did not spend extra time with them at practice. They did not advise the coaching staff on ways to integrate the new players into the lifestyle of college athletics. What they did was sneak up on McQueen, Charles, Walter "Dinky" Proctor, and sometimes even Thurl Bailey and tickle them.

"We would do whatever we could to separate them from the herd," said Perry, a reserve point guard who had transferred to NC State from Oklahoma and the team's most notorious practical joker.

Calling themselves the "Killer Bees"—so named because of the buzzing sound they made as they approached their targets—the trio of guards made the young players jumpy. Charles was particularly sensitive in the tickling department. "Sometimes, he couldn't control himself and you would find yourself flying across the room," Lowe said. "Lorenzo was so strong naturally, he could throw anybody up in the air. You had to be a little careful."

Their scare-and-tickle tactics helped bond the young players throughout a successful season, one in which the Wolfpack packed itself into a tight zone defense, let Lowe dribble the ball around as long as he could in a modified motion offense, and waited to get the right shot. The 1981-82 Wolfpack finished last in the ACC in scoring with just 57.5 points per game, but was second in the nation in scoring defense, allowing just 49.1 points per game. Of course, having 7-foot-5 senior center Chuck Nevitt in the lineup helped deflate the scoring.

But it was not a mentally tough team. Sometimes the team's behavior got out of hand. After a particularly disheartening loss at Clemson, Whittenburg blasted his teammates in the media. "We have no leadership right now," Whittenburg said through tears. "On the road, we play too tentatively and we don't come to play. And we joke around too much. We don't take it seriously enough. We lack intensity and we just joke around. This is serious business. We are just standing around out there like it's a social event."

Valvano's team managed to win 22 games in the regular season, finished third in the Atlantic Coast Conference, and absolutely flopped in the postseason, losing to North Carolina in the first round of the ACC Tournament for the second year in a row and to Tennessee-Chattanooga in the first round of the NCAA Tournament in Indianapolis, Indiana.

The last performance of the season, in which the Wolfpack quickly fell behind to the Moccasins and never recovered, was an embarrassment to Valvano, who threw in the towel midway through the second half and benched most of his starting lineup. It was an off-key performance that would have humiliated Indiana native Everett Case, NC

State's Hall of Fame coach who brought big-time college basketball to the South after winning five championships as a Hoosier high school coach. *Back Home Again in Indiana*, the state's theme song, was the last thing Valvano wanted to hear during the summer of 1982.

"If ever there was a team that was just satisfied to be in the NCAA Tournament, that was it," Valvano said.

The coach knew that Lowe, Whittenburg, and Bailey, who had vowed to go to a Final Four when they arrived to play for Norm Sloan in the fall of 1979, would not joke around in their final season with the Wolfpack.

DERECK WHITTENBURG

If bad things had not happened to Dereck Whittenburg in the winter and spring of 1983, good things would not have happened to NC State. Whittenburg's broken foot against Virginia on January 12 of that year—an injury thought to be career-ending—forced the Wolfpack to grow up and grow together. His airball from 30 feet in the finals of the NCAA title game against Houston turned out to be the perfect setup for Lorenzo Charles' game-winning dunk.

Whether he was in the lineup or not, whether he was draining long-range jumpers or not, Whittenburg was the heart of the Wolfpack's championship team. The mature leader wasn't afraid to kick a teammate in the pants, even with a cast on. He wasn't shy about intimidating an opponent with an icy stare during a game or a hard slap of the palm instead of a handshake during pregame introductions. He brought a hard edge that was a perfect complement to fellow senior Sidney Lowe's heady execution and Thurl Bailey's soulful emotion.

The Glenarden, Maryland, native and talented cousin of NC State All-American David Thompson was an undersized, high-flying, bombs-away shooter who infused a championship spirit into the Wolfpack. He came to Raleigh from Morgan Wootten's celebrated program at DeMatha Catholic High School in Hyattsville, Maryland, as a prep All-American. Still, it took him longer than Lowe to find his exact place in the Wolfpack's lineup, and he was frequently relegated to "the other guard" status, a secondary piece in the Wolfpack offense, because of his shooting inconsistencies. He was a reserve his first two seasons at NC State, playing behind Kenny Matthews. It was hard for Whittenburg, a streaky shooter, to keep a hot hand when coming off the bench. But when the ball started falling for him, he was a deadly weapon. "When Whit is on," Wolfpack head coach Jim Valvano once said, "there's nobody that I have more confidence in than him."

As much as he loved to fill up the basket, Whittenburg loved his role in shaping the Wolfpack more. He was an intense leader who wasn't all that pleasant to be around at times. "If somebody wasn't working hard, I would jump them," Whittenburg said with no small amount of pride. "If they weren't warming up hard, I would jump them. If they weren't lifting weights hard, I would jump them. I was much more of the in-your-face kind of guy."

There is no doubt he scared people, his own teammates and cheerleaders included. "Whit was a nasty son of a gun on and off the court," said Terry Gannon, whose post-practice shooting games against Whittenburg are legendary in the annals of Reynolds Coliseum. "I love him dearly, but he was downright mean. He would intimidate everyone. I remember we were in the hotel in Ogden, Utah, and he was walking down the hall. Our cheerleaders were at the other end, and when they saw Whit, they literally veered into the next hallway to get out of his way. But he was a great guy to have as a teammate. He would jump off a wall for you."

Measured at 6-foot-¼ and 193 pounds, Dereck Cornelius Whittenburg was a stocky package whose stature forced him to stretch his shooting range beyond conventional distances. That was fine with the unconventional Whittenburg, who played with his shirt untucked and his conscience unfurled. In his first three years at NC State, he longed for the ACC to adopt a three-point line, because he knew it would be a great weapon in his game. But he was a bit disappointed when the league adopted the experimental 19-foot three-point line his senior season. Any schmuck could make a jumper from there. Whittenburg was used to pulling up from 22 to 25 feet away.

Growing up, Whittenburg was a three-sport player on the outskirts of Washington, D.C. He played quarterback in football, third base and pitcher in baseball, and shooting guard in basketball. When it came time to pick just one sport, Whittenburg followed in the steps of his mother, Lillian, a 5-foot-9 basketball player in her younger days, rather than his father, Don, who had been a standout high school football player. By the time he enrolled at DeMatha as a sophomore, basketball was the sole focus of his athletic career. He had always been a natural scorer. "When I started playing at the Boys Club, I noticed I was the guy who scored all the points," Whittenburg said. "You watch a little league game and you'll see that kind of kid. I was that type. I could jump a little higher and run a little quicker than other guys my age."

Whittenburg's prep career was a preview of what he would do in college: as a junior, he and Lowe were reserves on a squad that went undefeated and was declared the best high school team in the country. As a senior, he suffered a broken foot that kept him out of action for nearly six weeks, but came back just in time to help DeMatha defend its city in the Maryland state championships. Even better, he finished off his All-America career by hitting game-winning shots in two star-studded high school all-star games.

Norman Sloan recruited Whittenburg to play for the Wolfpack as part of his D.C. trio of freshmen in 1979. Whittenburg was disappointed when the fiery coach left for Florida just after his freshman year, but he quickly took to Sloan's replacement, Jim Valvano. From their first meeting, the player and coach developed a bond that went well beyond his scoring average, his timely baskets, and his clutch free throws. The coach liked Whittenburg from the first time the young player walked into a team meeting with a briefcase and took a seat on the front row, two habits he brought with him from his regimented days at DeMatha. Whittenburg loved his battered briefcase. "It made me feel smarter," he said. And Valvano, the renaissance coach who did a little bit of everything, loved players who could follow more than just bouncing balls.

For years, as a player, a graduate assistant, and an assistant coach, Whittenburg treasured the hours he spent talking to Valvano about subjects unrelated to basketball, especially serious topics that Valvano loved to dissect: literature, economic theory, and politics. "The most vivid conversation I remember having with him was just prior to our senior year, when he showed me a nasty letter he got from a fan pertaining to the fact that we had an all-black starting five," Whittenburg said. "We talked about that extensively. What came out of that conversation was how important it was to get an education. He made me realize that I didn't want people to think I was just a dumb old athlete and that's all there was to me."

Whittenburg was one of the few members under Valvano's umbrella of followers who wasn't just around for the yuks. "I wasn't a funny kind of guy," Whittenburg said. "I wasn't there to tell jokes. I went to talk to him about life. I was interested in other things. He always told me that there is a lot more to [me] than bouncing balls. We talked about real stuff." The bond lasted until Valvano died of cancer in April 1993. Valvano chose Whittenburg as the only former player to be a pallbearer at his funeral. He has also been a part of Valvano's legacy as a member of the V Foundation's board of directors.

Whittenburg's relationship with Valvano inspired a detour from his intended path, the world of business. After one season working with NC State as a graduate assistant, Whittenburg caught the coaching bug—not because he wanted to win championships, but because he wanted to influence young people the way his coaches had influenced him. Whittenburg admits that he was a little too fiery as a kid and needed a guiding hand to keep his emotions in check. But even as an underclassman, he found joy in teaching young kids about the game of basketball.

Whittenburg's journey to become a head coach began not long after his playing days were over.

The Phoenix Suns took him in the third round of the 1983 NBA draft, in those euphoric days after NC State's fairytale run through the postseason. But Whittenburg wasn't destined to spend the next couple of decades in the NBA. He was given a brief shot, but his fire-plug body was not the prototype for shooting guards at the highest level of professional basketball. That came the next year, when Chicago selected North Carolina's Michael Jordan, the player who revolutionized the position and the sport.

It was obvious to Whittenburg that his future as a professional player was not guaranteed, at least not in the same way it was for the 6 foot, 11 inch Bailey, whose silky-smooth baseline jumper was a coveted skill for a big man. And Whittenburg was sure that he didn't want to follow the same path as his friend Lowe, who toiled for years in the Continental Basketball Association before getting a real shot at the NBA. "That is second rate to me," Whittenburg said in a 1985 story in the *Technician*. But Lowe's playmaking skills were always a valued commodity. Whittenburg was an undersized shooter and he was honest enough with himself to know that the CBA, the European leagues, and the NBA were all stocked with dozens of similar players. He spent a short time playing overseas in France, just long enough to realize he had no desire to trot the globe while waiting for a chance to sign a 10-day contract every now and then. "I didn't want to run down one long tunnel all my life hoping somebody would give me a chance," said Whittenburg. "Because what happens if it's a dead end? Then what do I do?" He wanted to get on with his life. Whittenburg enrolled at NC State for the 1984 fall semester to complete the 17 hours he needed for his business administration degree, thinking he would like to become a sales representative for a major corporation. Receiving that degree was always important to him. In 1985-86, he and Gannon joined Valvano's staff as graduate assistants. He outlasted Gannon, the son of a high school coach, in the profession when Gannon gave up his position to embark on his television broadcasting career.

Whittenburg had one-year assistant positions at George Mason and Long Beach State before he returned to NC State for a three-year stint as a fulltime assistant under Valvano. His career took some inevitable steps backward when Valvano was cut loose by NC State in the spring of 1990. The former player found a job at Colorado for three years, then moved back East with a one-year opportunity at West Virginia. In the spring of 1994, he found a way back to the ACC as an assistant coach for Georgia Tech's Bobby Cremins, a longtime friend of both Valvano and Morgan Wootten. "I did not know Dereck personally, but he showed me that he had a great enthusiasm for the game and a great work ethic," said Cremins, who is now the head coach at the College of Charleston. "I was impressed by his love of the game." The fact that Whittenburg's name was familiar to recruits and their families because of his role in NC State's national title didn't hurt. Whittenburg even helped the Yellow Jackets land sensational New York guard Stephon Marbury, a huge recruiting coup.

Cremins eventually recommended Whittenburg for his first head coaching job at Wagner College, a school on New York's Staten Island with no tangible basketball tradition. Prior to Whittenburg's arrival, it hadn't won a conference title in its 15 years in the Northeast Conference and had five consecutive losing seasons. His first team's only returning starter was a 5 foot, 9 inch point guard named Yves, for crying out loud. None of that mattered to Whittenburg, who guided the Seahawks to their first NCAA bid in school history in 2003. After four years of improving Wagner's record, he was hired to rebuild Fordham, a private school in the Bronx in need of a similar turnaround. In 2007, while his longtime friend Lowe led the Wolfpack to an appearance in the ACC Tournament title game and a berth in the National Invitation Tournament, Whittenburg guided his team to the most wins in school history and its first winning season in the Atlantic 10 Conference. "I am really proud of Dereck; he has done a fabulous job," Cremins said. "He has paid his dues." Lowe, who once offered Whittenburg a job as an assistant coach when he was head coach of the NBA's Vancouver Grizzlies, also believes Whittenburg will continue his successful coaching career. "We are cut from the same cloth—the way we approach the game, the way we think about the game, the players we like," Lowe said. "He does a great job. He's going to do well."

Whittenburg thinks so too, though winning a national championship is not his sole goal. Before he left Wagner, he watched six players make the Dean's List and his athletes record the highest grade-point average ever for the school's basketball team. "That's the equivalent of winning the national championship there," Whittenburg said. At Fordham, he has improved the team's record every year, including a 10-6 mark in the Atlantic-10 in 2007. But Whittenburg doesn't want to be measured simply by his team's on-court success. "I have a totally different agenda about why I coach," Whittenburg said. "I coach because I love coaching and what it does for kids, the impact it has on the kids, and what it is going to do for their lives. That's what does it for me. My experiences at NC State made me want to go out and be productive in life, to be an example out in the community. The real story is what you are doing after basketball and how did your experience help you be successful in something outside of athletics. I think college basketball has lost its way with that; it's 'win at all costs' and 'forget about the kids who graduate.' I think coaching is not about how many championships you win, it's about how many lives you empower and how many people you put out there who can be productive in society."

Still, Whittenburg doesn't believe his NCAA Tournament legacy is done, no more than he believed his playing career was over when he broke his foot in the winter of 1983. His Wagner team lost in its only NCAA Tournament game and he is still working to take Fordham there. It may take several more years and another rebuilding project to find the right team to replicate the Wolfpack's achievements in 1983. But he has worked too hard since his playing career at NC State ended with college basketball's most famous airball. His postseason story isn't yet finished. Lowe may have landed the dream job they both wanted, but Whittenburg is certain his years of preparation will lead him back to the enchanted territory on the game's biggest stage.

"I will be back [to the Final Four] someday as a coach," Whittenburg said.

4 "THAT WAS ENOUGH PUNISHMENT"

For 25 years, Lorenzo Charles has honorably taken the blame. Maybe that's why he was rewarded with the most fortuitous airball rebound and dunk in the history of the NCAA Tournament.

First, however, Charles became the game's most infamous pizza snatcher, though few people knew he had the help of three pepperoni-breath accomplices—if that's what you want to call them—on the night of May 30, 1982.

Charles, who had come to NC State as a still-impressionable 17-year-old freshman barely nine months earlier, was hanging out on the university's central campus with three additional athletes, including teammate Cozell McQueen. Some of the other basketball players had gone to see Rick James at Dorton Arena at the NC State Fairgrounds. But Charles, McQueen, Carl Hollingsworth, and Skip Hamilton were looking for other means of entertainment at one of the school's few women-only dormitories.

When they saw Domino's Pizza deliveryman Peter Gross carrying an insulated bag with two pizzas into the stairwell of Carroll, one of them yelled, "Hey, I ordered those pizzas." Gross turned around as someone other than Charles yelled, "Give me that pizza," and grabbed the insulated bag out of Gross' hands.

"I am sure the guy pees his leg and runs," said teammate Terry Gannon. "What was he going to do, chase after Lorenzo?"

They all scurried away. Hollingsworth and Hamilton left on foot, tossing the insulated bag into the bushes as they fled, while Charles and McQueen made their getaways on their trusty mopeds, legs dangling as they reached speeds of up to 15 miles per hour. The accomplices met up at the College Inn at the corner of Avent Ferry Road and Western Boulevard. It's hard to say which pair showed up first, the two football linemen running at full speed or the two lanky basketball players on their well-used mopeds. It would have been the most boring low-speed chase in criminal justice history, at least until O.J. Simpson tried to escape in a white Ford Bronco.

The four young college students shared the pizzas in Hollingsworth's room, though McQueen insisted he never ate a bite. For nearly two months, they laughed about their free meal, courtesy of the pizza deliveryman. But Gross happened to see Charles walking through the D.H. Hill Library on NC State's main campus in late July. He immediately recognized the well-cut, 6-foot-7 forward as one of his attackers seven weeks earlier. He drew up a complaint with NC State's Office of Public Safety on July 24, 1982. Later that day, Charles was charged with "larceny from person," a serious felony offense for which he could have been sentenced to 10 years in prison.

That fact was on his mother's mind when she flew down the next day to meet with her son and Wolfpack basketball coach Jim Valvano. Team manager Gary Bryant went to pick up Charles' mother at the airport and brought her back to Valvano's office at the Case Athletics Center.

"His mom was not happy," Bryant said. "She said, 'Gary, Coach, would you excuse us for a minute?' Coach V grabs me by the arm, leads me out, and closes the door. We hear the biggest commotion going on in that office you ever heard. We hear Lorenzo crying and his mother yelling.

"Coach V looks at me and says, 'I don't think we'll ever have a problem out of Lorenzo again.'"

And he didn't, thanks to the first of a series of fortunate breaks that led to the 1983 NCAA championship. Charles' good luck came from the fact that Wake County had just begun a felony diversion program. It dropped first-time offenders' charges if they completed a litany of probationary conditions within a year of entering the program.

Charles was placed in the program after he agreed to spend three 12-hour shifts in the Apex Municipal Jail, paying a total of $21 for his expenses while there. He agreed to pay Domino's Pizza $20 in restitution for two pizzas and an insulated bag. And he agreed to complete 300 hours of community service. For more than two months, Charles slogged away at his obligation, spending nearly 70 hours washing and waxing cars for the NC State Department of Public Safety. He didn't always show up on time or tidy up when he left, but Charles slowly worked off his debt, even as fall basketball practice began.

After giving both players heavy tongue-lashings, Valvano put Charles and McQueen on probation and promised school administrators he would immediately dismiss either of them if they were involved in any other matters on or off the court.

The incident received much attention around the Triangle, and Charles caught a great deal of grief. Valvano knew that the athlete would be in for a rough time on February 23, when the Wolfpack played at Duke. Blue Devil fans really were Cameron Crazies back then and were notoriously hard on opposing players who had run afoul of the law. In 1973, the Duke pep band greeted NC State center Tommy Burleson, who had been caught breaking into an on-campus pinball game, with a horn-heavy rendition of "Pinball Wizard." In 1984, the

Crazies threw panties and inflated condoms at Maryland's Herman Veal after he was accused of a sexual assault. The rich kids from Jersey loved looking down their blue-painted noses at NC State, the commoner's college just 25 miles away. Valvano, though, enjoyed their antics and figured the best way to neutralize them was to join in the fun. On his first trip to Cameron Indoor Stadium as the Wolfpack's head coach, he borrowed the starting offensive line from Monte Kiffin's football team and sat them behind the NC State bench in their red-and-white football jerseys. Another time, when he was greeted by a chorus of "Down with Jim! Down with Jim!" he ran into the stands—not to attack anyone, but to help start a new chant that even the Dukies could appreciate: "Down with Packer! Down with Packer!" referring to television analyst Billy Packer, who was calling the game that night. Valvano, the New York native, proclaimed many times that he loved the Duke fans because "they all talk like I do."

Valvano sat Charles down before the game and told him that the Duke students might have something special in store for him. The coach had been told by Duke officials that some students might drive up in a golf cart to deliver a pizza to the Wolfpack bench before the game. Valvano's only request was that it have pepperonis. But when Charles was introduced, the Duke students instead showered the court with dozens of empty pizza boxes, leaving the floor of Cameron Indoor Stadium ankle-deep in cardboard.

Charles was well prepared for a blistering reception, because it didn't come close to his teammates' ragging. They actually used the episode to create a little team chemistry.

"We had to take it seriously, of course, because it was an arrest and it brought bad publicity to the school," Gannon said. "But you think they gave him crap at Duke? It was nothing compared to what we did to him. Every situation we were in somehow came back to pizza or Domino's through some circuitous route. It was constant for the whole season."

NC State got the last laugh that night, thanks to outstanding performances by Charles, Lowe, and Bailey. Just days after upsetting North Carolina, the Wolfpack whipped the Blue Devils 96-79, with Charles scoring a then-career-high 13 points and grabbing five rebounds. At the time, it was Charles' best performance of the year.

Charles continued his community service responsibility throughout the season, but his duties became exponentially easier following the Wolfpack's NCAA championship. He was assigned to the North Carolina Department of Crime Control and Public Safety, with which he went to community centers around the Triangle to teach kids basketball skills and to talk to them about staying out of trouble. Those were particularly popular following the 1983 NCAA Tournament. In the end, Charles actually worked an additional 27 hours above and beyond his 300-hour requirement.

"He was the most visible client I've ever worked with," said C. Robert Sorrels, Charles' counselor in the felony diversion program, in the August 9, 1983, edition of the *Raleigh Times*. "That was put to good use. He is a magnet for youth. They swarm around him wherever he goes."

To this day, Charles has never publicly spoken of his three abettors in the pizza theft.

"That's just who Lorenzo is," said Sidney Lowe. "He wasn't going to tell on the other guys. No one had to sit him down and tell him that, either. He took the responsibility for being there that night, and V felt that was enough punishment."

LORENZO CHARLES

Early in the 1982-83 season, Lorenzo Charles would not have made the dunk that is remembered for capping off the Wolfpack's upset of Houston in the NCAA championship game. For one thing, Charles might not have even been around to try. For another, he needed an additional full season of on-court maturity before becoming bold enough to make such a play in a big game.

The powerful but timid youngster from Brooklyn, New York, came south to develop his body, his confidence, and his game. By the end of his career, Charles had transformed into an All-America and first-team All-ACC athlete who finished second in the ACC Player of the Year race to Maryland's Len Bias—an astonishing career for the most lightly regarded member of Jim Valvano's first full recruiting class.

Like so many other important advances during the 1982-83 season, the catalyst for Charles' improvement was Dereck Whittenburg's broken foot. With the senior guard out of the lineup for 14 games in January and February, Charles had no choice but to step up to provide other scoring options for the Wolfpack offense. Otherwise, he might have suffered a few broken fingers—not from a New York wise guy, but by a quickly zipped pass from point guard Sidney Lowe.

"What changed for Lorenzo is that we just started throwing him the ball more," Valvano said near the end of his team's postseason run. "At first, he tried to dunk everything. A little child would walk by and Lorenzo would try to dunk him. We had to get him to understand that he didn't have to."

By the end of the year, Lorenzo was begging for the ball, a welcome change for Valvano, who never understood shrinking violets, and for Charles' teammates. They helped goad him from a player who averaged exactly 6.0 points and 4.5 rebounds in the Wolfpack's first 22 games into a budding beast who nearly doubled that production over the last 14 games of the season (11.4 points and 8.3 rebounds), hitting double figures in points eight times and in rebounds five times. The change began shortly after Whittenburg's injury. Charles started arriving an hour early for practice to work on his basketball and mental skills. "I was not playing well early in the season because I wasn't concentrating," Charles said during the NCAA Tournament. "I wasn't concentrating. That's what I needed to do more than anything."

Charles did have a great deal on his mind. He was arrested in the summer before his sophomore year for stealing a couple of pizzas from a deliveryman on NC State's campus, a New York prank that had serious consequences in Raleigh. He faced felony charges and up to two years in prison, but was saved from the justice system due to a new program in Raleigh's Wake County that allowed each first-time offender to enter a felony-diversion program to expunge the arrest from his record. Otherwise, Charles may not have been on the team at all his sophomore year. He spent much of the preseason washing squad cars for NC State's Department of Public Safety as part of his 300 hours of community service.

"I think that helped me mature," Charles told Ira Berkow of the *New York Times* in the weeks after the national title. "Before that, I didn't take things as seriously as I do now. Like basketball. I began to concentrate more."

When the season began, Charles was in a fight for the starting power forward position with transfer Alvin Battle, a Rocky Mount, North Carolina, native who arrived in the off-season from Merced (California) Junior College. Battle was the reigning California junior college player of the year.

Valvano saw Charles' potential—not just as a rebounder and defender but as a shooter who could occasionally step away from the basket and make a big shot. And Charles had one big advantage over Battle—his incredibly soft hands allowed him the ability to catch Lowe's pinpoint passes in perfect scoring position.

But he did not always contribute. "To tell you the truth, Lorenzo wouldn't go all out all the time," said teammate Thurl Bailey. "He would accept the fact that someone blocked him out or that he got tired. We had to holler at him at times. There would be no expression on his face. We told him if he wanted to play, he had to take the ball inside and score. He knew we had to go to him. He knew we needed the inside game with Dereck out. At one time, he and Cozell were averaging about six points a game. Then, in the Carolina game we played at Reynolds, there was a point where Lorenzo went up for a shot and missed. He took it up three more times. I think that was the beginning of when things turned around for him."

By the time the postseason arrived, Charles was a scoring and rebounding machine—an inside force who relieved pressure from outside shooters like Whittenburg, Terry Gannon, Sidney Lowe, and Thurl Bailey. And he proved himself capable of performing in pressure situations.

In the first round of the ACC Tournament in Atlanta, Charles drew a foul from Wake Forest's Alvis Rogers with three seconds to play and the score tied at 70. He missed his first foul shot, but made the second to give the Wolfpack a one-point win. In Ogden, Utah, NC State trailed by a point against Virginia and mighty Ralph Sampson. Charles hit a pair of free throws for a one-point victory. And in the championship game in Albuquerque, Charles found himself in the wrong place at the right time with just seconds to play and stuffed home Dereck Whittenburg's 28-foot airball for the winning points against Houston. The shot will forever be associated with the drama and excitement of the NCAA Tournament.

Charles is surprised that the offensive rebound he made that snowy night in Albuquerque is still a conversation piece in college basketball.

"Here it is more than 20 years later, and people are still talking about it," he said. "When it happened, I thought I would have my little 15 minutes of fame and that would be it."

But between the time he dunked the ball and greeted a roaring crowd the next afternoon at Reynolds Coliseum, Charles had made another transformation: from a role player to a Wolfpack hero.

Charles, born in Panama, was a product of the Starrett City section of Brooklyn, New York. He was raised in much more of a middle-class section of the city than even Valvano, who grew up in the mostly Italian neighborhood of Corona in Queens. Charles' father, Herman, worked at a meat-packing plant and his mother, Sylvia, was a typist.

He was smart enough to secure a spot at Brooklyn Technical High School, a prestigious public school that specializes in engineering, math, and science for individuals who pass a rigorous testing process. He showed the potential to become a powerful basketball player, but recruiters were not wearing out the concrete to get to him. A handful of other basketball schools were interested in Charles besides NC State—most prominently Massachusetts, Maryland, DePaul, St. John's, and Syracuse. Valvano was mildly interested early in the recruiting season, but later backed away. A phone call from Wolfpack assistant coach Ray Martin in the early spring rekindled the athlete's interest in NC State. Charles was the sleepiest of sleepers when he signed as part of a recruiting class that included prep All-Americans Walter "Dinky" Proctor, Cozell McQueen, and Mike Warren, along with a baseball pitcher/shooting guard named Terry Gannon. But after he made himself bigger and better, Charles had a greater impact than any of his classmates.

He arrived in Raleigh as a baby-faced 17-year-old, immature in many ways. He had great strength, but it was all natural and undeveloped. And he was not in very good shape. "When he first came here," Valvano said during Charles' junior season, "he couldn't run up and down the court three times without grabbing a blow." Charles had never stepped foot in a weight room before he arrived at NC State and, even after his freshman season, rarely lifted weights.

But Charles, a natural introvert, needed to escape the spotlight following his game-winning dunk against Houston in the 1983 NCAA championship game. He retreated with McQueen to the weight room, where he became obsessed with improving his natural strength. He fell in love with squats, clean jerks, and pull-ups wearing a 50-pound belt. From the end of his sophomore season to the beginning of his junior season, Charles added 15 pounds of muscle to his already toned physique. At 6-foot-7 and 239 pounds, Charles no longer had reason to be timid. In fact, he became a beast.

Throughout the next two seasons, Charles was one of the ACC's most feared players, a powerful inside scorer and rebounder who had the ability to step outside and hit an 18-foot jump shot. Few other power forwards could guard him. As a junior, he was good enough to consider leaving early for the NBA, but opted to return for his senior year. He averaged more than 18 points a game those final two seasons and was twice named First-Team All-ACC.

"Lorenzo's story is a great one because he didn't come with all the credentials," Valvano told student reporter Scott Keepfer prior to Charles' senior season at NC State. "He was not that highly recruited. He was not everybody's All-America this or all-that team. He came to NC State basically undersized. Now . . . he's considered one of the best power forwards in America. I've seen Lorenzo grow and become a man. To watch him grow from that 17-year-old kid in Brooklyn to become the man he is today was really rewarding. That is something to live for—to see a kid develop. It is one of the most delightful parts of my profession."

Charles expected to make the same kind of impact in the NBA, just as contemporary Charles Barkley—an undersized power forward even shorter than Charles—was with the Philadelphia 76ers. And that's what others expected, too.

"I used to sit back and watch him when I was playing in the NBA and tell guys that I played with, 'You better watch out—Lorenzo is coming,'" said Sidney Lowe. "He had all the footwork, all the moves, all the mental aspects of the game. He just got better and better until he was a beast."

But Charles—taken by the Atlanta Hawks in the second round of the 1985 NBA as the 41st overall pick—was about three inches too short to make the kind of impact at power forward that Lowe had predicted. He was not quite quick enough to be an effective small forward. He was not such a tenacious rebounder as Charles Barkley, who overcame his 6-foot-6 height to become one of the game's most productive and popular players.

"Size is a big deal in the NBA, but I think desire is something you should measure a player on," Charles said. "In the NBA, everybody doesn't get an equal shot. When you are not drafted in the first round, you don't get as much opportunity to be successful. For me, going in the second round, opportunities for playing time were few and far between. You have to wait your turn, and sometimes that turn never comes."

So Charles went looking for it. He played only one season with the Hawks, averaging just three points and one rebound per game. He spent the next 12 years as a basketball nomad, traveling the globe in search of a team that needed his unique skills. He played in the Italian, British, Swedish, Turkish, Uruguayan, and Argentine professional leagues. He played for the Raleigh Bullfrogs in the short-lived Global Basketball Association and for the Rapid City and Quad City entries in the Continental Basketball Association.

"You more or less go where the job is," Charles said.

He retired in 1999 and returned to Wake Forest, North Carolina, about 20 miles north of the NC State campus. He drives a mini-coach passenger van for a Raleigh-based limousine service and is a regular fixture at Wolfpack basketball games, especially now that Lowe has returned as the school's head basketball coach.

Charles is as surprised as anyone that his 15 minutes of fame have not completely faded away. But his dunk will remain the video clip that defines March Madness.

"Lorenzo is famous *forever*," said former teammate Mike Warren. "No doubt that clip will always be shown when they play the NCAA Tournament."

Lowe believes it is fitting that Charles—whose bright, beaming smile is a welcome sight for his former teammates—is remembered for something other than a youthful mistake.

"Somehow, good things happen to good people," Lowe said. "It comes in different quantities and on different levels. But certainly making that dunk was something great that happened to Lorenzo. He will be remembered forever as the guy who dunked the basketball to win the national championship and not the guy who robbed a pizza delivery guy."

"A TEAM GOOD ENOUGH FOR THE FINAL FOUR"

5

O ther than Lorenzo Charles' pizza caper, the summer of 1982 could not have gone much better for Jim Valvano. The NCAA allowed each conference to adopt any number of experimental rules in an effort to spice up the game of college basketball. It was an unconventional reaction to the uproar caused by the 1982 Atlantic Coast Conference Tournament championship game, when two of the best teams in the country, North Carolina and Virginia, spent almost the entire game dribbling time off the clock. College basketball had become an overthought chess match, and fans were turned off by it.

In May, after heated debates at the annual meetings in Myrtle Beach, South Carolina, the ACC coaches adopted a set of experimental rules that clearly favored the Wolfpack: a 19-foot three-point line and a 30-second shot clock that would be turned off at the four-minute mark of every game. Valvano had long been a proponent of these rules, but he thought both the clock and the shot should be longer. North Carolina coach Dean Smith, however, liked the plan, and the rest of the league's coaches agreed, giving the ACC the shortest shot and quickest clock of any of the 14 conferences that adopted experimental rules in conference play. Strangely enough, Valvano became one of the two coaches who voted against the rules he had fought so hard for the league to consider.

Wolfpack senior Dereck Whittenburg, who had publicly lobbied the ACC for a three-point shot, was also a little disappointed at the proximity of the line, which dipped inside the top of the key and was just 17 feet, 9 inches away from the front of the rim. "Where the line is, inside the top of the circle, it's a normal shot for a lot of people," Whittenburg said. "There are a lot of players, forwards and centers too, in our league who can shoot from that range. I hope in the future they will move the line back to the 20-foot range. That way, it will really reward just the long-range shooter."

Still, everyone in the league knew Whittenburg would be deadly with the new rules. The picture on the Wolfpack's 1982-83 pocket schedule was of Whittenburg, along with the caption "Little D Bombs for 3."

Terry Gannon was excited. He read about the proposed rules while at home in Joliet, Illinois, and immediately drew a circle 19 feet from his backyard basket. For the rest of the summer, the son of a high school basketball coach took 1,000 shots a day from behind the arc he had drawn in the dirt. "Even my dad thought I was crazy," he said.

Valvano hired two new assistant coaches, Tom Abatemarco from Virginia Tech and Ed McLean from Raleigh's Needham Broughton High School. Abatemarco, known to be a dogged recruiter, was a member of Valvano's staff at Iona. During his 17 years at Broughton, McLean had coached both "Pistol" Pete Maravich and Phil Spence, a member of NC State's 1974 NCAA championship team. Another one of his high school All-America selections, Mike Warren, signed the year before to play for the Wolfpack. McLean was also closely tied to NC State as a longtime counselor at summer camps run by Everett Case, Press

Maravich, and Norm Sloan.

Thinking ahead, Valvano put together one of the nation's toughest schedules, including games against three of the previous four national champions: Michigan State at home, Louisville on the road, and North Carolina both at home and on the road. It also featured home games against Notre Dame and Memphis State and road trips to Missouri and the Meadowlands in New Jersey to play West Virginia. Valvano deemed it to be a perfect test for a veteran team.

"We don't have our all-Catholic schedule anymore," Valvano said at ACC's Operation Basketball. "Last year, we played St. Peter's, St. Francis, and Loyola of Maryland and got off to a nice 12-1 start. But it won't be that way this year."

It was a season of change for Reynolds Coliseum as well. The upper-balcony seats, dark green in color since the building opened in 1949, were painted bright red. The synthetic playing floor was resurfaced and repainted. And the scorers table and team benches were switched from the west sidelines to the east sidelines.

The Wolfpack played three red-and-white intra-squad scrimmages, one in Reynolds Coliseum, one at Rocky Mount High School, and one at Page High School in Greensboro. And Valvano felt just as strongly about the short three-point line afterward as he had in the spring.

"At halftime of our first red-and-white game, my mom came down out of the stands and hit three out of four," Valvano told the reporters at the annual Operation Basketball in Greensboro.

Because the Wolfpack's senior backcourt of Whittenburg and Lowe was so suited for the new rules and because senior Thurl Bailey was an excellent outside shooter, Valvano's team was picked to finish third in the ACC in a preseason media poll. The Associated Press had the Wolfpack ranked No. 16 in the preseason. So, despite the fact that some people swear NC State was picked to finish in the lower half of the ACC prior to the 1982-83 season, the team was actually expected to be Valvano's best in three seasons in Raleigh. The *Sporting News* even gushed, "The Wolfpack would likely be a preseason favorite in many conferences. Look for NC State to upset Virginia and North Carolina during the season." Little did anyone expect that the Pack would also knock off three other teams ranked ahead of it and two teams picked right behind it in the preseason top 20 poll.

"We had three seniors that were damned good players," Terry Gannon said in a 2006 interview. "We thought we would be pretty good. It was a team from the start run by those three guys. V really put a lot of responsibility on their shoulders. Thurl had yet to become the player that he was going to become. His senior year is when he really blossomed. We had two great college guards—as good a backcourt as there was in the country. I would take that backcourt to war any day against any team."

Late in the season-opening win against Western Carolina, Lowe was approaching the school record of 15 assists. The guy who owned the record, Max Perry, happened to be sitting on the Wolfpack bench in his only season as one of Valvano's graduate assistants.

Perry had transferred to NC State from Oklahoma after his freshman year to play for Norm Sloan, arriving as part of the same recruiting class as Lowe, Whittenburg, and Bailey. However, Perry left one distinguishing mark in his career. It came during Lowe's sophomore season, when the starting point guard missed two games due to a stress fracture in his foot. Perry stepped in as Lowe's backup to help the Pack beat East Carolina and Georgia Tech, a couple of highlights in an otherwise mediocre season. Against the Pirates, Perry dished out 15 assists to break the single-game school record.

So in the high-scoring opening game of 1982-83, played against in-state opponent Western Carolina using the ACC's experimental rules, Lowe had amassed double-digit assists, and Perry was on the sidelines sweating. "Any player who tells you he wants to see someone break a record that [he owns] is lying through his teeth," Perry said.

With just a few minutes left in what turned out to be a 103-66 blowout, Perry sidled up to Valvano on the bench. "Coach, I think you ought to get Sidney out of there before he gets hurt," Perry said.

"Maxie," Valvano said. "I will take him out—right after he breaks your record."

Lowe finished the game with 18 assists, a school record that lasted until 1991, when Chris Corchiani surpassed it by two. Gannon made the first three-pointer in ACC history, the first of 53 he would make in just 17 games using the experimental rules. Whittenburg made six three-pointers in the game and freshman Ernie Myers made his collegiate debut with a stellar 18 points.

The next two games were also big wins in Reynolds Coliseum: a 100-70 victory over North Carolina A&T (with the experimental rules) and a 57-49 win over East Carolina (without the rules). Freshman George McClain, Valvano's first backcourt player off the bench in the first three games, suffered a severely twisted ankle against the Pirates, opening up the door for Gannon, who saw more playing time than he had in the first three games.

Valvano was curious as to how his team would handle the next two games. Michigan State and Louisville had both won national championships over the last four years. The Wolfpack beat a Spartans team featuring Scott Skiles, Kevin Willis, and Sam Vincent at home thanks to a defensive play late in the game by little-used reserve Harold Thompson. But it lost at Louisville when the Wolfpack backcourt failed to convert Lowe's pair of steals into points. Still, Valvano saw something he had not expected: sophomores Lorenzo Charles and Cozell McQueen, who had combined to score just 17 points in the season's first three games, showed a spark against a frontcourt that featured brothers Scooter and Rodney McCray and center Charles Jones. The coach knew if his two young players were properly pushed, they would continue to improve.

When the team returned home after its loss to the Cardinals, Valvano gathered his players at midcourt at Reynolds Coliseum and told them something they could scarcely believe. "From what I saw from you guys in the game last night, this is a team that is good enough to make it to the Final Four," he said.

They just were not ready to believe him yet.

COZELL McQUEEN

Just the mention of Cozell McQueen still makes people smile.

Fans continue to remember those lasting images of the 6-foot-11 center from Bennettsville, South Carolina: his grimace after each foul called against him; that "thing" on his right shoulder; his stance atop the basket at the Pit in Albuquerque, New Mexico, immediately after the Wolfpack won the 1983 national championship, his arms stretched to the sky as his sister yelled, "Junior, get down from there. You're going to hurt yourself!"

No one smiles broader, though, than McQueen's former teammates. Whether he wanted to be or not, McQueen was the comic relief on a team full of comedians, starting right at the top with head coach Jim Valvano. They dearly loved to poke fun at the lanky, left-handed center with limited offensive skills but an unlimited capacity for challenging some of the biggest names in college basketball.

Valvano loved telling people that McQueen chose NC State because he always wanted to "go up north" to play college basketball. Former NC State history professor William Beezley remembers the day McQueen uttered that one-liner for the ages in his "History of American Sport" class, though McQueen denies he ever said it. In NC State player lore, the comment ranks right up there with Charles Shackleford's declaration that he could shoot right-handed or left-handed. "I am amphibious," Shackleford declared. Other recruiting stories have circulated about the 185-pound broomstick that he swears are not true. Like when the University of Houston called to recruit him and he asked what state the school was in. Or how he put off Valvano for an extra week before committing to the Wolfpack because he wanted to take another trip to a big city—Toledo, Ohio—before making his decision.

By the time he arrived in Raleigh, the Great Red North, in the summer of 1981, the affable McQueen had already assumed his role as a team punching bag—a gullible youngster from South Carolina's backwoods who always generated the opportunity for a good laugh. He never saw himself that way, of course. In his eyes, he was just misunderstood because of his Palmetto State roots.

"It seems to me that people think everybody from South Carolina is slow and behind," McQueen told student reporter Devin Steele in the fall of 1984, as the athlete was about to enter his senior season. "I know I am quite intelligent, or I wouldn't be here. I consider myself smarter than a regular student. Some regular students can't even do their work. People just say if you are from South Carolina, you are a dummy and you don't know what you are doing. If you come from a big city or something, people give you the benefit of the doubt. They don't know if you are dumb or not."

McQueen liked to remind people that he was not some South Carolina hick—he was actually born in Paris, France, where his father was serving a stint in the military. The family eventually moved back to Fayetteville, North Carolina, and spent a little time in Georgia. "I have lived all over the world," McQueen declared as he entered his final season with the Wolfpack. And that was certainly true. But the McQueen family settled down in South Carolina right after McQueen's father left the Army. Cozell, the international wanderer, was 18 months old. He spent the next 17 years there, realizing a prep All-America career at Bennettsville High School, until he headed north to become a favorite target of teammates and opposing fans alike.

When McQueen arrived the summer before his freshman season, he, Mike Warren, and Walter "Dinky" Proctor went to Fuquay-Varina to apply for summer jobs. While filling out the job application, McQueen was unsure of whom to list as personal references. These were wholly unnecessary, since the minimum-wage job was through a huge NC State supporter who liked employing Wolfpack basketball players to work in his textile mill. But McQueen didn't want any blank spaces on the application. "Yo, Mike," McQueen said to Warren. "Can I use your references, too?"

After the three received their first paychecks, Proctor went to Barnett Suzuki in downtown Raleigh and bought a top-of-the-line moped to ride around NC State's sprawling campus. McQueen was impressed. He asked Warren to take him downtown to pick one out as well. McQueen, who came from a retired military family of modest means, didn't have as much to spend, so he asked to see a used moped. According to Warren, McQueen picked out the dirtiest, most beat-up bike on the lot and negotiated what he thought was a fair price, about $200. When the deal was done, McQueen pulled out a new $10 bill.

"What's that?" the salesman asked.

"My down payment," McQueen said.

The salesman laughed, but agreed to finance the moped. McQueen spent the next four years chugging around campus with his feet on the pedals and his knees near his chin, only adding to his legacy as the class clown.

His teammates constantly preyed on McQueen's small-town gullibility. During the 1982 ACC Tournament, senior Scott Parzych called McQueen in his hotel room, pretending to be a sportswriter who had it on good authority that McQueen was about to be named ACC Rookie of the Year. Never mind that McQueen hadn't started a single game all season long, that he was averaging just 2.3 points and 2.4 rebounds a game, and that his primary competition was a newcomer at North Carolina named Michael Jordan. McQueen was convinced. He didn't discover it was a joke until the next day in a team meeting.

Just about every one of McQueen's former teammates has a similar story. Walk-on forward Tommy DiNardo remembers a discussion the players had before the 1983 season about the fun they were going to have on the road, staying in nice hotels and dining in elegant restaurants on the university's expense account. "I can't wait to order me a good T-bone," one of the players said. "I'm thinking about a nice ribeye," another said. "I'm going to get a filet mignon," chimed in another. "Man," McQueen chimed in, "I don't want none of that stuff. I'm getting a steak."

Sportswriters who covered NC State's championship season say that one of their favorite moments was running into McQueen late the night before the Wolfpack was scheduled to play Virginia in the NCAA East Regional championship game. McQueen had a girl under each of his extra-long arms and was enjoying what little Mormon-tinted nightlife there was in Ogden, Utah. "Cozell," one of them asked, "aren't you worried about playing Ralph [Sampson] tomorrow? Shouldn't you be back in the room?" McQueen didn't break stride as he said, "Let Ralph worry about me."

Apparently, Sampson didn't worry enough, even though he outscored McQueen 23-0 the next afternoon. After Cavalier forward Tim Mullen missed a shot that would have given his team the lead with just seconds to play, McQueen boxed Sampson completely out

70

of the picture and grabbed the rebound that secured the Wolfpack's trip to the Final Four.

In Albuquerque, McQueen put on a performance that is greatly overlooked, but was as important as anything else that happened that weekend to put the Wolfpack in a position to win the title. He grabbed a career-high 13 rebounds against Georgia. He held Bulldogs center Terry Fair to just two-of-nine shooting and five points. "He's an animal," Fair said of McQueen after the game. "He plays like an animal." Later, a reporter asked McQueen to name the ACC's best center. McQueen thought for a minute and declared himself the winner. "What about Ralph Sampson?" an incredulous reporter asked of the Cavaliers' three-time national player of the year. "Ralph ain't in the ACC no more," McQueen said.

Two nights later, McQueen went toe to toe with Houston's Akeem Abdul Olajuwon, grabbing 12 rebounds and playing a huge role in keeping Akeem from taking control of the game's tempo. "He played his tail off," said Sidney Lowe, the former State point guard who returned as the Wolfpack's head coach in 2006. "He wasn't afraid."

That was certainly the case when he volunteered to go in at the end of the Wolfpack's victory over North Carolina near the conclusion of the 1983 regular season. No one on the court could make the front end of a one-and-one, and a frustrated Valvano looked at his bench and screamed, "Can anyone here make a free throw?" McQueen, a 57.6 percent shooter that season, raised his hand. Sure enough, he drained a pair of foul shots to seal the landmark 70-63 victory—Valvano's first over North Carolina. And he never let the gravity of the Wolfpack's desperate times get the best of him.

"Me, nervous?" McQueen told Thad Mumau of the *Fayetteville Observer* during the Final Four. "I've never been nervous; I just go out and play."

Olajuwon played well early in the national championship game, but McQueen shut him down in the second half. The 7-foot All-America center made just one field goal and two free throws in the game's final 14 minutes, and McQueen outrebounded him 9-7 after intermission. After the game, "McQueen" was the first name Houston coach Guy Lewis mentioned. "He knows how to play defense," Lewis said. "In the last 10 minutes, he was our biggest problem."

Big performances against the game's biggest names were the hallmark of McQueen's four-year career with the Wolfpack: the left-handed shooter was never a threat to throw in 20 points, but he always rose to the occasion when he had to play defense and rebound against some of the nation's best big men. He went toe to toe with Sampson and Olajuwon as a sophomore. As a senior, he shut down Southern Methodist's Jon Koncak in a nationally televised upset at Reynolds Coliseum.

"The thing about Co is he is someone who didn't know any better," Lowe said. "When he stepped on the floor against Ralph, Co thought he was better. Consequently, he played that way. The great thing about him was that he always understood his game and his role—to rebound and play defense. He was always unselfish in that way. He didn't care about scoring."

Of course, McQueen would call for the ball on occasion, and every now and then Lowe would accommodate him. "He wanted to touch it every now and then," Lowe said. "That was all. We would come down the floor and I would say, 'You and me, big fella.' I would throw it in to him and he would do his thing where he pats the ball real hard, dribbles it once, and throws it back out. That kept him happy."

As a junior, McQueen played hurt after injuring his shoulder while lifting weights. As a senior, he and Lorenzo Charles played with Russell Pierre to give the Wolfpack an outstanding front line. Valvano's team returned to Albuquerque for the West Regional finals, but lost a heartbreaker to St. John's. McQueen never averaged in double figures throughout his collegiate career. In the summer of 1985, the athlete was the 91st pick in the NBA draft, taken by the Milwaukee Bucks as the 24th pick of the fourth round. Deemed an offensive liability, McQueen was cut in training camp and he headed to Spain to play in the European professional leagues. He spent some time in the Continental Basketball Association and once signed a 10-day contract with the Detroit Pistons, but his NBA career lasted only three games.

Yet McQueen was still good for a few belly laughs. Two NBA beat writers from North Carolina, John DeLong and Richard Walker, were in Corvallis, Oregon, in the early 1990s, covering a Charlotte Hornets-Portland Trailblazers preseason exhibition game at Gill Coliseum. McQueen was trying to make the Trailblazers' roster, and DeLong and Walker, both NC State graduates, naturally did a story on McQueen's return to the same floor on which he scored the famous basket off Dereck Whittenburg's missed free throw to send the opening-round game into a second overtime. As the reporters reminisced about the 1983 championship and NC State's victories over Pepperdine and Nevada-Las Vegas, McQueen appeared suddenly confused. He had no idea why they were bringing up such ancient history until one of them said, "Cozell, this is where you beat Pepperdine and UNLV; this is where it all started."

"Damn," McQueen said, looking around the locker room with a new perspective, "I thought this place looked familiar."

He enjoyed eight successful seasons overseas, including one year in his "native" France. When the championship team gathered for its emotional 10-year reunion at Reynolds Coliseum in February 1993, the day a dying Valvano said goodbye to his players in front of a sold-out arena, McQueen was near Venice, Italy, playing professionally. He sent 83 long-stem red roses to Pam Valvano to apologize for this absence.

Once his basketball career ended, McQueen settled in Cary, North Carolina, just outside of Raleigh. He has dipped his hands into many different business ventures, including youth basketball camps and a minor-league basketball team. In 1999, he promoted a heavyweight boxing match between James "Bonecrusher" Smith and Larry Holmes at the Crown Center in Fayetteville, North Carolina, an event that unfortunately shared the sporting spotlight with the first U.S. Open played at Pinehurst No. 2, a half-hour away. The event gained a little notoriety when the two boxers actually got into a fistfight over who had to weigh in first. (Neither of the heavyweights tipped the scales at less than 250 pounds.) Sadly, what sports fans tend to remember about that weekend is the late Payne Stewart's 25-foot putt for birdie on the 72nd hole to win the Open, not the fight between a pair of overweight codgers that had to be stopped in the eighth round because of Smith's shoulder injury.

Asked if it might have been a bad idea to schedule the fight on the same weekend as one of golf's four majors, McQueen gave a perfect Cozell answer: "They don't play golf at night."

McQueen's reputation as a class clown continues to endure for Wolfpack fans and the athlete's former teammates. But he remains connected to the program, especially since Lowe returned as head coach in May 2006. McQueen was one of a handful of members of the 1983 championship team who attended the press conference where Lowe was announced as the new head coach. McQueen declared on that day, "We are like a family again." Lowe, who had his share of laughs at McQueen's expense, appreciated the sentiment of his slap-and-pass teammate.

"Cozell wasn't really a punching bag for everyone," Lowe said. "He was just a guy who grew up in a smaller town who didn't know as much as the other guys in terms of being aware when someone was being sarcastic. You could always pull the wool over his eyes back then, which is why, I think, you can't get anything past him now."

While Lowe was shaking hands and greeting friends, a group of reporters asked McQueen if he could still climb on top of the backboard as he did on that glorious night in Albuquerque so many years ago. "Sure," McQueen said, and he began to demonstrate how he and Ernie Myers had pulled themselves up to a standing position on the rim. The reporters stopped him before he created a headline-stealing scene, but McQueen was confident that he could still do it.

Just as he guarded Sampson and Olajuwon on consecutive weekends in 1983, McQueen wasn't afraid to try.

HAROLD THOMPSON

It is not that Harold Thompson hides the fact that he was a member of NC State's 1983 national championship team. He wears his ring proudly. His office is loaded with NC State memorabilia. When he gets a little wistful for home, he winds up the miniature wolf on his office desk and listens to the school's fight song. But in Texas, where he has lived since 1994, most people are football fans. Many of them get excited when they see the burly 6-foot-5 former forward, thinking he might have been a linebacker in his youth. And the few who will admit that they are also loyal basketball fans were likely rooting for the Wolfpack's opponent in the title game.

Being a basketball transplant in a football world has afforded few opportunities for Thompson, a reserve defensive specialist on the 1983 team, to talk up his bit role in one of college basketball's lasting Cinderella stories.

The former junior high and high school basketball coach rarely mentions it, even when he is instructing dozens of kids each summer in his church's recreational league. And they receive pretty good instruction at Mt. Olive Baptist Church in Arlington, Texas: Danny Worthy, brother of Basketball Hall of Famer James Worthy, has also helped Thompson with the recreational team. But with work, community activities, and a new family—Thompson and his wife, Diane, have been married since 2000 and just welcomed their second child in March 2007—the athlete doesn't have much time to reminisce.

"I just have so many things going on in my life right now that are far more important that consume a lot of my time, like working at the church and serving in the community," said the relocated native of Raeford, North Carolina. "We do a lot in working with people who are less fortunate. And my job consumes a lot of my time."

Thompson is a senior admissions representative at Sanford-Brown Institute, the world's second-largest education provider, operating medical training programs at universities, colleges, institutions, and online schools in more than 20 locations throughout the United States. He's also been a teacher, a junior high and high school basketball coach, the head of the dropout prevention office at his alma mater, Hoke County High School, and the owner of his own security company.

But even if he doesn't bring it up very often, Thompson often thinks about that magical run to the national championship and his role in helping the Wolfpack get there. Though his playing time was limited—the Wolfpack only played seven players for most of the season and Thompson saw only two minutes of action in the entire NCAA Tournament—Thompson had a huge impact on two victories in 1983, over Michigan State and North Carolina in the ACC Tournament. And had he not made a quick defensive adjustment on Tar Heels star Sam Perkins at the end of regulation in the ACC semifinal game against North Carolina, the Wolfpack may never have received an invitation to the NCAA Tournament.

"I want role players to come in and execute their roles," Jim

Valvano once said of Thompson and the rest of his bench. "Harold does that. He comes in and plays excellent defense."

Depending on how you look at it, Thompson was either Valvano's first or Norm Sloan's last basketball recruit at NC State. Sloan originally contacted Thompson, a lifelong Wolfpack fan and Converse All-American at Hoke County High School in Raeford, to play for the Wolfpack before he left Raleigh for Florida following the 1979-80 season.

"My concern was that he was going to leave," Thompson said. "He told me he was not going to leave. At the last moment, he called me and told me he was leaving and he asked me if I would be interested in going to Florida with him."

Thompson turned down that opportunity, just as he had turned down then-Hoke County coach Rodney Johnson's offer to relocate to the North Carolina mountains when Johnson took the job at Asheville High School following Thompson's freshman year. When it came time for college, Thompson was not interested in straying too far from home. His father had just died on May 22, 1980, and Thompson, the youngest of 10 children, had to be convinced to leave his family at such a difficult time. But when Valvano, who had just been hired a week earlier to replace Sloan, came to visit Thompson's home, his mother gave her son the go-ahead to become the Wolfpack's only freshman that season.

Following 1979, which may have represented the greatest crop of high school talent to ever graduate to college basketball, Thompson's senior class was lean on talent. He was considered one of the ACC's top 10 recruits in 1980, behind North Carolina's Sam Perkins and Matt Doherty, Maryland's Steve Rivers and Charlie Pittman, and Clemson's Clarke Bynum.

Thompson's credentials were legitimate. He had averaged more than 22 points and 10 rebounds per game as a senior at Hoke County. As a sophomore and junior, he had played for another coach who would go on to win an NCAA championship. Former High Point College star Orlando "Tubby" Smith, who guided Kentucky to the 1998 NCAA championship in his initial season with the Wildcats, coached Thompson during those two seasons before embarking on his college coaching career as an assistant under J.D. Barnett at Virginia Commonwealth.

Smith advised Thompson not to go to NC State when he graduated, but Thompson refused to listen. He had grown up a diehard Wolfpack fan—how could a basketball player named "Thompson" not want to play for the Wolfpack after three-time national player of the year David Thompson (no relation) led the team to a pair of ACC titles and the 1974 NCAA championship?—even though he spent most of his summers and a few falls attending basketball camp and preseason practices at the University of North Carolina in Chapel Hill.

Smith and other coaches told the athletic Thompson, quite correctly in hindsight, that he would not flourish in Valvano's half-court system. His shooting liabilities made it difficult for him to contribute as a wing. However, Thompson was content to be a role player, someone who came off the bench to offer a couple of possessions of intense defense before giving way to more offensively gifted players.

As a sophomore, Thompson made two key steals that allowed the Wolfpack to come back from a 10-point deficit with 11 minutes to play against Wake Forest. "Harold is our best man-to-man player, but he's not confident taking the outside shot," Valvano said at the time. As a junior in 1983, Thompson took just 17 shots, scoring 13 points and grabbing 12 rebounds. But his defense in two particular games was critical to the Wolfpack's success.

Early in the season, the Wolfpack played a non-conference game at Reynolds Coliseum against Michigan State, which featured future NBA players Scott Skiles, Sam Vincent, and Kevin Willis. The Wolfpack took a two-point lead with 17 seconds remaining, and

Valvano inserted Thompson into the lineup to guard Vincent, the Spartans' top offensive threat. "I was trying to keep him [Vincent] from getting the ball," he said after the game. "Everybody in the Coliseum knew who it was going to. I was just trying to beat him to it. And that is what I did. I saw him going for the ball, and out of the corner of my eye, I saw that the guy throwing it in had released [the ball]. I stepped in and tapped it."

Later on, in the ACC Tournament semifinal against North Carolina, the game was tied in regulation with less than 30 seconds to play. The Wolfpack was setting up for the final shot, but on the drive, Sidney Lowe had the ball stripped out of his hands by UNC's Curtis Hunter with two seconds remaining. Valvano inserted Thompson, his most reliable man-to-man defender, into the lineup to defend Doherty. It was his only appearance in the game. After a series of timeouts by both teams, the Tar Heels got the ball to Perkins for a 30-footer at the buzzer.

"Perkins got open out on the wing about 30 feet from the basket," Thompson recalled. "Someone had blown their assignment. I jumped out there and I did hit his elbow a little, but the ref didn't call a foul. I don't really think it affected the shot. The horn blew and Perkins was looking at the referee, looking for a foul."

The shot rolled around and dipped into the basket's cylinder, but popped back out, sending the game into overtime. In the additional five minutes, Dereck Whittenburg took over, scoring 11 of his 15 points in the extra period. The Wolfpack outscored the Tar Heels 15-2 in the final two minutes for a 91-84 victory, one that might not have come had Thompson not nudged Perkins on the elbow at the end of regulation.

"Sometimes I wonder how different things would have been if the referee had made the call," Thompson said a quarter-century later. "I suppose they would have been a lot different."

Then again, Thompson might also have had a much different

career had he listened to Tubby Smith and other coaches who told him that NC State wasn't the right fit for him.

"Overall, going to NC State was a very positive experience, even if I didn't play that much throughout my career," Thompson said. "The question you ask yourself is, 'Would you trade being on a national championship team versus going to some other place where you could play?' I tell you, I was hounded a lot about leaving. I would go work these summer camps and coaches would ask me, 'Why are you there?' My high school coach thought it was a bad deal from the beginning."

Playing for Valvano, however, taught the reclusive and shy Thompson to come out of his shell. Now, he makes his living speaking to prospective students, both in groups and individually.

"When I got to NC State, I wanted to change my personality," said Thompson, who gave himself the nickname "World" and corrected any teammate who called him something else. "Never would I stand up in front of a group of people and speak. That is one of the main things I do now. A lot of what I do is what I learned from Coach Valvano. I wanted to become a well-rounded person. I think that part of it was more than fulfilled. Sure, I anticipated having a better college basketball career than what I had. Sometimes, though, it's not always about having the greatest career on the court. I don't know if I would have wanted to score as many points as David Thompson at another school and not live through the experience of winning a national championship. It was that much fun."

6 "DON'T DRINK AT THE SAME BAR"

Christmas 1982 was sandwiched between two big road games—the pre-holiday loss at Louisville and a win over West Virginia at the Meadowlands in East Rutherford, New Jersey. It was a neutral-site game Valvano scheduled specifically because his team had performed so poorly in the NCAA Tournament the year before, losing in the first round to Tennessee-Chattanooga in Indianapolis, Indiana. Valvano chose West Virginia as an opponent because the Mountaineers had won 27 games the previous season.

Of course, it was also a chance for him to see his family. Rocco and Angelina Valvano were in the stands, seated right behind the bench.

The players, who had a three-day rest for the holiday, did not even have enough time to eat leftovers. That was OK—Christmas came in April that season.

While on break, freshman George McClain developed a case of bacterial spinal meningitis, a swelling of the membranes around the spine and brain that is highly contagious. On Christmas Eve, he nearly died in a Greenville, North Carolina, hospital as his temperature soared to 106 degrees.

With McClain laid up in his hospital bed, the team reconvened in Raleigh for their trip to Valvano's home turf. Because no one ever discovered how McClain had contracted meningitis, all the players on the team, as a preventative measure, were prescribed a dose of antibiotics—most likely Cipro, according to team trainer Jim Rehbock.

Two days after Christmas, the team left school for a short bus ride to Raleigh-Durham Airport. All the players, save Cozell McQueen, were in their seats waiting to depart when they began to talk about the biggest side effect of the antibiotic treatment: it turned their urine Gatorade orange. The players figured McQueen—a frequent target of everyone's practical jokes—would not handle this sudden change in his bodily functions very well. So they decided to act like it was a symptom of spinal meningitis instead. That was all anyone could talk about when McQueen finally strolled onto the charter bus, found his seat, and sat down. He overheard someone a couple of rows in front of him say that orange urine was one of the first signs McClain noticed after he contracted meningitis.

A panicky McQueen shot straight up out of his seat and immediately headed to the front of the bus in search of Rehbock.

"Yo, Rehbs," McQueen said frantically, "I think I got the shit."

The whole bus collapsed in laughter, and McQueen knew he had been had. Again.

For Valvano, the New York homecoming was both a blessing and a curse. Like his wife and three daughters, he had grown to like homey feel of North Carolina. At the time, Raleigh had a small-town atmosphere, Interstate 40 was still under construction, and the only thing that resembled a major thoroughfare was the Cliff Benson beltline. Valvano had gone to New York before Christmas for a press conference to promote the West Virginia game, which was one of six doubleheaders at Brendan Byrne Arena that season. The gleaming white edifice across the river from downtown Manhattan was still brand new, having opened the year before with three consecutive Bruce Springsteen concerts. Primarily, it has been one of the nation's top sports arenas; home of the NBA's Nets and the NHL's Devils, it is capable of seating 20,500 fans per basketball game.

After the pregame press conference, Valvano had to fly home to Raleigh. He left the Meadowlands at 4 p.m. hoping to catch a 7 p.m. flight from LaGuardia, some 20 miles away in northern Queens across the Hudson River. He waited in the back of a taxi for more than two and a half hours without traveling more than 10 miles. On his cabbie's advice, he decided to try a 9 p.m. flight from Kennedy in southern Queens instead. He made it with just a few minutes to spare.

"I was in a car over four hours to go 35 miles," Valvano said in his book, *Too Soon To Quit*. "This was one coach who was glad to get back home to North Carolina."

West Virginia, like Louisville, was an excellent test for the Wolfpack. Valvano used the Mountaineers as a barometer to see just how good his team might be. In those days, every conference was playing by different rules regarding the shot clock and three-point line distance. West Virginia, in its first year of competition in the new Atlantic 10 Conference, played with a 40-second shot clock and a three-point line similar to the one used in college basketball today— tangent to the top of the key at 19 feet, 9 inches. The Wolfpack was still adjusting to the ACC's experimental rules, which included a too-short three-point arc of 19 feet and a 30-second clock. Valvano and West Virginia coach Gale Catlett agreed to use a 35-second shot clock and the A-10 three-point line, though no delineating markings were added to the court until after the doubleheader opener between St. Peter's and Arkansas. After that game ended, the facilities crew slapped down some temporary tape roughly 19 feet, 9 inches away from the basket.

Valvano had told his players that they were good enough to make it to the Final Four when they came back from Louisville. Now it was time to prove it against a team that Valvano believed would be similar to those his squad might face in the first or second round of the NCAA Tournament.

The game was close early on, at least until the Wolfpack scored 16 straight points in the final minutes of the first half. After intermission, Dereck Whittenburg hit three three-pointers and the Wolfpack scored another 10 unanswered points, leading by as many as 15 points. But the Mountaineers kept the game close. Then, with less than a minute to play, freshman Ernie Myers scored on a dunk from Sidney Lowe, pushing the Wolfpack's lead to eight points. Assistant coach Tom Abatemarco stood up from his seat on the bench, raised both his arms in a classic three-point signal, and yelled, "It's over!"

That was a bad move. The ever-superstitious Valvano never wanted anyone to declare a game over, no matter how big the lead. He grabbed Abatemarco by the neck and took him down behind the bench. Horrified assistant Ed McLean jumped up to shield his two combative coworkers—Valvano on top, Abatemarco on the floor—from the television cameras broadcasting the game, which ended with a pair of dunks by Lowe and West Virginia's Lester Rowe. Fortunately, no one ever saw the fracas, either on television or at the arena.

"I thought he was going to kill him, literally," said one individual who witnessed the fracas from the bench. "It wasn't like he was just grabbing him and pushing him—he had him down on the floor, giving it to him good."

After the game, Valvano and Abatemarco continued their fisticuffs in the hallway that led to the Wolfpack locker room. Valvano's father, Rocco, a former high school coach in New York, couldn't believe what his son had done.

When things quieted down, Rocco asked, "What did you do that for?"

"The game isn't over until the horn goes off," said Valvano, whose Italian temperament led to almost as many heated confrontations with his staff as it did late-night comedy routines. "What if we blow that game because this idiot jumps up?"

Remarkably, few people saw the outburst, but it is one of McLean's favorites from his five years as a member of Valvano's staff. The game started at 9 p.m. and didn't end until the witching hour. Most of the reporters at the matchup were either back in the press room filing their stories or sitting on press row, furiously typing on a 20-pound Port-O-Ram word processor or a Tandy TRS-80 Model 100 portable computer, which was little more than a keyboard with a four-line dot-matrix display. Both machines were early precursors of the ubiquitous laptops reporters use nowadays to remain connected to their offices for web surfing and lonesome pregame solitaire.

Abatemarco, who has a fiery Italian personality similar to Valvano's, confirms that his boss had him on the ground and was beating the crap out of him. And he wasn't all that bothered by it.

"We used to have a lot of fun together," Abatemarco said. "We really did. We had fun. We joked. We laughed. We cried. We did it all."

After the game, the players went back to the hotel—but not for long. A handful of them—Ernie Myers, Mike Warren, Quinton Leonard, Walt Densmore, Mike Warren, and Tommy DiNardo, along with former teammate and New York native Phil Weber, who was serving as host—got dressed up and piled into the back of Weber's parents' station wagon. They dropped Myers off at his home in Spanish Harlem, which at the time might have been one of the roughest neighborhoods in the country, especially for a wagon full of white college kids. It was well after midnight, and Myers told them not to make eye contact with anyone they might pass in the street. Then, he jumped out of the car and dashed toward his mother's apartment building.

"Ernie isn't normally so fast," Densmore said. "But he was that night."

For senior Quinton Leonard, going out on the town in New York was an eye-opening experience, especially since the team had chosen to visit one of the most famous discos in the country, Studio 54. It has had bad karma for NC State basketball since Wolfpack legend David Thompson fell down its back stairs in the spring of 1984, tearing his knee ligaments and ruining his spectacular basketball career.

Watching the half-dozen basketball players, none of them under 6-foot-1, climb out of the family wagon at 254 West 54th Street must have been similar to witnessing the McCaughey septuplets' birth.

Leonard, who saw little action on the court but much off of it, wasn't what you would call cosmopolitan. He stood with his back to the wall most of the night, particularly when the song "It's Raining Men" blared from the speakers. The famous disco was nothing like he had ever seen on his family's 1,000-acre farm in Louisburg, North Carolina.

"It was Quinton's first experience seeing gay people," said Laura Leonard, Quinton's widow. "They were following them around this club and he and Tommy and someone else went to the bathroom where there was this big urinal. He was really uncomfortable because these guys were staring at them—until they started peeing bright orange."

No one pursued them the rest of the night.

When the players left the club, however, they found that the Weber family station wagon had a flat tire. They waited more than an hour for AAA to arrive and fix the flat, so they could return to the team hotel before anyone realized they weren't in their rooms. The bus that would take the team to the airport was leaving early the next day, as NC State would return for a New Year's Eve practice prior to its January 3 game against Fairleigh-Dickinson. The group got back to the hotel well after 4 a.m. Not that anyone was waiting for them to return—Valvano famously didn't believe in player curfews.

"He had two basic rules while we were on the road: don't let your nightlife affect the way you play, and don't drink at the same bar that he did," Rehbock said.

In New York, no one had trouble obeying those guidelines.

GEORGE McCLAIN

For Christmas 1982, George McClain had been promised a new car. He needed something to replace the $100 green AMC Hornet he had been driving for the last three years. But instead of a car, McClain received a weeklong stay in the hospital, where he nearly died of spinal meningitis.

McClain was a freshman point guard on the NC State 1982-83 roster, another all-star player from Rocky Mount (N.C.) High School who had led his team to back-to-back appearances in the North Carolina High School Association 4-A championship game. He was a talented scorer who averaged 25.4 points and 3.5 assists as a senior, leading his team to a 28-2 record and the state 4-A title and winning Most Valuable Player honors at the state finals and at the East-West All-Star game later that summer. Still, he was rather small at 5-foot-11 and wasn't added to NC State's recruiting class until late April, choosing the Wolfpack from a list that included Maryland, Georgetown, East Carolina, and, interestingly enough, Houston.

"I thought about going to North Carolina, and probably would have if James Worthy had stayed in school," said McClain, who followed all-star players Phil Ford and Buck Williams at Rocky Mount High. "But when I met Lorenzo Charles and saw him play, I thought, 'Shoot, me and him could take over the ACC with him inside and me outside.'"

McClain's early efforts as a freshman drew compliments from Wolfpack head coach Jim Valvano, who called the young guard the biggest surprise of the season's first month. In the Pack's first two games, McClain averaged 10 points, three assists, and 16.5 minutes as he made the transition from shooting guard, which he played in high school, to point guard, playing behind senior Sidney Lowe. He made 10 of his first 17 field-goal attempts. He played exceptional defense, which is usually a weakness for most freshmen. He seemed to be a strong candidate to take the court with seniors Dereck Whittenburg and Lowe when Valvano went to a three-guard rotation. In both early games, McClain received more playing time than sophomore Terry Gannon.

"I had Terry Gannon so far on the bench he couldn't get off of it," McClain remembered 25 years later.

But McClain suffered an ankle injury in the third game of the season against East Carolina when teammate Alvin Battle tripped over his leg. He missed the Wolfpack's next two contests, but was ready to resume practicing when the team dispersed for a short Christmas break. For McClain, that brief break turned into a fight for his life.

After spending the afternoon two days before Christmas playing pickup basketball at Rocky Mount High School, McClain went to a downtown bar with some old friends for a little holiday cheer. He remembers buying a drink and leaving it on the bar so he could dance with a girl he had just met. When he came back from the dance floor, he took another couple of sips from his drink. Soon after, McClain was spitting up blood.

He went home to rest, leaving his new acquaintance behind. He developed a raging headache and high fever. The next morning, Christmas Eve, McClain couldn't move his legs. His mother, Redessa Bynum, rushed him to Nash County General Hospital, where he was told he had a virus and was sent away with a few pain relievers. Later that day, as his fever approached 107 degrees—the point at which the human body begins to suffer brain damage—McClain went to see his family physician, Dr. William Cooper, who directed Mrs. Bynum to get her son to Pitt County Memorial Hospital in Greenville, North Carolina, some 50 miles away. There, he was properly diagnosed with bacterial spinal meningitis, a highly contagious and sometimes fatal illness that causes swelling in the membranes surrounding the spinal cord and brain.

The doctors packed McClain in wet towels filled with ice. They put him in a small room with no windows. He remembers hollering his lungs out from the pain and the cold.

"I was not thinking I was really as sick as I was," McClain said. "But everybody else knew. They thought I was about to die. I never really thought I was going to. I kind of looked at it like our team was that year—I wasn't going to give up."

McClain's fever finally broke as the antibiotics the medical staff pumped into him finally took effect, but not before he spent Christmas and New Year's Day in the hospital, enduring rounds of penicillin, IVs, spinal taps, and more ice baths. He slowly began to recover and regain his strength. On January 3, he listened to the radio as his teammates beat Fairleigh Dickinson 111-76 at Reynolds Coliseum. When the announcers gave the final statistics, he heard that Gannon had scored a career-high 17 points.

"Uh-oh. It's time to get on up out of here," McClain said to himself.

Remarkably, McClain was out of the hospital later that week. He stayed at home another few days, regaining his strength and stamina. And he was back in Raleigh on January 12 for the start of the spring semester. He never missed a day of class because of his illness. But Valvano, who had never redshirted a player in his 16 years as head coach, wanted McClain to sit out the rest of the season. McClain, as weak as he was, wanted to return to the lineup. It was one of several instances throughout McClain's NC State career in which he didn't see eye to eye with the coach.

McClain eventually won this particular argument and returned to the Wolfpack lineup against Georgia Tech, the game that immediately followed the Virginia contest in which Whittenburg broke his foot. But McClain's game was never really the same. He suffered from fatigue and dead legs. He couldn't get up and down the floor very well because his injured ankle still had not completely healed. Like all the role players on the bench, he continued to contribute, seeing action in 25 of the 36 games during the championship season. But with Whittenburg out of the lineup, Valvano called on Gannon and another freshman guard, Ernie Myers, to fill in.

McClain still made some important plays along the way. He is especially proud of the pass he made to a streaking Thurl Bailey in the second overtime of the NCAA first-round game against Pepperdine, a critical part of the Wolfpack's miraculous comeback.

"Without that pass, we might not have won the game," McClain said. "And if we don't win that game, we might not have won the whole thing."

Valvano accurately predicted, "He'll never throw a better pass than that one in his career at NC State."

McClain saw limited action in the games against Nevada-Las Vegas, Utah, and Virginia, but he did not play in either game at the Final Four, something that bothered him greatly at the time. But Valvano, knowing just how sick McClain was over the holidays, was greatly appreciative of everything McClain contributed.

"This was our miracle number one," Valvano wrote in his book, *Too Soon to Quit*. "It came early. Dereck's [foot] injury was much more publicized, but George came back from a bad ankle injury and spinal meningitis to help us win the national championship. He had an outstanding year despite incredible adversity."

When McClain returned his sophomore season, he still had not completely regained all his strength and stamina. He played even less than he did as a freshman. It didn't help that Valvano had recruited 5-foot-6 point guard Anthony "Spud" Webb from Midland Junior College to run the Wolfpack's offense over the next two years. In McClain's junior season, Valvano recruited Nate McMillan from Chowan Junior College and Quentin Jackson of DeMatha Catholic High School as his future point guards. McClain believed he had never had a fair chance to be the starting point guard, so after his junior season, he left NC State.

"Valvano never gave me the opportunity to play," McClain said. "He recruited Spud and Nate and Quentin and gave all of them the chance to start. He threw them out there, and I was killing them in practice. They couldn't stop me. Yet he gave them the job. I was disappointed, and it just didn't work out. I don't have any hard feelings about it, but I was disappointed with my playing career."

McClain returned to Rocky Mount after his junior season, intent on transferring to a CIAA school for his final year. But he got a good paying, first-shift job at a textile manufacturing plant in his hometown and never returned to school. After a couple of years, he took a position at a group home in Rocky Mount and spent 17 years working with the at-risk kids who lived there.

McClain regrets that he gave up his senior season of college basketball. "It hurt me more than it hurt them," he said. "I wish I would have stayed. I would probably be better off, but just from the basketball point of view, I didn't think I was being treated fairly. And if I had stayed, I might not have my family. I love my family. I probably would have never met my wife [Michelle] if I stayed at State."

McClain stayed in his hometown and became a terror in the industrial and recreational leagues, playing with many of the same guys he helped lead to the high school state championship in 1982. He proudly wears his state championship ring on the middle finger of his left hand and his national championship ring on the ring finger of his right hand. He also passed his love of sports to his two daughters, Ashley Smith and Tiffany McClain, who followed in his basketball footsteps at Rocky Mount High. Both became college athletes: Ashley played basketball at Methodist University in Fayetteville and Tiffany was a cross country and track standout at UNC-Charlotte. Both helped their teams win conference championships.

"They got their rings, too," McClain said proudly.

He's pleased that Ashley went back to school after having his first grandchild, Isaiah, in 2006. She sat out the 2005-06 season and then returned in 2006-07 for her senior year, while McClain and Michelle took care of their grandchild.

In 2003, McClain became a sales representative at a car dealership in Rocky Mount, and by 2005, he was named the salesman of the year. So he's now in a position to get a new car whenever he wants since he never did receive the one he was promised for Christmas in 1982.

DINKY PROCTOR

It was early one morning in the parking lot of Reynolds Coliseum, just days before the Wolfpack's fateful ACC home opener against Virginia. Walter "Dinky" Proctor had borrowed roommate Harold Thompson's car and was pulled over by campus public safety as he eased into a hidden parking lot at the three-way intersection near the back of the arena. Proctor was in a tight spot because he knew that the registration in Thompson's car was not valid, and the last thing he needed was an encounter with a campus officer. Proctor, the bad boy of the 1982-83 championship squad, always had reason to sweat encounters with the police, especially since he was driving with a revoked license at that precise moment.

"What's your name, son?" the officer asked.

"Cozell McQueen," Proctor answered.

There was a long pause.

"Now look here, I am an ACC fan and I like State," the officer said. "I have seen them enough to know that is not your name.

You had better call Mr. Valvano and see if he can tell us who you are."

So at 2 A.M., Proctor called his coach to come bail him out of the situation. "That fucking Proctor," Valvano said, "is always into something." The next five games—Virginia through Memphis State—the sophomore forward sat the bench on an unannounced suspension for disturbing Valvano's insomnia.

Valvano wasn't always so cold to Proctor, the coach's first real recruit after arriving from Iona College. At one time, the coach believed that the 6-foot-9 guard from Somerset, New Jersey, was going to be the cornerstone of his program. Just about every major school in the country wanted Proctor, hailed by the New York media as the "next Magic Johnson" because of his combination of size and graceful ball-handling abilities. In his final two seasons at Rutgers Prep High School, Proctor nearly averaged a triple-double in points, rebounds, and assists. He chose NC State over Johnson's alma mater, Michigan State, as well as Louisville, South Carolina, DePaul, Maryland, and Rutgers.

Proctor had a special place in his heart for NC State. He idolized David Thompson. He saw the Wolfpack play live at Madison Square Garden during the 1978 National Invitation Tournament semifinals and finals. And the first recruiting letter he ever received following his freshman year in high school was signed by Norm Sloan's assistant coach, Marty Fletcher. Valvano declared that if the sterling guard signed on with the Wolfpack, NC State would win a national championship at some point in his career. Noted ACC basketball writer Al Featherston, then working for the *Durham Sun*, also predicted immediate success for Valvano's first big-time catch: "NC State recruit Walter 'Dinky' Proctor gets my early vote as Freshman of the Year in the ACC next season, even though Carolina's Mike Jordan is the most talented player entering the league. Proctor will get to play a bigger role with the rebuilding Wolfpack than Jordan will play with the overloaded Tar Heels. In fact, Maryland's [Adrian] Branch may be Proctor's chief competition—he ought to end up as the league's freshman scorer."

Branch did indeed lead all freshmen in scoring that year, averaging more than 15 points a game. Jordan hit the jump shot that won Tar Heels coach Dean Smith his first NCAA championship. Proctor, meanwhile, scored 28 points in 23 games of mostly mop-up duty.

Problems appeared the moment Proctor arrived on campus, stemming, he says, from the fact that he had injured his knee prior to his junior year of high school and never had it treated. But the multiple assessments of Proctor's abilities were pretty clear: Proctor was not fast, could not jump, and did not have the consistent outside jump shot needed to play guard in the Atlantic Coast Conference. He was only suited to play power forward in college, and he had no experience at the position. It did not help that his freshman season was limited because of a hand injury.

"I got away with the injury my last two years of high school, but once you get to that next level, you have to bring something else," Proctor said. "It caught up with me. It hurt me to my heart to not be able to do what my mind was telling me to do. But my body wouldn't let me do it. It was the worst feeling in the world."

Proctor's sophomore season was no better as he watched Lorenzo Charles and McQueen, two players who were mostly afterthoughts in his recruiting class, start almost every game of the season. And Alvin Battle, a junior college transfer, played in twice as many contests (33) as Proctor (16). Of course, none of them were as troublesome to Valvano as Proctor.

Proctor continued to play leftover minutes as the regular season ended. In the ACC Tournament, however, Valvano gave the sophomore forward a chance to contribute, inserting him in the first half of the semifinal game against North Carolina. But on a fast break, Proctor tripped over the clumsy feet of Tar Heels center Warren

Martin while passing the ball to Charles. He actually heard the ligaments in his left knee shredding as he fell to the floor. "It sounded like someone ripping up a stack of newspapers," he said.

Proctor never played for NC State again, even though he spent another two years on an athletic scholarship.

As disappointing as his injury was—and Valvano announced later that week that Proctor was done playing for the year—nothing compared Proctor for the shock he received when NC State loaded buses for the airport on its way to Albuquerque. Proctor had stayed behind, along with graduate assistant Max Perry and some other regular members of the traveling squad, during the Pack's trips to Corvallis, Oregon, and Ogden, Utah, hosting game-day parties in his dormitory room at the College Inn for each of his team's first four NCAA Tournament victories. He had assumed that he would be on the trip to the Final Four.

But assistant coach Tom Abatemarco came up to Proctor on the bus and told him he wasn't making the trip. Those words turned Proctor's heart cold.

"They had told me that if we went to the Final Four, everybody was going," Proctor said. "Abatemarco told me to call V."

That conversation didn't go particularly well. The coach insisted he could not travel with the team, but offered to fly him to Albuquerque the day before the semifinal contest with Georgia. Proctor hung up the phone and went back to his dorm room, where he, along with some of his closest friends, watched the Wolfpack beat Georgia and Houston.

"It was me, Emmett Lay, Chuck Nevitt, Art Jones, and a bottle of Wild Turkey," Proctor said.

As soon as the game was over, Proctor hobbled out of his room, jumped on his moped, and rode to Hillsborough Street to watch others celebrate the championship Valvano had so often predicted. He could not walk and could not take his crutches on the moped, so he stayed on his bike until it became too hard to maneuver through the thousands of partiers.

Proctor remained on campus for two more years, rejecting opportunities to transfer elsewhere. He saw himself as the team's missing link, particularly in 1985, when the Wolfpack came within one game of returning to the Final Four. But he admits now that staying was a poor decision. "I regret not transferring," Proctor said. "I could have gotten away, got my leg straight, and contributed."

Instead, he fell into a cycle of drug and alcohol abuse that all but ended his athletic career and distanced him from his former teammates. "I used to love to smoke a little weed," Proctor admits. "I outgrew that when I got to State and graduated to other stuff. It got pretty bad. I broke some laws."

Proctor tried to resurrect his basketball career for a brief time at Brandon University in Manitoba, Canada. Although that didn't work out, he at least escaped the drugs and alcohol that had brought him down. "Going to Canada was like going to rehab for me," Proctor said. "The stuff just wasn't available." He came back to financial and legal problems in the United States, which he blames on the student loans he took out to pay his out-of-state tuition after his scholarship money ended in 1985. He was convicted in 1989 of credit card fraud and sent to prison for the first time. "It took that—getting locked up—to set me straight," Proctor said. "The first time you get locked up and they close them doors, it ain't pretty."

When he got out, Proctor joined his brother in the Army, spending three years at Fort Bragg just outside of Fayetteville, North Carolina. He never mentioned his knee injury, which was why he was allowed to make 25 jumps out of an airplane before hurting himself again. It must have been funny back then to see a 6 foot, 9 inch paratrooper—someone whose college career was derailed in part because he could not jump—floating down to the ground.

After leaving the Army in 1992, Proctor spent some time in

Atlanta and Greensboro, North Carolina. He did not attend the 1993 reunion at Reynolds Coliseum, when a dying Valvano made his famous speech in front of a cheering crowd and his tearful players. But Proctor said he did make peace with his former coach. "When I heard he was sick, I sent him a card," Proctor said. "It was kind of sarcastic because I didn't know how sick he was. But I told him, 'We have been through a lot of things, but the one thing we never did was give up. Now it is your turn. Don't give up.'"

Proctor returned to school at NC State in 1997 under a program created by then-NC State athletic director Les Robinson to bring former athletes back to school to pursue their degrees. He spent more time in jail during that period for driving with a permanently revoked license and failure to pay child support. He went through several jobs, including working at a convenience store, serving as a plant manager for a small manufacturing company, and working at Amedeo's, the NC State-themed Italian restaurant on Western Boulevard.

In 2001, Proctor finished the last class he needed for his degree in sociology. Shortly thereafter, he moved back to Greensboro, where he works for a small renovation and repair company he started with some friends. His dream is to open a group home for troubled youth and people who are looking to rebuild shattered lives.

Some might say that Proctor—who is without regular employment, estranged from his family that lives across town, and missing his two front teeth—must first shore up his own foundation. In the spring of 2007, Proctor had gone years without talking to anyone from NC State. He didn't even know that Quinton Leonard, one of his favorite teammates, had died of a heart attack some 14 months earlier. But he's happily living his life with his girlfriend and trying to spend time with two daughters from other relationships.

"I am not a kiss-ass kind of person," Proctor said. "Never was and never will be. That is why it took me so long to get where I wanted to be. But to be honest, I don't give a shit. I am just going to be me. I'll die that way. I am just too strong-minded. They couldn't break me. I have kind of learned over the years to pick my battles. I can't completely be the same way. But I haven't changed too much."

For years, Proctor was bitter that he did not play a bigger role in college basketball's most famous fairytale. He was bitter, in general, about the way the school honored the members of the team and, specifically, about how Valvano treated him. It didn't help that he saw many of the same players he used to dominate in high school and in AAU tournaments playing in the NBA. "I couldn't even watch basketball on television," said Proctor.

But that bitterness faded not long after he received his diploma. The next Magic Johnson may largely be forgotten, but he has no more regrets.

"I let it all go," Proctor said. "My final chapter with all of that was getting that piece of paper that said I graduated. Me, of all those assholes on that team, I graduated from college! Once I got that, I closed the door. It was what it was, and it is no more."

"HE TOLD US TO GO TO HELL RIGHT THERE"

There was only one way to stop Dereck Whittenburg on the night of January 12, 1983. Virginia had to find some way to get the senior guard off the floor. Taking advantage of the ACC's experimental three-point shot, Whittenburg scorched the Cavaliers with seven long-range baskets and scored a career-high 27 points in the first half alone. Thanks to Whittenburg's totals, the Wolfpack led the second-ranked Cavaliers by as many as 16 points.

"Whittenburg was unconscious," remembered then-Virginia coach Terry Holland. "That was one of the first games we played that year with the new rules. We could not stop him."

With All-America center Ralph Sampson, Virginia was the one ACC team that eschewed the experimental rules, preferring to rely on its inside game instead of its perimeter shooting. And why not? Sampson was the most dominat big man in the country and the Cavaliers were intent to ride him to a national championship. Besides, the ACC's new regulations would not be in effect during the NCAA Tournament, and

Holland wanted to make sure his team was playing its best in the post-season without having to worry about rules unlikely to be around the next year.

It was a rollicking Wednesday night game in Reynolds, played just days after Sampson had the biggest emotional outburst of his career. In a physical contest at Maryland, a frustrated Sampson slammed the ball down on the court and chased after game official Joe Forte. He received two technical fouls—an automatic ejection these days. Afterward, Maryland coach Lefty Driesell said Sampson should have been thrown out of the game; Holland claimed that too many opponents were trying to stop the nation's best player with physical play and the tantrum was justified.

In the first 20 minutes against Virginia, Whittenburg discovered another way to neutralize the nation's best player: by hitting outside shots worth 50 percent more than Sampson's dunks. It appeared the only way the Cavaliers could slow down the emotional Whittenburg was to annoy him. So Holland inserted reserve guard Ricky Stokes into the game with almost the sole purpose of getting under Whittenburg's skin. With three minutes to play in the first half, Stokes goaded Whittenburg to retaliate against a little physical play in the backcourt, drawing an away-from-the-ball foul 50 feet from the basket. When Whittenburg complained about the call, he was hit with a technical. Stokes made three straight free throws and Sampson threw down a monster dunk to complete the five-point possession. The Cavaliers, down 50-34 at one point, were back within striking distance. They scored the final seven points of the half, cutting the Wolfpack lead down to six at intermission. With 102 points between the two teams in the first half, this was hardly the kind of stall ball that both Virginia and the Wolfpack had become famous for in the days before the experimental rules.

But Whittenburg came out cold in the second half, perhaps still bothered by his own temper tantrum. He went up one more time for a long-range shot from the corner and cringed as it bounced off the rim for his fourth straight miss. He never looked down to see Virginia guard Othell Wilson between his feet and the rubberized surface of the Reynolds Coliseum floor. He landed awkwardly on Wilson's foot and tried to limp down the floor to play defense. Instead, he crumpled to the ground, taking NC State's championship dreams with him.

As Whittenburg lay on the floor, one of the officials came by to tell team trainer Jim Rehbock to attend to the injured player. Rehbock and Valvano rushed to Whittenburg's side to comfort him and check him out. "What the fuck are you doing here?" Whittenburg yelled at them. "I'm fine."

He wasn't. He had broken the same fifth metatarsal he had fractured as a senior at DeMatha High School, the injury he pressed to come back from a little too early in the Stags' quest to repeat as city and state champions. As Rehbock, Valvano, and Whittenburg walked off the floor, the athlete poured all of his emotions into a string of vile profanities aimed at the team trainer. "He was just cussing up a storm," Rehbock said. "I sort of had him by the arm and was trying to get away from him a little bit because he was just letting me have it." Whittenburg didn't stop berating Rehbock from the time he left the foul line until the two were in the locker room, when he sat down on a table to be examined by team physician Don Reibel.

"You know, with this kind of injury, you are probably out for the rest of the season," Reibel told Whittenburg. That didn't go over very well. "He basically told us to go to hell right there," Rehbock said. The doctor's fears were confirmed after a quick trip to nearby Rex Hospital for X-rays. The bone was definitely broken.

Upstairs, things were falling apart for the demoralized Wolfpack. It made only nine of 32 points, scored only half as many points as it did in the first half, and failed to score at all in the game's final four minutes and 49 seconds. What had started out as the greatest night of the Valvano era ended with the coach berating the referees for calling another questionable away-from-the-ball foul on junior Alvin Battle, who was in a shoving match with Sampson. Virginia scored the game's final eight points for an 88-80 victory.

Long before anyone received a medical update, frustration was obvious in the Wolfpack locker room after blowing the 16-point lead. "We've lost some tough ones," said senior guard Sidney Lowe said. "It seems like in the four years I've been here, we can never get that big win, the one that can get us started down the road. We always play well and we never win. When we do, it's going to make a big difference. It's coming. It's got to."

More than 30 minutes after the game ended, Whittenburg returned from Rex sporting a new pair of crutches. Dr. Reibel gave his grim report to associate athletic director Frank Weedon, who pulled Valvano away from the media collected in the hallway outside the training room. Weedon said two words: "It's broken."

"Oh, that's wonderful," Valvano said. "Oh, my God. That's it."

Weedon ushered Valvano into the training room and closed the door so they could examine the three X-rays hanging on the wall. The coach let the news sink in, then slammed the bottom of his foot against the door. He walked out without saying a word and disappeared down the hallway.

The players were just as devastated as their coach and their teammate. Suddenly, the loss to the Cavaliers became irrelevant.

"We felt awful for him because we all thought his career was over," said reserve Walt Densmore. "Everyone felt awful for him. A lot of guys were upset. It was a bad night all the way around."

No one was more upset than Sidney Lowe, who had not played without Whittenburg for any significant amount of time since the pair's senior year at DeMatha, when Whittenburg missed nearly two months of action for the same injury.

"The night Dereck went down, it was just like somebody died in your family," said ACC associate commissioner Mike Finn, who was a sports information assistant at NC State from 1979-83. "You just had this horrible feeling that everything you were hoping could happen that whole season was all of a sudden gone. And, for a while, it was."

The next day, as the news slowly spread throughout campus and to the outside world, Valvano tried to gather his thoughts. He had just lost the team's leading scorer and its most vocal leader, the "holler guy," as the coach liked to call him, who was not afraid to kick his teammates in the pants if he needed to. In a meeting with the media, team trainer Craig Sink said, "The quickest I have ever heard of someone come back from this type of thing is three to four weeks. But it could be longer. He could be out for good."

At practice that Thursday afternoon, Valvano knew he had to address the situation with his players, who knew all too well how important Whittenburg was to the team.

"Last night, we lost a great ball player," Valvano began. "We lost a great leader, a young man we were counting on to help us reach all our goals this season. When it happened, we were on our way to a great victory. Now a lot of people are writing us off. They are saying our season is over. I'm telling you I believe something good is going to happen to us. I'm telling you it's too soon to quit. We're not going to forget Dereck, but if we stop working, I can guarantee you we won't win. Even if we continue to work, I can't tell you we're going to win, but our chances will improve. That's the only shot we have."

Oddly, the person least upset was Whittenburg, perhaps because he never believed the doctor's prognosis. "It had happened before," Whittenburg said. "I knew what to expect." He was disappointed that he might not reach a few personal goals—he wanted to average four or five three-point baskets a game. He wanted another chance to beat North Carolina. And he wanted one more chance to succeed in the ACC and NCAA Tournaments. He never stopped believing those things would happen.

Days later, as Valvano's speech began to take root, the team was given some much-needed levity. As usual, the coach provided it. He came to practice proudly waving a letter he had just received from a concerned fan. He was giddy with excitement as he read it to the team. "Dear Coach Valvano, I am writing to express the disappointment I have in the lack of compassion shown by your trainer to one of our injured players in the Virginia game." Apparently, the newspaper pictures of Rehbock helping Whittenburg off the court did not include a soundtrack of Whittenburg's profanity. The coach, who had heard every vile word Whittenburg spewed as he hobbled out of the game, made Rehbock sit down and write a note of apology for not being sympathetic enough to the guy who was calling him every name in the book.

WALT DENSMORE

Being an end-of-the-bench part of NC State's 1983 championship team was the highlight of Walt Densmore's shortened basketball career.

Densmore, a 6-foot-7 forward from Tuscaloosa, Alabama, came to NC State basically on a lark. He made an unofficial visit to Reynolds Coliseum to see some of his buddies from the University of Alabama play North Carolina in the East Region semifinals of the 1982 NCAA Tournament, a game the Tar Heels won 74-69 en route to the national championship that season. Densmore grew up in the shadow of Alabama and Southeastern Conference football, but always wanted to play basketball in the ACC, just as his father, Walt Densmore Sr., had. He spent the weekend hanging out with some high school friends who were enrolled at St. Mary's. By the time he returned home, he knew that he would be part of fun-loving Jim Valvano's program.

"I came up here for that tournament with no intention of going to school at NC State," Densmore said. "But after that weekend when I got off the plane back at home, my mom said she looked at me and knew I was gone."

Few ACC coaches spent much time courting Densmore, despite his impressive statistics as a senior at Tuscaloosa Central High School: he averaged 18.3 points and 9.6 rebounds per game, shooting 56.3 percent from the field on a team that went 27-5 his senior year. But Alabama, Vanderbilt, and Mississippi were all interested.

Like teammate Tommy DiNardo, who would join the team in October after an open tryout camp, Densmore wanted to become a second-generation ACC player. DiNardo's father, Phil, played for Everett Case at NC State in the late 1950s, about two years before Walt Densmore Sr. played at Virginia. So when the younger Densmore found an opportunity to play in what was hands down the best league in the country, he jumped, joining Ernie Myers, George McClain, and junior college transfer Alvin Battle as part of Valvano's second full recruiting class.

Unlike the others, Densmore did not really have an opportunity to contribute immediately. He was stuck playing behind Lorenzo Charles, Thurl Bailey, Alvin Battle, and Harold Thompson. He appeared in just six games that season and never scored a field goal. His only points came from four made free throws in wins over Fairleigh Dickinson, Clemson, and Georgia Tech. The only time he played in the postseason was in the 75-56 blowout over Utah in the West Region semifinals, grabbing one rebound in one minute of play.

Densmore saw even less action as a sophomore, playing in just one game in the fall of 1983 before he was declared academically ineligible by the university. Densmore admits that his grades suffered during the Wolfpack's month-long run to the national championship and that he had little chance to get back into good standing at NC State. He opted to return home to Alabama with hopes of playing at a smaller school like Samford or Birmingham Southern.

The summer after he left NC State, Densmore sat down with Alabama coach Wimp Sanderson, whose son, Scott, was Densmore's high school teammate, to talk over his options. "Alabama had offered me a scholarship out of high school," said Densmore. "He told me when I met with him, 'Walt, we would love to have you, but unless you are 100 percent sure you want to do this—not 80 or 85 percent sure—I don't want you.'"

By this time, Densmore was not sure if he even wanted to continue playing college basketball. How could he ever top being part of the Wolfpack's odds-defying championship? Densmore talked over his options with his father, who was the director of business services at the University of Alabama. "As long as this is something you don't have regrets about in 20 years," the elder Densmore said, "then you have made the right decision."

So Densmore enrolled at Alabama and began pursuing a degree in communications, advertising, and public relations. A girlfriend he met at NC State eventually joined him in Tuscaloosa to enroll in graduate school. After graduation, they returned to Greensboro, North Carolina, got married, and had two children. That marriage ended after the family moved to Charlotte, North Carolina, but Densmore was remarried in 2000. He and his wife, Ann, lived in Charlotte until the fall of 2006. Just months after former teammate Sidney Lowe was named NC State's head basketball coach, Densmore and his blended family moved back to the Triangle.

With more than two decades of hindsight, Densmore says he has no regrets about the decision he made to give up basketball.

"I really didn't miss it that much," Densmore said. "Playing basketball is very time-consuming. I just focused on getting my degree and enjoying college life at Alabama."

But Densmore treasures his experiences as a member of the 1983 championship team, even if he never saw much playing time. He was a frat-house celebrity during his remaining college years and is a regular at all reunions with his Wolfpack teammates. He saved everything he collected on the team's whirlwind ride, from the St. Christopher's cross someone handed him at the airport on the way to Albuquerque to the Final Four pennant his mother had signed by every member of the team.

"At the time, I was like, 'C'mon, Mom,'" Densmore said. "Now I wish she had three or four more of them."

He also has videotapes of the original broadcast of all nine post-season games, along with several locally produced television specials about the team. He pulls them out from time to time to relive the incredible final month of his college basketball career. They have survived long enough to be copied onto DVD, even if they are a little grainy and choppy.

"The one I like to see the most is the Pepperdine game," he said of the 69-67 double-overtime victory in the first round of the NCAA Tournament. "You can stick a fork in us, because we were done. Without the three-point shot, without the shot clock, we had no chance to win that game."

It was a game Densmore almost did not see in person. He was nearly sent home shortly after the team arrived in Corvallis, Oregon, because of a severe case of the flu. He spent all of his free time holed up in the dumpy hotel where the Wolfpack stayed and was too sick to participate in the team's double-decker bus tour around Corvallis following the win over Nevada-Las Vegas.

Densmore nearly had a big impact on the Wolfpack's championship hopes: Dereck Whittenburg and Jim Valvano both caught the same flu bug two weeks later at the Final Four in Albuquerque, New Mexico. Whittenburg missed two of the team's practices prior to the Georgia game, and Valvano had a 101-degree temperature during the championship game.

Even though he saw action in only seven games during his Wolfpack basketball career, Densmore cherishes his association with the championship team, especially now that he has returned to the Triangle after more than 15 years in Charlotte. He attended several basketball games during Lowe's first season as the Wolfpack's head coach and is a regular at special events the school holds for former basketball players.

"You have to be a pretty big NC State fan to even know I was on that team," Densmore said. "But I have been surprised at how many people know about it, especially now that I am back in Raleigh. The great thing is that the championship season grows with each passing year, and it will continue to do so as long as Sidney is the head coach."

"WE ARE NOT GOING TO WIN A NATIONAL CHAMPIONSHIP"

The day after Dereck Whittenburg had surgery to insert a screw in his broken right foot, the Wolfpack played again in Reynolds Coliseum, handily beating Georgia Tech in a game that was supposed to prove the team would be all right without its senior shooting guard. The good news began when freshman George McClain returned to practice, still weak from his bout with spinal meningitis and still hobbling from the ankle injury he suffered against East Carolina in the third game of the season. He was at least an additional practice player to take Whittenburg's spot.

But the responsibility of replacing Whittenburg in the lineup rested on the shoulders of freshman Ernie Myers, the high-scoring newcomer from the playgrounds of New York. Myers had already impressed his teammates by scoring 18 points in his first collegiate game and 25 points against Clemson in his first ACC game. For Myers, putting points on the board was easy. "Coach called me in his office after Whitt got hurt and said, 'Ernie, we need you to do what you have been doing, just more of it,'" Myers recalled in 2007. "That was fine with me. That's what I came down here from New York for."

So it really was not that surprising that Myers, a classic playground scorer, stepped in and immediately tallied 27 points against the Yellow Jackets. Not only did he hit 10 of his 16 shots, he also canned a pair of three-pointers, showing a shooting touch that typically wasn't part of his game. Maybe things would turn out okay after all.

"If [Ernie] continues to play this way," predicted Georgia Tech coach Bobby Cremins, "NC State will not suffer from the loss of Whittenburg."

But that was hardly the case. The team still had its head, with Sidney Lowe running the point. It still had its soul, with the pensive Thurl Bailey offering everyone a shoulder to cry on. What it needed, however, was a new heart, someone who could not only score points but also kick his teammates in the seat of their shorts.

Valvano knew that heart would be hard to find in the two weeks immediately after Whittenburg went down. After the win over the Yellow Jackets, the Wolfpack had a three-game stretch in five days, including a trip to Chapel Hill, North Carolina, to play the reigning national champion Tar Heels followed by back-to-back games against Wake Forest in Greensboro, North Carolina, and Memphis State in Reynolds. When he set the schedule the summer before, this stretch of games was meant to mimic the challenge of the postseason, when teams must play difficult opponents in a quick turnaround. With Whittenburg out of the lineup, Valvano wished he had stuck with his all-Catholic lineup of opponents.

Even though the competition was tough, Valvano did not like the way his team played in the first two contests. He ripped into the Wolfpack after it lost by 18 points in Chapel Hill. The coach detected a hint of surrender from a team that was clearly feeling sorry for itself.

"If you can't have the same dream I have, then get the hell out of here, because I don't want you playing on my ball club," Valvano told his team after the game. "Whether it's three people left, five people left, or whatever, that's all we'll continue with. You better get your act together or go play somewhere else. We lost a player, but that's over with. That's done. I'm telling you when I say we can get it done, we can get it done. I didn't promise that it would be easy. I didn't promise it would be overnight. I told you it would be a long, hard struggle against what seemed like insurmountable odds and obstacles. I believe we can do it. Now, do you?"

Apparently not. Three days later, the Wolfpack looked, if possible, even worse against the Demon Deacons, committing 15 turnovers in another 18-point loss. Myers had his second straight rough night: the freshman missed 17 of his 25 shots against North Carolina and Wake Forest and failed to score in double figures in either game. Following the bus ride home from Greensboro, Valvano gathered his players in the locker room in the basement of Reynolds Coliseum for another frank assessment.

"You guys know I never bullshit you," the coach said. "I tell you the truth. We are not going to win a national championship this season. I don't know that we will make the NCAAs. We have to set our sights on making the NIT. It would be really nice if we could make it to the finals so I could go home. I always dreamed about playing the late game at Madison Square Garden. It would be kind of nice to raise a banner from there."

His players were shocked. Not 10 days earlier, Valvano had told his team to keep working hard, that something good would happen, and that it was too soon to quit. Now it seemed he was all but writing off the season less than 12 hours before NC State would play a top-five opponent on national television.

"Of all the locker-room speeches he gave that season, that is the one few people remember: 'We have no shot at the national championship—let's go to New York,'" Terry Gannon said.

But the speech made an impact, if only that it upset the right people.

"I was pissed about that," Sidney Lowe said. "I didn't like it. None of us liked it. What I think he was trying to make us do was face the reality that Dereck wasn't there anymore and we needed to figure out what we could do to have a successful season. But in my mind, I didn't like him telling us that we weren't good enough."

The next day, Whittenburg hobbled over to Reynolds Coliseum, the place where his career had supposedly ended, for the Sunday afternoon game against Memphis State. But he was stopped as he tried to enter the side door of the arena without a ticket. It only took a few minutes before Whittenburg found someone who recognized him to let him in the door, but it was a depressing situation for the 22-year-old guard. "How soon they forget," Whittenburg thought. "How soon they forget."

Valvano's speech the night before seemed to have some effect against the Tigers, who had All-American Keith Lee on the court and an assistant coach named Lee Fowler on the sidelines. The Wolfpack led throughout the game and had a chance to win it, but what Valvano believed to be a handful of bad officiating calls doomed the team in the contest's final three minutes. Memphis State guard Phillip "Doom" Haynes, who hit a driving lay-up with 51 seconds to play, can also take some credit for the Tigers' win. Thurl Baily actually blocked Haynesk's shot from his help-side position, but the ball bounced off teammate Lorenzo Charles' outstretched arm and into the basket. Clearly, the Wolfpack could not catch a break. With nine seconds to play, Lee hit a pair of free throws to finish off the Wolfpack's third defeat in just five days.

"We feel snakebit," Valvano said after the game. "This is not my year right now. I don't know what more can happen to this team."

For one, the Wolfpack could read its obituary in the paper the next morning. *Durham Sun* columnist Frank Dascenzo wrote, "NC State's 1982-83 basketball team died yesterday in Reynolds Coliseum of severe discouragement and depression. Funeral services will be delayed so coach Jim Valvano can finish the season, one that carried a horizon of high hope but now shows burning ashes."

Valvano was certainly in mourning: "I don't think I ever saw Coach V as despondent as he was when we lost to Memphis," said Max Perry, a graduate assistant that season. "He said there were things we should have done differently. I don't think he slept, literally, for three days after that game. Of course, that wasn't all that unusual for him."

As the season progressed, however, Valvano began to view the loss to the Tigers as something of a turning point. Since the game was played without the ACC's experimental rules, Valvano chose to play the entire game in a 2-3 zone defense, trying to control the tempo and protect Myers' inexperience on defense. That was a mistake, the head coach later admitted.

"We stayed in that same defense the entire 40 minutes, and the game went right down to the wire," Valvano said. "I decided from that point on we would not play another game against a team and not make them play against man-to-man pressure or against a half-court trap. We needed to play more aggressively."

Two things cheered Valvano up after that loss. First was a phone call from his old coach, Bill Foster, who had watched the loss to Memphis State from a hospital room, where he was recovering from quadruple bypass heart surgery. "He was calling me to cheer me up," Valvano said.

Secondly, Valvano got a little pick-me-up from the university. After making the NCAA Tournament in 1981-82, Valvano asked for a big contract extension to show his commitment to the school and the school's commitment to him. The day before his team hosted Duke in Reynolds Coliseum, Valvano signed a 10-year contract, upping his annual income from the school and his numerous outside activities to a reported $300,000 a year.

The Wolfpack celebrated their coach's renewed commitment to the school with an important win over Mike Krzyzewski's rebuilding Blue Devils, which had four freshmen in its starting lineup. Myers, who had struggled with his shooting touch against North Carolina and Wake Forest, gained some confidence when he scored 18 points versus Memphis State. Against the Blue Devils, Myers exploded offensively for 35 points, breaking the ACC freshman scoring record.

But Myers' 15 points were not enough when the Wolfpack went to Maryland on what should have been Whittenburg's final trip home of his college career. Lowe didn't have a very good night in front of his home crowd either, making only two of eight shots and scoring six points. Only Thurl Bailey, the least well known of the Wolfpack's Washington trio during his high school days, played well, scoring 18 points and grabbing seven rebounds. Maryland's Stevie Rivers controlled this game, hitting 11 three-pointers and scoring 29 points for the Terrapins.

With the defeat, the Wolfpack's record dropped to nine wins, seven losses. The prospects for a second consecutive trip to the NCAA Tournament were looking bleak, an unimaginable scenario when the season began just two months earlier.

ERNIE MYERS

One thing Ernie Myers wants everyone to know is that he was a big part of NC State's 1982-83 season before Dereck Whittenburg suffered a broken foot. And he was an important part of the program for three years afterwards as well.

It seems, though, what people remember most when they talk—and talk and talk and talk—to Myers is that he stepped in from nowhere as a 14-game fill-in and then kind of disappeared.

"People always think I just came in when Whittenburg got hurt," Myers said. "I could have sworn I was playing before then, scoring a lot of points. It seems like that's what people remember: Dereck got hurt and here came this guy who was a freshman who had just been sitting on the bench before. But I guess that's how it goes."

Myers has good reason to be a little miffed. The former Parade and McDonald's All-America selection scored 18 points against Western Carolina in his college debut in November. "I was thinking, 'This isn't that hard,'" Myers said. He had 25 points in his Atlantic

Coast Conference debut against Clemson in early January. He was averaging 11 points through the Wolfpack's first 10 games of the season. "I didn't come to Raleigh from New York to sit on the bench," Myers said. "I wanted to play and to show Coach [Jim] Valvano everything that was being written about me was true."

But things changed dramatically after the Wolfpack's ACC home opener against Virginia, the game in which Whittenburg broke the fifth metatarsal in his right foot and opened a new door for Myers. From that moment on, the freshman went from a role-playing reserve to a starter who had to assume the scoring responsibilities of the team captain. Myers, a free-spirited scorer, loved it.

In the Wolfpack's first game without Whittenburg, Myers scored 27 points against Georgia Tech. He struggled with his shooting soon afterwards, but was a dynamic player, capable of putting a dozen points on the board whenever he suited up. In a late January game against Duke, Myers broke free for 35, the most points ever scored by an ACC freshman. He finished the season with 391 points, which at the time was second only to the 420 scored by Hawkeye Whitney for an NC State freshman.

"I did not think I played a whole lot differently during that stretch than I did before," Myers said. "I was just playing a lot more minutes and the team needed me to score more. I really didn't think I turned on some kind of switch after Dereck got hurt and came completely out of the blue. But I hear that a lot."

Fans are not mistaken when they say that Myers practically disappeared over the final 12 games of the season after Whittenburg returned to his regular starting spot in the lineup and the Wolfpack went back to playing without the ACC's experimental 30-second clock and three-point line. What people do not understand is that Myers was not sulking on the sidelines. He just had to do what the rest of the reserves, other than Terry Gannon and Alvin Battle, had to do the final month of the season: wait for his number to be called in a situation he was needed.

For Myers, those situations did not come up very often. He saw extensive action in the Wolfpack's opening-round win over Wake Forest in the ACC Tournament, but played only four minutes and did not score in the other two games. He barely moved off the bench in the double-overtime game against Pepperdine, the close victory over Nevada-Las Vegas, and even the blowout win versus Utah. He did not play at all in the semifinal win over Georgia and was in for just 30 seconds of the championship game. In all, he scored only 12 points in the Wolfpack's nine-game run to the national championship. But, as he quickly points out, he was enjoying every minute of the championship run.

"I think people expected me to be angry and mad about that, but I wasn't," Myers said. "We started winning. How could I be angry about that? It was different coming off the bench again, but I still felt confident. The team just started playing differently. When we got to the NCAA Tournament, there was no three-point shot and no 30-second clock. It was like every possession was life and death. You lose the ball and the game is over. That was Whit's kind of game. It wasn't my game."

Fortunately for the Wolfpack, Myers recognized and accepted that the Wolfpack was a better team with Whittenburg back in the lineup. This is not a poor reflection on Myers, but a testament to how much all the other components matured while Whittenburg was gone. Lorenzo Charles was more aggressive. Cozell McQueen played up to better competition. Terry Gannon gained even more confidence in his shot.

"I'd like to think I had something to do with that," Myers said. "They saw how I played when I got my chance, that I wasn't scared to play. I thought they played a little nervous before Whitt got hurt. They saw me play and said, 'This freshman from New York, he can't be better than I am,' and they worked harder to get their shots."

In his book, *Too Soon to Quit*, Valvano wrote, "Ernie stepped in and performed brilliantly when Dereck was injured. He did a magnificent job. He was our leading scorer during that stretch and had some incredible games. He was the unsung hero of our 'season within a season.'"

But the way Myers handled his reduced role may have been as important to the Wolfpack's postseason success as his scoring was during Whittenburg's absence.

"We always felt when Dereck came back, it would make us a better team," said assistant coach Tom Abatemarco. "Mainly because we always knew that we would have Ernie as instant offense off the bench. It might have bothered Ernie at the time, but he took it like a trooper. He helped us in the games and was a better player for it."

As a sophomore, Myers admits that he took his position in the starting lineup a little too much for granted. He did not work quite as hard in the off-season, came back a few pounds overweight, and continued to press on when his shot didn't fall. That is what scorers like Myers do—miss a shot and shoot again. But what he did not realize was how quickly things would change after Whittenburg and Sidney Lowe left the program. Valvano became much more dependent on inside players like Charles, McQueen, Russell Pierre, Chris Washburn, Chucky Brown, and Charles Shackleford. Valvano needed shooters on the wings, not a scorer who could slash into the lane and make things even more congested inside for his big men. Myers never pretended to be an outside shooter. When Myers missed his first 17 shots his sophomore season, it was easy for Valvano to pencil Terry Gannon's name into the starting lineup at shooting guard, even though the ACC no longer had a three-point line.

As a junior, Myers started in 25 of 33 games as a small forward, averaging a career-low seven points a game as the Wolfpack returned to the Elite Eight. When his senior season began, Myers was the only remaining player on the roster from the national championship team. The rest of his recruiting-class buddies—George McClain, Dinky Proctor, Walt Densmore, and Alvin Battle—had either left school voluntarily or flunked out. But even though he remained a crowd favorite, Myers was no longer the centerpiece of NC State's offense. "We played a different kind of game, more pound it inside," Myers said. "And [Valvano] wanted me to do different things." He was expected to rebound, to make passes, and to be a team leader rather than a leading scorer. Myers shared his playing time with too many similarly sized competitors at the shooting guard and small forward positions—Nate McMillan, Bennie Bolton, Vinny Del Negro, and Walker Lambiotte—to be the star he expected to be after his freshman season.

What makes Myers different than many high school All-Americans whose NBA dreams did not come true is how he handled it.

"When you look at my career, it wasn't what I expected, but it was better than a lot of people," Myers said. "And we did something that was special. People will remember me forever as part of NC State's basketball legacy."

Even if they do not get all the little details correct.

Like many kids who learned basketball on the New York City playgrounds, Myers expected the game to be his way out of a difficult life at the corner of 123rd Street and Lexington Avenue. He grew up in the heart of Spanish Harlem, where hookers and pushers staked out their territories not far from where Myers' uncles taught him the basics of basketball. Before he was a teenager, he saw a disagreement between two men playing cards. One of them pulled a knife, the other pulled a gun. Myers was only 20 feet away when the man with the gun shot and killed the other.

In such a place, the basketball courts could keep some young people safe. "If we weren't doing nothing else, we were playing basketball," Myers said. "It kept us out of trouble. We would get a group of guys together from our housing complex and go around to all the other housing complexes and play against their best five guys. It became a vehicle to get me out of where I was, to lift my family up."

He also learned about other parts of the country. He would spend some of his summers with his grandmother in Florence, South Carolina. He stayed with other members of his mother's family in New Bern, North Carolina. That made his decision to play at NC State much easier.

When he was 14, Myers and his mother, Marie Lovell, moved to a safer neighborhood, closer to downtown Manhattan. He became involved with the Riverside Church Hawks, an AAU basketball program coached by New York legend Ernie Lorch. Traveling the globe to play basketball made Myers worldlier, whether he was drinking water from a mountain stream in Utah, viewing the Grand Canyon, or going head to head in a best-of-seven road series against the Russians in Moscow.

"I saw a lot of things kids in Harlem would never see," Myers said. "Our coach would make sure we didn't just go places and play basketball. He would make it a learning experience."

Myers also faced stiff competition attending all-star basketball camps. As a contemporary of guys like Michael Jordan, Len Bias, and Johnny Dawkins—all of whom became stars in the Atlantic Coast Conference—Myers knew he could play *against* the best players on the planet. He could play *with* some of the best players as well. His Riverside Church teammates included Kenny Smith, Bruce Dalrymple, Chris Mullin, Walter Berry, and Ed Pinckney. "When I got down to NC State, I was like, 'Hold up, I've played against some of these guys already,'" Myers said. "So it was no big deal for me to play against them again. I came to NC State very confident."

To be honest, though, Myers' dream was not to play college basketball. He wanted to play in the NBA like his childhood heroes, Walt Frazier, George Gervin, and David Thompson. "I liked guys who could jump high," Myers said. "I liked guys who had a lot of flair. I liked guys who scored a lot of points."

As a sophomore, Myers met a dynamic young coach who liked the way he played. The coach had a special connection to Tolentine—his father had been the coach at the Catholic school for years during the 1950s and '60s. Myers' coach at Tolentine, Bob Austin, had even played for the coach's father way back when. After visiting a Tolentine practice to recruit Myers' teammate, Mike Moses, the coach told Myers, "You wait right here for two more years and I'll be back to get you." His name was Jim Valvano from Iona College.

After leading Tolentine to three consecutive New York City championships, the high school senior was one of the top-rated high school prospects in the country. Valvano had moved on to NC State, but he did not forget about the young player who was averaging nearly 30 points and 10 rebounds per game. The Wolfpack was one of 250 schools that sent Myers recruiting letters. The young player did not forget that Valvano was the first coach to show interest in his game, and he eagerly headed south to play for the Wolfpack.

Myers knew he was not going to be a basketball junkie his entire life. He worked hard in pursuing his degree in communications, staying at NC State an extra year as a student assistant coach to finish his degree requirements and become the first member of his family to graduate from college. He spent one year playing professional basketball in Innsbrook, Austria, before returning to New York to begin his career as a social worker in Brooklyn, where he tried to reach out to kids growing up in the same kind of community that he did. It was a rewarding but mentally and emotionally challenging job, especially for a single parent.

After he returned to New York, Myers was married briefly. The union produced a son, Ernest Marquise Myers. About two years after his divorce, the elder Myers gained custody of his seven-year-old son and assumed the responsibility of sole caretaker with plenty of help from his mother, his grandmother, and the rest of his family.

"It's a hard job," admitted Myers, who had a limited relationship with his father before he died in 1985. "You have got to do every-thing: be the mother and the father. You have to compensate for the loss of one of the parents, going to all the parent meetings, taking him to the doctor, staying at home with him when he is sick, and still get all of [your] work done. It was a rough situation."

But Myers established a successful career path after he left his job as a social worker. He worked for a while as a sales representa-tive for the Miller Brewing Company. He now works for a New York company that sells litigation databases, shuffling back and forth between Manhattan and Atlanta, Georgia, and his new—and old—home, Raleigh.

Myers lived one more dose of destiny when his old teammate, Sidney Lowe—the player who hosted Myers on his recruiting visit to NC State—was named the Wolfpack's 18th men's basketball coach in the spring of 2006. Two days before the announcement was made, Myers was walking down a street in Manhattan when he received a phone call inviting him to join other members of the 1983 champi-onship team at the Saturday afternoon press conference in which Lowe would be officially introduced.

When Myers heard that Cozell McQueen and some of his other teammates were planning to be there, he decided to make his way south from New York one more time. He could not catch a flight out of any of the three airports in the New York area, so he took a train to Philadelphia, where he almost missed his plane. He arrived in Raleigh just in time to reach the Dail Practice Facility before the 4 p.m. press conference.

While spending time with the familiar faces that surrounded him that afternoon—McQueen, Alvin Battle, Tommy DiNardo, Max Perry, and Quentin Jackson—Myers said hello to NC State's Hall of Fame women's basketball coach Kay Yow. Standing beside her was NC State's assistant athletic director for media relations, Annabelle Vaughan.

Days after the press conference, Vaughan was asked to write a magazine story on either McQueen or Myers. She randomly picked Myers and set up a telephone interview with him after he returned to New York. After that hour-long phone call, the two began dating. Within months, Myers transferred his office to Raleigh, and five months after they met, the two were married.

"He loves being part of NC State and the basketball program again," Annabelle Myers said. "There are so many of them together again. He went to football games all fall and to some of the basketball games that I didn't even go to."

So many little details could have derailed Myers' entire trip to Raleigh that fateful afternoon. What if Lowe's press conference had been on a weekday instead of the weekend? What if he had not decided to take the train to Philadelphia? What if he had missed his plane? What if Coach Yow was standing alone?

It almost seems like, well, some kind of destiny.

"I prefer to think of it as God's plan, but His plan is my destiny," she said. "All the factors came together to bring us together, and if just one of them had not worked out, we would have never met. We think about that all the time. I think it is a great story."

And it's one that seems strikingly familiar for someone who lived through NC State's miracle run of 1983.

9 "MY DREAM SITUATION"

Terry Gannon wanted to beat one team on NC State's schedule more than any other. And it was not one of the usual suspects like North Carolina, Virginia, Maryland, or Duke.

Growing up in Joliet, Illinois, Gannon had the same dream as every other Irish-Catholic schoolboy who had picked up a football, basketball, or baseball. "I went to bed for 12 years praying I could play for Notre Dame," Gannon said. He regularly went to South Bend, Indiana, to play pickup games with a kid from his hometown, a hustler who had wormed his way into living in the residential portion of the Athletic and Convocation Center, Notre Dame's basketball arena, by working as an equipment manager for the football team. A journeyman in his 20s and a pre-teen gym rat who both dreamed of one day playing for the Green and Gold teamed up time and time again to play against college students in the darkened arena.

Against all odds, one of them accomplished that goal. Gannon's friend, Daniel Ruettiger, had spent time in both the Navy and at an area junior college. He then spent two years handing out socks and towels in the equipment room before he talked the Irish coaches into adding him as a non-scholarship practice player. On November 8, 1975, his lifelong dream came true when he saw action in the final two plays of Notre Dame's win over Georgia Tech. That brief appearance spawned the inspirational movie *Rudy*, as Ruettiger was known as to all his friends.

After that now-famous game ended, Rudy handed his golden helmet to a 12-year-old kid in the locker room and said, "Terry, sneak this out of here." Later that evening, when his teammates' chants had died down, Rudy said goodbye to his parents and went out to dinner with the Gannon family at a South Bend restaurant. (Gannon held on to that helmet for years, saving it from a scrapheap in 2006 during a mother-in-law cleaning spree. "It's a little banged up and scuffed," Gannon said. "I figured after the movie came out I should probably stop playing backyard games in it and put it up.")

Gannon longed to have a similar experience as a Notre Dame hero for Digger Phelps' basketball program. He had all the connections a young player could hope for: because of his dad's status as the head coach of a major Catholic high school in the Chicago-land area, Gannon was in the locker room during every Notre Dame home football game from the time he was five years old until he left for college. Rudy even put in a good word for him with Phelps. "[Digger] took one look at Terry and said, 'He is too small,'" Ruettiger said. "I told him, 'You gotta see him shoot. He can shoot the eyes out of the basket.' Digger said, 'What the hell do you know about basketball, Rudy? You make one tackle and all of a sudden you are an authority?'"

By Gannon's senior year, he was 6 feet tall and 170 pounds. He was also Joliet Catholic High School's all-time leading scorer, a deadly outside shooter who was also an all-state pitcher on his high school baseball team. But Phelps wanted someone bigger. He signed Dan Duff as his only shooting-guard recruit that year, sending Gannon on a search for a new dream. He could have gone to any of a handful of Midwestern mid-major schools, like Marquette or Loyola of Chicago, but he was intrigued by the possibility of playing basketball in the Atlantic Coast Conference—especially at NC State, where a good friend was already playing baseball.

Pitcher Mike Pesavento convinced Wolfpack baseball coach Sam Esposito to talk to basketball coach Jim Valvano about Gannon. Esposito was a former assistant basketball coach under Norman Sloan and had once found another two-sport star named Tim Stoddard, an integral part of NC State's 1974 NCAA championship team. Esposito, who later became one of Valvano's most trusted advisors, was persistent about this Gannon kid, perhaps because he had won eight straight games and pitched a two-hitter the day Esposito went to see him play. Valvano eventually dispatched one of his assistants to Joliet for a state playoff game, and Gannon turned in an impressive 42-point performance.

When Valvano offered him a scholarship, he also mentioned that the Wolfpack still had two games remaining in a four-year contract with the Fighting Irish.

Gannon's freshman year, the Wolfpack whipped Phelps' team by 20 points, though Gannon contributed little to the victory. He was hoping for a much bigger role when the Irish came to Reynolds Coliseum on February 12, 1983. The Wolfpack finally seemed to have rebounded from Whittenburg's absence and demoralizing losses to North Carolina and Wake Forest.

Freshman Ernie Myers had found his rhythm again, senior point guard Sidney Lowe was beginning to take additional offensive responsibilities, and the big sophomores down low, Cozell McQueen and Lorenzo Charles, were becoming more confident in their abilities. Gannon continued to provide instant offense off the bench as an outside shooter, whether the Wolfpack was playing with or without the ACC's experimental rules. The team had reeled off four straight wins over Georgia Tech in Atlanta, Furman and The Citadel in a North-South doubleheader in Charlotte, and the Tigers at Littlejohn Coliseum in Clemson.

The game against the Fighting Irish was the Wolfpack's last chance to gain a victory over an intersectional opponent to impress the NCAA Selection Committee. Valvano knew it would not be easy: senior forward Thurl Bailey had been suffering from the flu all week and had a bad reaction to some medication he had taken before the game. He was playing at half-strength, at best.

An hour before the contest started, however, the crowd received an unexpected surprise when Whittenburg stepped onto the court wearing a suit with an open-collared shirt, one sneaker on his injured right foot, and a dress shoe on his left foot. For 15 minutes, he thrilled—and, to some extent, saddened—the early arrivals at sold-out Reynolds Coliseum by hitting a handful of jump shots in his street clothes. "I just wanted them to know I was getting ready," Whittenburg said. "Getting ready."

However, he could not contribute just yet. Gannon was sure he could provide whatever outside punch the Wolfpack needed, since his point totals had also improved during Whittenburg's absence and he had twice led the team in scoring.

The game settled into another old-style, slow-down contest dominated by tempo-controlling point guards. Wolfpack senior Sidney Lowe, who also grew up wanting to play for the Fighting Irish, had not fully forgiven Phelps for signing prep All-American John Paxson instead. The two floor leaders went at each other all game long.

Duff, the player Phelps had chosen over Gannon as his shooting guard, missed two of his three free-throw attempts in the final 90 seconds of the game. Gannon had the perfect opportunity to be a hero. On the game's final possession, Valvano called for a play that put Gannon on one wing, Myers on the other, and the two big sophomores beneath the basket. Lowe's job was to penetrate and create a shot for himself or get it to one of his open shooters on the wings.

Gannon was wide open and Lowe hit him with the perfect pass. But the 18-foot jumper with five seconds to play bounced off the rim and into the hands of a waiting Tim Kempton. "You couldn't ask for a better shot than that," Valvano said after the game. Gannon left the court with his head slumped down. "I had been waiting for this game for a long time," Gannon said in the locker room. "It was my dream situation: a jump shot to beat Notre Dame on national television. I'd love to have the chance to take that shot again tomorrow."

For days, he was inconsolable. "He was really bad after that game," said Lowe, remembering the occasion years later. "He had his head down. We all knew he wanted it so bad. But the thing is, he bounced back."

"That game still eats him up," said Gannon's one-time roommate, Mike Warren. "It's like the lowlight of his life. It was the exact same play we ran so many times at the end of the game, where we work it around and get the ball to the open shooter."

But this time, it didn't work. This NC State version of *Rudy*—a Grade B script at best—never made it off the cutting-room floor.

The Wolfpack had only six regular-season games remaining to make a strong impression, and Whittenburg wasn't ready to make shots in anything other than a dress suit. With reigning national champion North Carolina on its way in less than a week, Valvano and his team needed to find inspiration elsewhere.

TERRY GANNON

When watching him on television—at the British Open, the Belmont Stakes, the World Figure Skating Championships, or a weekly college football or basketball game—it's hard to believe that happy-go-lucky Terry Gannon is such a bitter man.

But bring up the last play in NC State's improbable national championship, and the ABC broadcaster with the boyish good looks is ready to spit on the grave of his NC State teammate and post-practice nemesis, Dereck Whittenburg—even if it is not filled yet.

"I just want Whit and the whole world to know that he has cursed himself to a lifetime of ridicule by me to everybody I come in contact with in every walk of life," Gannon said. "I will tell them all that I could have been immortalized but for one asshole who wouldn't throw me the ball."

Gannon is convinced he would have been the hero of the 1983 NCAA championship game against Houston. He was standing wide open on the wing when Whittenburg let fly college basketball's most famous airball with just seconds to play.

"Why in the hell would I pass the ball to him?" Whittenburg said. "Number one, I'd just made three 25-foot jump shots. Number two, I don't pass. And number three, I ain't passing it to a fucking sophomore."

The irony, of course, is that Whittenburg did exactly that: his 30-foot shot from the left wing was two feet short and landed right in the hands of sophomore forward Lorenzo Charles, who dunked the ball as time expired.

"Any time I am sitting around with the guys I work with when that play comes on," Gannon said, "they all say, 'Hey look, there's Gannon standing wide open on the wing.'" And that's where he stood to watch the dunk that gave the Wolfpack the impossible 54-52 victory.

"Life could have been very different," said Gannon, with real wistfulness. "I could have been on all the posters instead of Lorenzo."

It's been 25 years, but Gannon and Whittenburg can't stop taking mostly good-natured jabs at each other, just as they did while playing countless post-practice games of "H-O-R-S-E" and "Tips," a Jim Valvano-created shooting and rebounding contest.

In reality, though, Gannon has no complaints about the path his life has taken, away from the steel-mill town of Joliet, Illinois, and his preordained career as a high school basketball coach like his father to a globetrotting basketball player and network television commentator.

Gannon grew up in a gym, watching his father's high school basketball teams practice and play. Jim Gannon was a successful boys' high school coach at Joliet Catholic, until health problems forced him out. He eventually returned to coaching for a local girls' high school program. Dinner-table conversation always revolved around sports, and Jim Gannon spent many weekends with his only child enjoying baseball games at Comiskey Park, horse racing at the Arlington Park racetrack, and college football at Notre Dame Stadium. Terry spent time with his mom, a professional dance instructor, as well, but he rarely mentions his four years of tap-dancing lessons when talking to his buddies in the sports world.

Despite a diminutive frame, Gannon excelled in baseball and basketball. At 12, he was a pitcher on a team that went to the Boys Baseball World Championship, the Midwestern equivalent to the Little League World Series. As a high school shortstop and pitcher, he was good enough to catch the eye of NC State baseball coach Sam Esposito, who had signed Joliet Catholic High School pitcher Mike Pesavento to play baseball for the Wolfpack two years earlier.

When Valvano came to visit Gannon's parents, they were smitten with the coach's energy and enthusiasm. Valvano sat in the kitchen discussing basketball with Jim Gannon for most of that visit while Terry climbed the living room walls, unable to hear the conversation that would decide his future. By the time Valvano left that evening, Gannon knew that his dream would lead him south. He admits he was a little leery about heading to North Carolina. "I had never been south of Comiskey Park in my life," Gannon said. "I remember thinking, 'What's it going to be like? Are there a bunch of plantations?' That's how naïve I was."

As a freshman, Gannon played both basketball and baseball. He contributed little to either, however, and decided afterward to concentrate just on basketball. As soon as the ACC adopted its experimental 19-foot three-point line before his sophomore season, Gannon knew he would have a larger impact on the Wolfpack. Arguably, no player has been a bigger force beyond the arc: Gannon made 53 of his 90 shots from the three-point distance, setting an ACC record of 58.9 percent that still stands nearly a quarter-century later.

Saddled with the all-too-obvious nickname "Gannon the Cannon," he blossomed as a shooter as his confidence grew, particularly after Whittenburg broke a bone in his foot and was declared done for the season. While his shooting may have been diminished when the Wolfpack entered the NCAA Tournament—when the ACC's super-short three-point rule was no longer in effect for the Wolfpack—Gannon continued to make contributions, displaying strong ball-handling skills, making clutch free throws, and playing unexpected defense. In the ACC title game, he stripped the ball out of Virginia star Ralph Sampson's hands with less than a minute to play. The smallest guy on the court took the ball away from college basketball's biggest giant to preserve yet another unlikely victory. In the double-overtime win over Pepperdine, Gannon's outside shooting allowed the Wolfpack to tie the contest in regulation. In the NCAA title game, he took the first-half charge that gave Houston's Clyde Drexler his fourth foul, a play that perhaps had the biggest impact on the game outside of Charles' dunk.

The rest of Gannon's career, played without the three-point line, wasn't quite as productive. (The NCAA adopted a permanent three-point line in 1986-87, two years after Gannon graduated.) He was the team's second-leading scorer in 1984, when the Wolfpack missed the NCAA Tournament. As a senior, Gannon suffered from a staph infection in his left leg, missing the first week of practice and completely losing his rhythm. He started only three games that year as Valvano relied more on Nate McMillan and Spud Webb in the backcourt. With a disappointing 41.4 shooting percentage from the field, Gannon finished sixth on the team with a 6.5-point scoring average. But Gannon, who maintained a 3.5 grade-point average, became NC State basketball's first Academic All-American his junior year and repeated the feat as a senior. He was awarded the 1985 Alumni Athletic Trophy as the school's top senior athlete and was the recipient of a $2,000 NCAA post-graduate scholarship.

But Gannon had already lived his greatest conceivable dream as part of the '83 championship team and didn't really know what he wanted to do with his life other than follow in his father's footsteps as a coach. He was finishing his degree in history education as a student teacher at Apex High School. In 1985-86, he and Whittenburg joined Valvano's coaching staff as graduate assistants. The grunt work consisted of little more than stocking Valvano's office with pizza, Church's Fried Chicken, cigars, and cheap wine for the coach's late-night, postgame bull sessions with his staff, his posse, and an occasional opposing coach. Gannon enjoyed being part of the fun, but was itching for more. He had received a few calls about the possibility of playing professionally in Europe, an idea that intrigued him, if only to see the world.

In the winter of 1986, Gannon visited Valvano for some career counseling. Jefferson Pilot Broadcasting had approached him to do some locker-room reporting from the ACC Tournament. Gannon believed he was at a crossroads in his life and was looking for some sage advice. Valvano told him to drop by the office the next day.

"So I get there and he's on the phone," Gannon said. "I am waiting about five minutes and he looks up and says, 'Terry, what do you need?' He's still talking to the guy on the other line. I say, 'Well, Coach, we are going to talk about my life, map out my future. Should I go to Europe? Should I coach? Should I pursue this broadcasting thing?'

"He told the person to hold on for a second and said, 'Terry, you're white, you're slow, you can't run, you can't jump. Who the fuck are you going to be, the next Walt Frazier? Get on with your life. Go do the broadcasting. If you don't like it or if you stink, come back and coach for me. I'll always have a job for you.' That kind of took care of my life in about 35 seconds."

In theory, anyway. Gannon had to hustle his way into the profession, first by doing some interviews at the 1987 ACC Tournament. He

136

made $50 a contest broadcasting Triple-A Charlotte Knights base-
ball games, but the gas used to take the five-hour round trip from
Raleigh ate up all his wages. Gannon filled in for Valvano on his
morning radio show and did a couple of scholar-athlete segments on
the coach's weekly television show. He filled in for UNC network
broadcaster Woody Durham on the *Morning Zoo Sports Report*. He
was paid by the segment to do sports features on the now-defunct
syndicated show *PM Magazine* with WRAL cameramen Jay Jennings
and Jeff Gravely.

"I would edit, produce, be the talent for the whole thing," Gannon
said. "If it was good enough, they ran it. If they ran it, they would pay
me. I wiggled my way into doing the radio broadcast for the Charlotte
Knights. I did some features on something called *ACC Sports Center*,
driving to Clemson or Georgia Tech or wherever, shooting the whole
thing, and putting it all together. I was on my own. But I learned every
aspect of the business and paid some dues."

For five years, Gannon did color commentary for basketball
games on Raycom and Jefferson Pilot weekly broadcasts. When
Valvano was diagnosed with cancer in 1992, Gannon traveled with
his old coach, prepared to step in whenever Valvano was too sick to
go on the air. He officially signed on with ABC in 1992. Two years
later, on a sunny September Monday afternoon, ABC executive pro-
ducer Mark O'Hara asked Gannon if he would do the upcoming North
Carolina-Georgia Tech game. "Sure," Gannon said, "but basketball
season is still three months away." But O'Hara wanted Gannon to do
play-by-play for the Tar Heels-Yellow Jackets football game.

"I had never been in a football press box in my entire life,"
Gannon said.

At that moment, Gannon took everything he ever learned from
Valvano and accepted the challenge.

"I put the phone down and started scrambling to find out how
the hell I was going to do play-by-play for a college football game,"

Gannon said. "I called every play-by-play guy I knew and asked them to send me their boards for preparation."

But he needed some experience in the press box. So he called two buddies—former basketball teammate Mike Warren and Pesavento, the baseball pitcher who first recommended Gannon to Wolfpack baseball coach Sam Esposito—to see if he could horn in on their weekly high school football telecast on the nonprofit Victory Television Network, which served about 35,000 viewers in western Wake County.

"I did the Apex-Cary football game on a Thursday night with Mike Warren and Mike Pesavento as co-hosts," Gannon said. "On Saturday, I did North Carolina and Georgia Tech on ABC in Atlanta. It was a helluva week."

But it also reinforced one of Valvano's greatest lessons: never be afraid to take chances. That philosophy has led Gannon, the little shooting guard who wanted nothing more than to coach high school basketball in Joliet, Illinois, to a high-profile, diverse broadcasting career far removed from his original dream. Among his worldwide travels for athletic events, Gannon has been to the Goodwill Games in Russia, the Tour de France, the World Cup in Los Angeles, the World Figure Skating Championships in Bulgaria, the British Open golf tournament, and the Arlington Million horse race right in his backyard near Chicago.

He's lived in Raleigh, Charlotte, Los Angeles, California, and New Jersey. He shares his profession with the former Lisa Sherrill, the daughter of a high school basketball coach who he met while at NC State. They now live on the West Coast with their three children.

"I have never been a goal person," Gannon said. "Jimmy taught me to be a dreamer, but if I had set goals, it would have limited me. He made me think that I should have an open mind and take the opportunities that came my way. So I took those opportunities to go do different sports and go do everything instead of mapping out my career as a college basketball or college football announcer. You can argue about what is more successful or what is a better career move, but for me, I really love covering a lot of different sports. One day, I am sitting next to Jerry Bailey, a Hall of Fame jockey, covering the Arlington Million or the Belmont Stakes, and two days later I am sitting next to Nick Faldo and Paul Azinger covering a major golf tournament, and the next week I am sitting next to Peggy Fleming and Dick Button covering a major skating championship. That's a pretty exciting way to cover sports."

Living this way has brought Gannon some great payoffs. One of his co-workers is former Notre Dame basketball coach Digger Phelps, who once determined that Gannon was too small to play college basketball and signed Dan Duff instead. Gannon loves working in the studio with him now.

"Hey, Digger, do you have your ring on?" Gannon sometimes asks. "Oh, that's right, you don't have one."

"He calls me every name in the book and we go from there," Gannon said. "But the point is if Digger Phelps had taken Terry Gannon instead of Dan Duff, right now I am coaching high school basketball in Joliet and probably very happy doing it. But how different would my life be?"

Gannon admits his life turned out pretty well. But maybe, just maybe, it could have been better.

In 1985, the Wolfpack was sent back to Albuquerque, New Mexico, for the first weekend of the NCAA Tournament. As soon as Gannon stepped off the bus for the team's first practice at The Pit, he grabbed a basketball and found the exact spot on which he was standing two years earlier in the national championship game, wide open while his teammates scrambled to get off a decisive shot.

He took the uncontested shot and watched it fall quietly through the basket.

"I buried it just so I could tell everybody forever, 'I would have knocked it down,'" Gannon said.

Of course he made the shot. By then, Gannon was a senior.

"I DON'T THINK ANYTHING COULD FEEL BETTER"

10

Greg Hatem and Mark Ciarrocca had a plan—they just needed a little help from a friend in Chapel Hill. It was two days before NC State played North Carolina in Reynolds Coliseum, generally the biggest game of the year for NC State students, alumni, and fans. The *Technician*, NC State's student newspaper, was in the process of putting together its annual spoof of the *Daily Tar Heel*, UNC's student newspaper. The competition between the papers—one stocked by plucky reporters who were more likely to be studying engineering against one staffed by students from a renowned journalism school— was intense. Their parodies of one another, which frequently jumped on the other side of good taste, were along familiar themes: NC State usually made fun of Chapel Hill's liberal, hoity-toity atmosphere, while UNC poked fun of NC State's down-home, low-brow background.

The rivalry has always been defined as culture versus agriculture.

So on Thursday, February 17, less than 36 hours before the game's tip-off, Hatem and Ciarrocca headed to Chapel Hill with a back-page photo idea. Hatem had a camera; Ciarrocca had a basketball. They met a buddy on UNC's campus and went to one of the famous bars on Franklin Street for a couple of beers. Afterwards, they walked to Carmichael Auditorium, home of the UNC men's basketball team from 1965-86. How did they get into the locked arena? "It's amazing how many doors will open if you pull on them hard enough," Hatem said.

They only spent a few minutes inside. While Hatem framed a perfect picture, Ciarrocca stripped naked, plopped down smack in the middle of the light blue UNC logo at center court, and positioned the basketball over his privates. After only a few snaps of Hatem's camera, they gathered up their things, rushed back to NC State, and headed for the third floor of the student center, where the newspaper offices were located. In the days before the picture-altering computer program Photoshop, Hatem still found a way to produce the image he wanted by photographing a page from the UNC media guide, reducing the picture to a size proportionate to what he already had, carefully cutting out a head, and pasting it right on top of his picture of Ciarrocca's body.

The next morning, students at both campuses were greeted with a newspaper called *The Daily Tar Heal*, featuring a back-page picture of UNC coach Dean Smith lying naked at center court of Carmichael Auditorium—a perfectly fake picture of the famous Coach Gone Wild.

The picture illustrated a bogus editorial about *Playboy Magazine*, which had created a stir on both campuses for recruiting coeds to participate in an upcoming "Girls of the ACC" spread. Both campuses held multiple protests over the sexist nature of the advertising, though the outcry was a little more vehement in the more politically correct Chapel Hill. The editorial complained that no males were recruited for the layout and offered up Smith—the outspoken liberal who had just filmed a series of regional ads calling for a nuclear freeze—as a prime model for this kind of exposure.

Fifteen thousand copies of the fake edition were distributed on NC

Jim Valvano
Courtesy of Roger Winstead

The 1983 seniors. Front row: Karen Brabson, Angie Armstrong, Sherrie Lawson. Back row: Sidney Lowe, Dereck Whittenburg, Jimmy V, Thurl Bailey, Kay Wow, and Quinton Leonard. *Courtesy of Greg Hatem*

Terry Gannon.
Courtesy of Roger Winstead

Ralph Sampson (left) with Cozell McQueen. *Courtesy of Greg Hatem*

ABOVE: Jimmy V.
Courtesy of Roger Winstead

LEFT: Thurl Bailey.
Courtesy of Greg Hatem

ABOVE and BELOW: A celebration ensues on the Brickyard after NC State's ACC Tourney championship. *Courtesy of Roger Winstead*

ABOVE: Ed McLean, with Valvano over his shoulder.
BELOW: Lorenzo Charles (43) gathers a rebound.
Courtesy of Greg Hatem

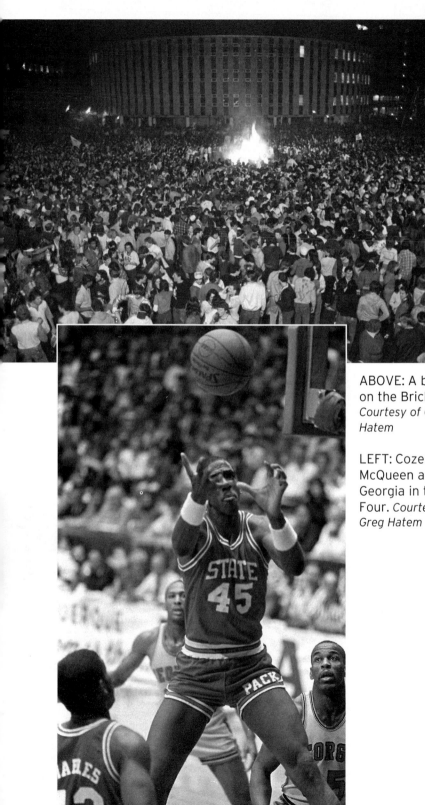

ABOVE: A bonfire
on the Brickyard.
*Courtesy of Greg
Hatem*

LEFT: Cozell
McQueen against
Georgia in the Final
Four. *Courtesy of
Greg Hatem*

RIGHT: "The D.C. Three," (left to right) Whittenburg, Bailey, and Lowe. *Courtesy of Greg Hatem*

LEFT: Valvano and Whittenburg.
Courtesy of Greg Hatem

RIGHT: Sidney Lowe at the 2007 ACC Tourney.
Photo by Bernard Connelly

Jim Valvano
Courtesy of Roger Winstead

State's campus, while another 10,000 went to Chapel Hill, replacing that day's real edition of the paper. News of the unauthorized center-fold spread quickly on local radio stations and in the afternoon news-paper, *The Raleigh Times*.

The spoof—with the usual amount of sophomoric humor, a strong dose of homophobia, and an extremely racy fake advertisement for the Peace Corps—was just one of the sparks that ignited an NC State fan base desperate to beat UNC in any sport. The Wolfpack football team hadn't won against the Tar Heels since 1978. The basketball team hadn't beaten Smith's squad since 1980, when Norm Sloan was head coach and Dereck Whittenburg, Sidney Lowe, and Thurl Bailey were lit-tle-used freshmen. That game ended in spectacular fashion as Wolfpack forward Charles "Hawkeye" Whitney received a between-the-legs pass from Clyde Austin for a game-ending dunk to cap off his final regular-season game at Reynolds Coliseum.

Jim Valvano, in his third year as NC State's head coach, had never beaten the Wolfpack's biggest rival, a fact that he was reminded of every time his team faced the Tar Heels. Other than an early season win over Wichita State in his second year, Valvano had yet to record a major upset against a higher-ranked team. NC State and UNC had met three times in each of Valvano's first two seasons, with UNC winning both regular-season games and eliminating the Wolfpack from the ACC Tournament in 1981 and 1982. Even though Valvano's predecessor, Sloan, had lost his first 10 games to UNC, Valvano was beginning to feel the pressure to prove himself against Smith. Never mind that the Tar Heels had a much bigger national reputation and a bigger cadre of bas-ketball talent at the time. Publicly, Valvano laughed off his lack of suc-cess against Smith. "I might not be able to beat Coach Smith, but I know I will outlive him," Valvano said. At the time, it was funny.

Earlier in the season, in the Wolfpack's second game without Whittenburg, the Tar Heels routed NC State 99-81 in Chapel Hill. The loss infuriated Valvano, because he thought his team was feeling a little too sorry for itself and was not buying into his belief that something good was on the horizon. He ripped into his players after the loss, essentially drawing a line in the sand and telling everyone who didn't share his dream of a championship to leave. Everyone stayed.

But after several close losses earlier in the season to Louisville, Memphis State, Virginia, and Notre Dame, the Wolfpack desperately needed a confidence-building win over a good team, even if Whittenburg was still sidelined with his injured—but quickly healing— foot. At that time, there was no better program in the country than the Tar Heels, who had given Smith his first national championship the year before with a last-second win over Georgetown at the Superdome in New Orleans. But the defending national champions were on a rare two-game losing streak, and the full Wolfpack nation was ready to hand Smith's team its third loss in a row for the first time since 1970.

So there was something different about NC State's campus when the sun rose on the morning of February 19, 1983.

"That day was incredible," said Sidney Lowe. "The atmosphere was unbelievable. For two or three days leading up to that game, it was just crazy on campus. Everybody was talking about that game, how they were going to be there, and what they were going to do. What I remember is that when we got to Reynolds that day, hours before the game started, there was just this electricity on campus among the people walking by. It was one of the wildest days I remember from my college career."

The tip-off was set for 2:30 p.m. as part of a regionally televised ACC tripleheader. Duke played Wake Forest in Greensboro in the lead-off game and Clemson played at Maryland afterward, but there was no doubt as to which game was the headliner that day. The Tar Heels, led by incomparable sophomore Michael Jordan, were in no mood to fiddle around with a pesky rival. A week earlier, the Tar Heels had suffered a defeat to Villanova, ending their 18-game winning streak. Three days later, they had lost their first ACC contest of the season at

Maryland. They didn't want it to happen again, especially after it was announced before game time that Smith had been elected for induction to the Naismith Memorial Basketball Hall of Fame, a rare honor for a still-active coach.

The Wolfpack, of course, had its own motivation. North Carolina's seven straight wins against NC State marked the longest winning streak by either team in this series since the Wolfpack had won nine in a row over the Tar Heels from 1972 to 1975. That was the David Thompson era, when the Pack was one of the most dominant teams in the nation. The Wolfpack had been looking to reinvigorate the rivalry for years without much success. The three senior starters had experienced only one win over their fiercest rival in their four years on campus, the 63-50 victory in 1980 in which Whitney made 11 of his 12 shots and scored 26 points to close out his NC State home career. It was one of the most memorable senior night performances in school history—at least for a few more weeks.

Reynolds Coliseum was buzzing by tip-off time, full of fans who believed the premises offered by Raleigh's two newspapers the day before ("Are the Tar Heels ripe for Wolfpack picking?") and the morning of ("Upset-minded Pack takes on Heels") the big game. However, that enthusiasm immediately waned when the Wolfpack turned the ball over on three of its first four possessions. The start was frustrating, especially for senior Dereck Whittenburg, who sat helplessly on the bench throughout the entire game. Though his broken foot was healing quicker than expected, he wasn't ready to play just yet. His only duty that afternoon was to keep young Stephanie Swiney, the North Carolina poster child for Easter Seals, company on the bench.

The Wolfpack's execution did not come close to matching the emotional intensity in the building, and with 3:17 remaining in the first half, the Tar Heels led 31-24. When Sam Perkins went up for one of his trademark jump hook shots, it appeared that the game was on the verge of disaster.

But NC State sophomore Cozell McQueen, who always played his best against better competition, came from the opposite side of the lane and tipped the shot, preventing the Tar Heels from taking a nine-point lead. Everyone on the North Carolina bench, most notably Smith, was sure the shot was going down when McQueen tipped it and that he should have been called for goal tending. The Tar Heels coach was enraged, and this time he bared his emotions at midcourt. Smith was already upset with Jim Burch for calling two touch fouls on Jordan earlier in the game, and according to the newspaper accounts the next day, Burch had already told Smith to "sit down and shut up." When Smith complained loudly about the lack of a goal-tending call, Burch quickly hit him with a technical foul from the other side of the court.

Smith charged at Burch, but was intercepted by official Charlie Vacca just as referee John Housman hit him with another technical foul. It was not a Hall of Fame moment for the newly elected member, who was roasted afterward with the following newspaper headlines: "How do you spell 'Smith'? With two Ts" and "Dean loses clothes on Friday, cool on Saturday."

The Wolfpack didn't waste this golden opportunity. Terry Gannon stepped up to the line and made four consecutive free throws, no small feat on a day that the Wolfpack shot an exceedingly poor 23-for-39 from the line. On the ensuing possession, sophomore Lorenzo Charles was fouled and cut the lead down to just one point by hitting both of his free throws. After UNC's Matt Doherty threw a pass out of bounds, Charles powered past Sam Perkins for a short jumper to give the Wolfpack its first lead of the game. In a span of just 22 seconds, the Reynolds Coliseum crowd went from laconic to explosive. The noise meter in the rafters of the building, which was about as real as the bogus student newspapers distributed the day before, was flashing red with regularity the rest of the afternoon as the Wolfpack took a 37-36 lead into halftime.

When the teams returned for the second half, Valvano's team

looked much more like a championship squad than the Tar Heels. Smith's team shot poorly from the field, couldn't rebound against the likes of McQueen, Charles, and Thurl Bailey, and whined incessantly about the officiating, especially on calls that went again Jordan. "The referees didn't do an adequate job throughout the game today," UNC point guard Jim Braddock said in the locker room after the game. Smith was again furious when Jordan picked up his fifth foul for charging into Lowe. It's a call the retired Smith—after another national championship, four additional visits to the Final Four, and four more ACC titles—still recalls vividly. "The thing I remember most about that game is that Michael is up in the air and Sidney moves underneath him," said Smith, sitting in his cramped office in the basement of the Dean E. Smith Center in the winter of 2007. "Jordan is called for his fifth foul, though it was obviously a foul on Sidney. Housman came up to Michael after the game and apologized for the call Burch made." Even current UNC coach Roy Williams, who was an assistant to Smith in 1983, couldn't let that call go a quarter-century later. "Sidney stepped right in front of Michael and Michael was already airborne. I can show you on tape if you want. It wasn't even close. They disallowed the basket and it was Michael's fifth foul."

The call sent the Reynolds crowd into a riotous frenzy. Valvano's stringent defense and a slightly slower tempo worked masterfully throughout the game. "It's the best job defensively we have ever done," he said after the game. "That was the plan. If we were going to lose the damned game, we were going to lose it playing aggressively." The Tar Heels never did get into a good offensive rhythm. Twice, they were called for shot-clock violations. Several more times, they rushed bad shots as time expired on the 30-second clock. The Wolfpack, which went deeper on its bench by inserting both Harold Thompson and Dinky Proctor into the lineup for significant minutes, simply ran the Tar Heels ragged. But Lowe stayed in the game, chewing up precious minutes off the clock. By the time Jordan exited the game, Lowe's legs were as heavy and burdensome as the seven-game losing streak to the Tar Heels. He had woken up at 4 a.m. that day to pick up his father, Willie, at the bus station. He then headed to the airport to pick up his brothers, James and Edward, at 6:30 a.m. "I told Coach V I was dead," Lowe said after the game. "And it was all their fault."

Lowe wasn't too tired to sink a pair of free throws to give his team a 58-56 advantage. The lead stretched to as many as seven points with three minutes to play, thanks to a couple of Terry Gannon three-pointers. However, Lowe's teammates seemed even more fatigued as they missed the front end of five consecutive one-and-one opportunities over the game's last four minutes. That is no way to beat a team like North Carolina, but the Wolfpack managed to hold on to the lead, thanks to the two minutes Lowe killed once the shot clock was turned off with four minutes left to play.

Finally, the Wolfpack victory was sealed by one of the unlikeliest of all heroes—McQueen.

Valvano, frustrated by his team's inability to make any free throws, screamed on the sidelines, "Can anybody here make a free throw?" McQueen, out of the game in favor of slashing freshman Ernie Myers, raised his hand. "Put me in, Coach," McQueen said. "I can hit it." As much as Valvano wanted to believe him, the statistics didn't lie: McQueen was just a 57.6 free throw shooter that year. Still, with the game on the line, Valvano needed someone with confidence, something McQueen never lacked. So the coach took Myers out of the game and put McQueen in.

With less than a minute to play and the Wolfpack holding on to a thin lead of 66-63—only one three-pointer away from a tie ballgame—Bailey missed another front end of a one-and-one. McQueen hauled in the offensive rebound and was immediately fouled. Smith called a timeout to force McQueen to think about the situation, but the joke was on Smith. "My mind was a total blank," McQueen said. Valvano encouraged the young player, saying, "Co, you are going to make these free throws. Co, you are going to make these free throws. Co, you are going to make these free throws." But Valvano had to have been less than convinced.

By the time the horn sounded for the teams to return to the court, McQueen was thinking again—about how sweet it would be to beat North Carolina. "That's all I ever heard about when I got here, the Carolina rivalry," McQueen said. He was a little nervous on the first shot, but when it bounced off the rim and fell through the basket, all the pressure fell from his shoulders. He sank the second shot with ease.

After McQueen made the free throws, the only thing to do was wait for the celebration. It began with seven seconds still on the clock when Lowe and Bailey brought down the house with a game-ending play similar to the one they saw from Austin and Whitney as freshmen. Lowe grabbed the ball on a long rebound and led the break down the court, with Perkins in pursuit and Bailey trailing him. Lowe figured the only way to keep Perkins from blocking his shot was to bounce the ball between his legs to Bailey.

"That's really not me," Lowe said in January 2007, the day before he joined Everett Case, Press Maravich, and Les Robinson among the modern NC State coaches who have beaten North Carolina in their first attempt. "I was just trying to get it to [Thurl] and that was the only way I knew how. If I tried to shoot it, Sam would have probably blocked it. I didn't want to be embarrassed. I saw Thurl trailing and I felt the only way I could get it to him was to pass it behind me between the legs.

"I wasn't trying to hot dog or anything like that. That is not really my style."

The play was the perfect punctuation mark on a landmark victory. Students and fans were tossing souvenir cups up into the air in the end zones, making Reynolds Coliseum look like a giant popcorn popper. That image will always stick out in the mind of Sarah Sue Ingram, who was an assistant sports information director with the NC State athletic department. She had lost her father in November and had tried for months to help her mother overcome the depression of losing a husband. She gave her mom a ticket to the game, but when the crowd went crazy, Ingram immediately became concerned. "I looked up in the stands and she was standing there throwing cups up in the air with everyone else," Ingram said. "I think it was first time I remember her smiling after Daddy died."

In so many ways, it was a healing victory for the Wolfpack. "This is something we needed, the school needed, the students needed," Valvano said in his postgame interview. Smith was the first person to congratulate Valvano when the final seconds ticked off the clock. "I told him I was happy for him, and I meant it," Smith said. "It had to get old always hearing that he couldn't beat North Carolina." Whittenburg jumped off the bench and ran to Lowe at midcourt, hugging his teammate of the last seven years just as he did when the two led DeMatha to the national high school championship their junior season. Bailey stood on the sidelines with tears streaming down his face as students, fans, and alumni rushed the court for an hour-long celebration that spilled over from Reynolds, spread all over campus, and ended on Hillsborough Street as car horns blared deep into the night.

Ron Morris, who covered NC State for the *Durham Morning Herald*, began his game story in the next day's paper like this: "NC State won its national championship on Saturday, or at least it seemed that way."

Beating the Tar Heels that afternoon was that important and that emotional.

"I don't think anything has come close to that in my lifetime," Bailey said a couple days after the victory. "Nothing has ever made me that emotional. We had struggled so long and so hard this year, and we deserved a game like that. When the buzzer went off, I closed my eyes and threw my hands up in the air. I felt hands tugging at my jersey. I opened my eyes and I was surrounded. So I surrendered. I was trying to hold back, but I just let the tears go.

"I don't think anything can top that feeling. Even if we go to the NCAA, even the Final Four, even if we won it all—at that point, at that moment in the game, I don't think anything could feel any better than that."

The win meant more as the events of the next six weeks unfolded—more than anything else, that win taught the newly developed team that it didn't have to depend solely on its three seniors to win games. Charles, who was maturing with each passing game, could make a difference. McQueen, who had 12 rebounds against Perkins that day, could make a difference. Gannon, who had 15 points in the game, including three critical second-half three-pointers, could make a difference.

The players cut down the nets after the game, a celebration that was introduced to college basketball by NC State's Hall of Fame coach Everett Case, the Father of ACC Basketball who brought the Indiana high school tradition with him when he became NC State's coach in 1946. Whittenburg, wearing a brown three-piece suit, was lifted up to cut away the final strands. Valvano—after drying the tears of joy that he couldn't hold back as the final seconds clicked away, after talking to the press for more than an hour after the game, after accepting a congratulatory phone call from Virginia head coach Terry Holland's wife, Ann, for knocking the Tar Heels out of first place in the ACC— begged everyone's pardon.

"I have never seen a celebration after a State game," Valvano said. "I am going to go see what it looks like."

More were to come, and they may have been even bigger. But nothing meant more to the Wolfpack family than beating the Tar Heels on February 19, 1983, the day Valvano's Pisces horoscope read, "Journey can be completed. Mission can be accomplished. Relatives, visitors, calls make this a busy time. Don't scatter forces. Remember resolutions concerning health, diet, and nutrition. You will have more recognition and a wider audience in a legitimate chance to grab the brass ring."

"That's the day that the national championship run started, without a doubt," said Gannon in a 2006 interview. "Never in my life, to this day, have I heard an arena that was louder or heard more bedlam than there was at the moment that game ended. Other than the national championship game—because of what it meant and how it changed my life—that day was my favorite moment of the whole season. You could take that game and show it to someone who had never seen a game before and say, 'That is what ACC basketball is all about.' It would tell them everything they needed to know. The rest of that day, there wasn't a second that a horn wasn't going off somewhere on campus. The students were rolling every inch of the campus with toilet paper. Traffic was stopped on Hillsborough Street. As a college kid, to be part of something like that, to know that you brought that much happiness to that many people, it was just unbelievable."

Plenty of people played a role in the most emotionally charged contest of the season, even a couple of cat burglars who took a few nude pictures two days before the game.

"If it gave the fans a boost and the fans gave the team a boost, then yeah, I guess [the picture of Dean Smith] had an impact on that game," said Hatem, who is now the president of Empire Properties, a downtown Raleigh real estate redevelopment company. "The reaction was pretty amazing."

And the celebrations only got bigger as the season and the march to the NCAA championship continued.

ALVIN BATTLE

Like the rest of his teammates, Alvin Battle was motivated by a dream. Unlike so many others, however, Battle was not longing for championship rings and trophies. From the day he arrived at NC State, his goal was to fulfill a promise he made to his grandmother, Olivia Battle, to become the first member of his family to graduate from a four-year university.

"She was the biggest inspiration of my life," Battle said. "I still get tears in my eyes thinking about her, because I loved her more than life itself. One of the dreams she always had for me was to graduate from college and to inspire all of my brothers and sisters, cousins, and nieces and nephews to do the same thing."

But the 6-foot-7 forward from Rocky Mount, North Carolina, suffered two crippling blows following NC State's 1983 national championship that nearly broke that promise for him. First, Olivia Battle died just weeks after watching her grandson hug Lorenzo Charles on national television following the game-winning dunk against

Houston. Less than nine months later, Alvin was declared academically ineligible by NC State, ending his Wolfpack playing career after just three semesters.

Without his team and without his inspiration, Battle was left to follow his dream unsupervised. "It was one of the most trying times of my life," Battle said some 25 years later.

The serious-minded Battle arrived at NC State in the fall of 1982, in time to contribute to the Wolfpack's uneven regular season and its mad dash to the NCAA championship. He transferred to Jim Valvano's program from Merced Junior College in California after a two-year exile to the West Coast. Battle came from an area in North Carolina that had already sent All-American Phil Ford to North Carolina and Buck Williams to Maryland and had been a coveted player through his junior year at Rocky Mount's Northern Nash High School. But he suffered a knee injury early in his senior season, and the two surgeries needed to repair the damage scared off college recruiters who had once eagerly attended his games.

During his two years at Merced, however, the athletic forward showed that he was healthy and talented enough to play big-time college basketball. After his second season there, he was named California's top junior college player, with dozens of schools clamoring again to recruit him.

Valvano desperately needed Battle because the Wolfpack was woefully thin on inside players. After Scott Parzych and Chuck Nevitt completed their eligibility following the 1981-82 season, the Wolfpack was left with only senior Thurl Bailey and inexperienced sophomores Cozell McQueen and Lorenzo Charles. Bailey, though 6-foot-11, was more of a wing forward than an inside banger. Neither Charles nor McQueen had distinguished himself as a freshman. So Valvano thought Battle would be a key component if the Wolfpack had any hopes of being something other than a guard-dominated team with no low-post presence. Specifically, Valvano wanted Battle to tussle with Charles for the starting power forward position.

Battle's assets included natural rebounding and shot-blocking abilities, especially for someone with relative height limitations. However, he did not have soft hands like Charles to enable him to become a good scorer inside. For most of the 1982-83 season, Charles and Battle split the power forward position. While Charles was almost always in the starting lineup, Battle came off the bench right after backcourt reserve Terry Gannon.

Battle didn't like being a reserve, but he made his contributions count. He was particularly impressive when playing against Virginia All-American Ralph Sampson, the reigning national player of the year whose mere 7-foot-4 presence often intimidated his opponents. "I liked being a Sampson-stopper," Battle said. "It was nothing against him personally at all. But it was my job and I wanted to take him down, because he was one of the best players in the nation at the time."

Battle also enjoyed the role of Charles-pusher. The young player from Brooklyn was notoriously shy during his first season with the Wolfpack, but competing against Battle brought out the monster in him. "Coach Valvano told us at the beginning of the season that the position was up for whoever could play it the best," Battle recalled. "Evidently, Lorenzo was the better player at the time. But he and I would battle in practice. He made me a better player and I definitely made him a better player. I like to think that I contributed to his growth."

Battle's own season was also uneven. He started out well, averaging more than 15 minutes a game through the non-conference season. But soon after Whittenburg was hurt, Battle lost his confidence and his minutes dwindled. By the time Whittenburg was ready to return, Battle became a contributor again. His rebounding and defense were key in the postseason, particularly in the ACC championship game against Virginia, the double-overtime win over

Pepperdine, and against Sampson in the West Region final. He played only four minutes, all in the first half, against Houston in the title game.

But Battle was not cut from the same cloth as his fun-loving teammates. He arrived at NC State as a mature 20-year-old, a born-again Christian for some four years. Early on, he had a serious girl-friend, Debbie Shugart, who was a member of Kay Yow's women's basketball program at NC State. He rarely partook in the fun his teammates were having. "I was always real serious—probably too serious," Battle said. "But inside, I had a great time at NC State."

At least until his senior year. Battle was cruising along on the basketball court, but being a junior college transfer was tough on him academically. Three days after Christmas, the school announced that he and teammate Walt Densmore had "failed to fulfill universi-ty standards at the academic level" and were declared ineligible. He could have pursued playing basketball overseas, as so many other American players were doing at the time. It would have been tough to leave his girlfriend, but the money was attractive. Yet keeping his promise to his grandmother was even more compelling. "She was holding me close to NC State to complete that degree," Battle said. "I am glad I took that path. A lot of guys don't get that degree and they go overseas and get hurt, and what do they have to fall back on? I sat down and I prayed and asked the Lord what I needed to do. Something just kept telling me to stay at NC State, get a degree, and do what Grandma wanted. I pretty much understood that if I didn't stay in school then, I would never come back."

Valvano helped Battle land an unpaid internship at WRAL-TV in Raleigh, where the coach taped his weekly television show. Battle spent a half-dozen years working as a freelance photographer for the local station before taking a job with Accounting Machine Systems, a small company in Fuquay-Varina, North Carolina, where he learned the ins and outs of computer systems. After nine years at

AMS, he went to work as an information technology specialist at two Triangle-based banks. For the last six years, he has been a senior lead computer programmer for First Citizens Bank. He and Debbie wed a few years after they graduated from NC State. It is the only known marriage between former Wolfpack men's and women's basketball players. They live in Apex, North Carolina, with their two daughters.

And just as he promised, he inspired more than a dozen members in his family to follow his path of going to—and staying in—college. "I am proud that my example catapulted my brothers and sisters and cousins to do what I did," Battle said. "I was probably voted 'Least Likely to Succeed' in high school. But I graduated from NC State, just like I promised I would do. Ever since that time, it has been the norm in my family that when you graduate from high school, you go to college."

Battle's time playing for the Wolfpack was brief, but his celebrity as part of the 1983 championship team lingers. Living in the Triangle, he is frequently recognized by NC State fans. People who do not recognize the 6-foot-7 former athlete often ask when and where he played basketball. "I tell them from 1982-84, at NC State," he said. "Then I just wait and see if they figure it out. They usually do pretty quickly."

Battle coaches one of his daughters' traveling AAU basketball team and is often asked to talk to local teams or groups of kids about his experiences as a basketball player. His message is always clear: make sure you have a backup plan in case basketball does not work out. Battle has also helped with a prison ministry at the Wake County Correctional Facility through his church. No one would be willing to listen, he said, if he had not been part of the 1983 championship team.

"Young boys, especially—when they hear I was All-State, I was the California junior college player of the year, that I played on the

1983 national championship team—their ears perk up a little bit,"
Battle said. "It opens up some doors for me to tell them some other
things, like how important it is to go to school."

Battle believes he was fortunate to be part of one of college basketball's most enduring Cinderella stories, but he has been even
more blessed in his life after basketball. Nothing made that clearer
to him than the summer of 2006, when he got a staph infection from
a cortisone shot in his elbow and missed three months of work.
"They were seriously thinking about amputating my arm," Battle
said. "But after three surgeries in five days, they were able to get
the infection under control."

When he was healed and back at work, Battle sat down and made
a list of the doctors, nurses, friends, neighbors, co-workers, and
Bible-study partners who had taken care of him and his family during that time. He came up with 87 names. "You never know how you
will get through something like that until it happens," Battle said. "I
feel blessed and fortunate that I had such a strong network of people to help me."

MIKE WARREN

As Mike Warren sits in his office in Raleigh's Cameron Village surrounded by bits and pieces of memorabilia from his NC State basketball career, he has a lone regret.

"Terry Gannon and I have always said we should have taken better notes," said Warren, the president of First South Corporation, a small financial services company that sells wholesale life insurance, handles employee benefits, and dabbles in personal financial planning. "We should have had the foresight to have written all this stuff down."

Still, Warren can spend hours spinning yarns about the events that occurred both during and after the Wolfpack's magical run to the 1983 NCAA championship. While he does not necessarily have a favorite story, he can recite chapter and verse the familiar highlights of the season and many of the behind-the-scenes stories that never made it into Jim Valvano's after-dinner or motivational speeches. Some of those memories are beginning to fade, of course, but Warren always jumps at the opportunity to relive the best year of his life.

"There was so much stuff going on throughout the course of that year; there is no way one person can remember it all," Warren said. "There was always something fun happening."

As Valvano immediately predicted when the team returned from Albuquerque following the national championship, the scope of their accomplishment has grown over the years. It returned to the forefront when Sidney Lowe was hired as the Wolfpack's head coach in the spring of 2006 and continues to grow even more as the team celebrates the silver anniversary of that unparalleled season.

"V told us at the time, 'You can't possibly grasp what this championship means,'" Warren said. "And at the time, we didn't. I am so glad I was a part of it. I knew early on I wasn't going to be a professional basketball player. I could have gone to another school and played more. But ultimately, you are going to end up in the same position, graduating and going to work, regardless of where you go to school. To be able to say I was connected to this team and to all of my teammates is something I will always have."

Warren was a prep All-American at Needham Broughton High School, Raleigh's Inside-the-Beltline public high school where Pete Maravich once played. Warren was coached by Ed McLean, who moved across town along with the athlete in 1981 to become one of Valvano's assistant coaches. As the only Raleigh native on the 1983 championship team, Warren always had a special connection to the Wolfpack. At the age of 11, he watched in wide-eyed wonder from a seat in Reynolds Coliseum as the 1974 team won the ACC and NCAA championships. To see his own team's banner hanging beside the one won by David Thompson, Tommy Burleson, Monte Towe, and company means a great deal to Warren.

Warren's dad, Wiley, played baseball and junior varsity basketball at Wake Forest. He was a member of the ACC's first College World Series in 1952 and represented the United States in the first

Pan-American Games. Mike was also a two-sport star at Broughton, but his only dream was to play college basketball for the Wolfpack. He considered scholarship offers from other schools, especially Appalachian State and UNC-Wilmington, but when Valvano offered him a chance to play for the Wolfpack, there was no doubt where he would go.

Choosing State cost the 6-foot-7 Warren the opportunity for significant playing time. Although he performed at center in high school, Warren had to move out to the wing to play college basketball, and he always had a more accomplished recruit in his way. He spent four years with the Wolfpack as a career reserve. As a sophomore in 1983, Warren played in only 10 games, scoring 14 points and grabbing 10 rebounds. But like the other reserves in the program at the time, he never felt like an outsider.

"It was never like that," Warren said. "Even in all the years afterwards, we are all just members of the team who all had specific roles. Some of us just played more than others. That was one of the reasons that team was so special. None of the teams I played on afterwards was like that. We had some fun times, but never like we did in 1983."

Valvano was so appreciative of Warren's contributions to the team that the coach offered him a position in JTV Enterprises after the athlete received his degree in accounting in 1985. Warren instead took a job with Deloitte and Touche, spending two years with one of the world's largest accounting firms.

"I was as proud of our young people who did not play that much in games as I was of those who were getting all the headlines," Valvano wrote in his book, *Too Soon to Quit*. "We could have never gotten the job done without the Mike Warrens on our basketball team. He was always ready to practice and play hard. I've always said that if you want to see how strong a program is, don't talk to the stars, talk to some of the kids who aren't playing. They will give you a good indication of what the morale is on the ballclub."

For Warren, being on the end of the bench paid great dividends throughout the season. He and Alvin Battle were the first players to reach Lorenzo Charles after the sophomore forward made the dunk that won the Wolfpack the national championship.

Warren remained on the team the next two years primarily as a reserve, relegated to end-of-game duties. As much as he would have liked to contribute more, Warren never gave a thought to going elsewhere. "I wouldn't have done anything differently," he said.

Even in high school, Warren knew he would pursue a degree in accounting. After leaving Deloitte and Touche, he spent three and a half years working as a stockbroker for Merrill Lynch. In 1991, he returned to his basketball roots as an assistant general manager of the Raleigh Bullfrogs in the Global Basketball Association. He was eventually elevated to general manager of the Wolfpack-flavored organization (Lorenzo Charles and Chris Corchiani were the top players on the team, which was coached by former Wolfpack point guard Monte Towe) until the league folded in late 1992.

Since then, he has formed two financial services companies, striking out on his own with a company he named First South Financial.

Warren pondered the simple question of how his life was changed by being a part of the 1983 championship team for a few seconds.

"I can't say that it changed the actual course of my life," Warren said. "I kind of always knew what I wanted to do. But it sure as hell changed my perception of the world and people's perceptions of me. It has always been a constant conversation piece for me. I am 6-foot-7, so people are always going to ask me if I played basketball. When I say I did, the conversation usually continues from there until they realize I was on the '83 team.

"Without fail, everybody says, 'I was here and I was doing this.' They all know what they were doing and where they were when that game was on. I never grow tired of hearing those stories."

Who needs good notes when so many people are willing to help Warren relive the most exciting year of his life?

11 "I GOTTA GET TO PRACTICE"

O n the day of the Wolfpack's landmark win over North Carolina, Dereck Whittenburg sat on the NC State bench with Stephanie Swiney, the state's 1983 poster child for Easter Seals. They were just two people familiar with crutches, caught up in the excitement of the game.

As Whittenburg helped his teammates cut down the nets, he gingerly ran up and down the court, something that did not go unnoticed by thousands of fans who lingered in the building for the hour-long postgame celebration. Rumors began to circulate on campus and in the media that the senior guard's career might not be over after all.

On Monday afternoon, just two days before the Wolfpack traveled to Durham, North Carolina, for its annual game at Duke's Cameron Indoor Stadium, NC State student Todd McGee happened to be playing a video game in the annex of the D.H. Hill Library, not too far from the wide expanse known as the Brickyard. He was surprised when he looked up from his game of Omega Race to see Whittenburg playing PacMan next to him.

"Hey man, what time is it?" Whittenburg asked.

"About 2:30," McGee answered.

"Uh-oh," Whittenburg answered. "I gotta get to practice."

Whittenburg took off running toward Reynolds Coliseum and McGee took off running for his dormitory suite to tell all his friends that Whittenburg, after three weeks in a cast and six weeks out of the lineup, was about to make an unexpected return. Later that afternoon, the official word came from team trainer Craig Sink. "The X-rays looked good this morning," Sink told the media. "He will go back to gradual activity. We'll see how he comes along."

Sure enough, Whittenburg was in uniform for the game against the Blue Devils. Few people noticed, however, because they were too busy dodging the shower of pizza boxes that rained on sophomore forward Lorenzo Charles during pregame introductions. It was Charles' first visit to Cameron after his arrest the previous summer for stealing a pizza from a Domino's deliveryman.

Everyone knew that the Devils fans would find some creative way to make fun of Charles, but the young forward had had plenty of time to grow up while washing all those public safety cars as part of his 300 hours of community service. He took the Blue Devils' taunts in stride, playing the best game of his career to date with 13 points and five rebounds in a 96-79 victory. He even took the time to sign a couple of pizza boxes for his teammates and some Wolfpack fans after the game.

Valvano's team had three more games remaining in the regular season: Virginia, Maryland, and Wake Forest. It needed at least two more wins to make a strong case for an NCAA bid.

But it was a touchy time in the Case Athletic Center basketball offices. Valvano had told those in his inner circle and a few members of the media that he did not want to put Whittenburg back in the lineup if he was less than 90 percent healthy. He also insisted that Whittenburg would have to play at least two regular-season games so he could adjust to the Wolfpack's new emphasis on its inside game now that Charles had turned into a more consistent scoring threat down low. It was a completely different team than the one Whittenburg left as he hobbled off the court against Virginia.

Freshman Ernie Myers had averaged 18 points during Whittenburg's absence, helping the Wolfpack win nine of its 14 games. Terry Gannon's long-range contributions off the bench had become even more important. The baby-faced Charles had grown up significantly. Sidney Lowe was averaging nearly five more points per game with Whittenburg out of the lineup.

"The team we had at the beginning of the season was one-dimensional," Valvano said. "It was a good team and deserving of a top ranking. But it was a rebound, run, and three-point shooting team. We had no inside game at all. Then, with Dereck's injury, Gannon got to play, and he got to play a lot. And every time we put him out there, he played better and gave us an even better outside game than before. Secondly, we had to start throwing the ball inside. We got to the point we had to. So we told Lorenzo, 'Whether you like it or not, here it comes. It's coming to you.' So he improved. And Sidney Lowe elevated his whole game."

But Valvano also realized that if Whittenburg returned, Myers' court time would be diminished, and the coach did not relish the thought of having to tell the happy-go-lucky freshman that he would have to take a back seat, something Myers had never had to do before.

To this day, Myers can recount, nearly verbatim, the conversation he had with the coach two days before the Wolfpack played at Virginia.

"Ernie," the coach began, "Dereck wants to come back, and I am going to start him. He only has a couple of games left. The team is yours after this. You've proved that you can play in this league. You've got three more years ahead of you."

Myers had no choice but to accept the decision with dignity. "I didn't come to NC State to take Dereck's spot," Myers said in a 2007 interview. "I was trying to create a spot for myself. I was all right with it. But when he returned, it took all the rhythm out of my game. I didn't lose confidence; I just wasn't playing the same way."

But Valvano also gave Whittenburg some instructions. The Wolfpack no longer had to rely only on its three seniors to carry the load. The team now had a greater inside presence and a deeper, more productive bench. Things were not going back to the way they used to be.

"Dereck," Valvano told his senior tri-captain, "you have to adjust to the team we have become. We don't have to adjust to you."

Whittenburg returned to the starting lineup against Virginia, of all teams, in a game at University Hall. Whittenburg needed all of two minutes to find an open three-pointer, which he swished with ease at the top of the key. But his comeback euphoria did not last: he missed nine of his final 12 shots that night. Privately, Whittenburg knew he was not completely healthy. "It was only about 80 percent healed," Whittenburg revealed. "But I did not care. I was still consciously thinking about the injury. I didn't complain about it. I never thought, 'I can't do this; I can't do this.' I just went out and played."

Whittenburg was a little out of shape and the Wolfpack offense was a disorganized mess. No one could make a basket against the Cavaliers, as the Wolfpack shot 35.6 percent from the field for the game and only 31.8 percent from three-point range. After his team fell behind by 18 points late in the contest, a disgusted Valvano put Whittenburg and Charles on the bench. Sidney Lowe fouled out for the first time all season. Gannon and Myers had been ineffective all night long, scoring only six points between them. The coach turned to a lineup of Myers, McQueen, Thurl Bailey, George McClain, and Alvin Battle— the Wolfpack's tallest combination—and his team went on a tear to cut Virginia's lead down to just six points with less than a minute to play. The Cavaliers held on for an 86-75 victory.

Near the end of the game, Virginia students began to chant, "N-I-T! N-I-T!"—their prediction for the Wolfpack's postseason destiny. Freshman Walt Densmore, whose father had played for the Cavaliers in the late 1950s, leaned over to one of his teammates on the bench and said, "Man, I'd like to pay them back for that in a big way."

Just three days later, the Wolfpack met Maryland to decide third place in the ACC regular-season standings. The Wolfpack was still a little dazed and confused now that Whittenburg was back on the court. Lowe, who had played so well in Whittenburg's absence, seemed to forego his new emphasis on scoring. He missed seven shots in the game and had three turnovers against the Terps. The Wolfpack played terribly on offense in the second half, making less than 35 percent of its shots and scoring only 23 points. Valvano watched on the sidelines as his team let a 35-31 halftime lead turn into a 67-58 defeat.

"We were chaotic," Valvano said. "In those couple of games, we lost our rhythm. We quit looking inside. I explained to Whit and to the ball club that we are a better team, a more versatile team, and he had to find a way to fit in."

The Wolfpack needed a direction-changing catalyst. The win over Carolina in a frenzied Reynolds Coliseum wiped away the disappointment following Gannon's missed jump shot against Notre Dame. Giving the Wolfpack's crowd the opportunity to say an emotional goodbye to Lowe, Whittenburg, Bailey, and walk-on forward Quinton Leonard might just lead to similar inspiration. It was also the team's one chance to repay Wake Forest for an 18-point loss earlier in the season—the game after which Valvano suggested to his players that the National Invitation Tournament might just be the best they could do in the postseason.

Following an emotional, tear-filled introduction of the four seniors, the Wolfpack put on an all-out blitz. Whittenburg and Gannon each scored 25 points. Bailey added another 23. Lowe, Myers, and Charles joined them with double-digit scoring, and Leonard, the forgotten senior, made the final basket of the day. The Demon Deacons scored 89 points in the contest—and still lost by a whopping 41.

The Wolfpack, which had finished last in the league in scoring the previous season, scored 130 points that afternoon, a record that still stands 25 years later as the most ever by one team in an ACC game.

"It was a special day," Bailey remembered. "We just got rolling. We only thought about how good we played, not how badly we beat them."

For Valvano, it was a return to the way the Wolfpack had played in early January, right before Whittenburg was hurt. Only the coach now had more options that would allow his squad to compete against the best teams in the country. "I couldn't have written a better script," the coach said.

This, Valvano believed, was a team that could win championships.

QUINTON LEONARD

He was the forgotten senior, a walk-on who made few contributions during games but for two years was an essential component at Wolfpack practices, where none of his teammates could stop his deadly 12-foot baseline jumper.

Quinton Samuel Leonard III was just a farm boy from Eastern North Carolina who dreamed of one day receiving a degree from and playing basketball for NC State. As a walk-on member of the team, he became the leader of the Secondary Pack—the hard-partying reserves who rarely played but were always ready for a little action before or after a game. Leonard fully enjoyed the rewards of the Wolfpack's grand run to the 1983 national championship.

But like his coach, Jim Valvano, Leonard was unable to relive his experiences into old age: on March 14, 2006, Leonard became the first member of the Cardiac Pack to reach his final destiny when he was found dead of a heart attack in his pickup truck. "It just doesn't seem real that he is not with us anymore," said his close friend and five-year college roommate Tommy DiNardo. Leonard was 44, three years younger than Valvano when the coach died of cancer. "That's way too early for us to lose one of our teammates," said fellow reserve Mike Warren.

Warren and DiNardo were among many former Wolfpack players who attended Leonard's memorial service in Apex, North Carolina, where Leonard owned a residential tree-cutting service. Dereck Whittenburg, the head basketball coach at Fordham University, rerouted his travel plans during a recruiting trip to attend the service, waiting for two hours in his rental car in the parking lot to give condolences to Leonard's wife, Laura, and his young son, Quinton Samuel Leonard IV. "What a great kid he was," Whittenburg said. "He could have played at several smaller schools, but he loved NC State and always wanted to be part of that program."

Leonard certainly gave the Wolfpack a down-home flavor, one that offset his fast-talking, New York-bred Italian coach. "He was very country," Sidney Lowe said. "V used to joke that he never understood a damned word he said."

Leonard almost missed his chance to be a part of history. He never played organized basketball—the game he fell in love with as a child—until he was 16 years old, primarily because of his responsibilities on the family's 900-acre cattle and sheep farm nestled in the flatlands less than 40 miles northeast of Raleigh.

When his parents finally allowed him to go out for the high school team, he suffered a broken leg prior to his junior year and was unable to participate. As a senior, however, Leonard was good enough to earn a scholarship to his hometown school, Louisburg Junior College. That's where he first met Tommy DiNardo, whose father, Phil, was a Wolfpack basketball co-captain under Hall of Fame coach Everett Case in the early days of the ACC. They shared a dream to one day play for the Wolfpack. Thanks to a little hard work and a little good fortune, both eventually saw that dream come true. Leonard had solid offers to go elsewhere, but chose to enroll at NC State hoping to join Valvano's basketball team as a walk-on.

But just before the open tryouts were slated to begin, Leonard hurt his shooting shoulder during a pickup game, forcing him to play left-handed throughout the week-long tryouts. After he impressed Valvano enough to make the team, Leonard had a team doctor look at his injured arm. "It had been dislocated the whole time," Warren said. "Needless to say, Quinton was a physically tough guy."

Leonard was content in knowing that he would never be more than a practice player, but like all the other players at the end of the bench, he was an integral part of the team's chemistry. He played only 17 minutes in eight games for the Wolfpack during its championship season. The final two of his 11 points that year came in the only game he ever started, the Wolfpack's 130-89 senior day whipping of Wake Forest. Leonard took the first shot in the game and missed badly. But he was back on the floor in the contest's waning moments. As the surrounding crowd cheered for Leonard to score, Warren threw him a pass in the lane. He canned the little turnaround jumper he had made so often in practice to finish off the highest scoring game ever between two ACC opponents.

"He was always very appreciative of that pass because he said no one else would throw him the ball," Warren said. "I probably wouldn't have either if it had been anyone other than a senior playing his last home game—we all wanted to score during those late-game times."

But "Q-Dog," along with DiNardo, Warren, Walt Densmore, and Harold Thompson, knew his primary duty was to help the starters prepare for opponents, a job that can lead to dissension in the ranks. Valvano always appreciated that the championship team never had any issues over lack of playing time. "They are either going to be positive or negative forces," Valvano wrote in his book, *Too Soon To Quit*, following the championship. "If they hang their heads, they can become divisive in times of stress. But if they are upbeat, positive, and supportive, they can keep the team together when things get tough. The quality practice time they give us is so important, too. They are pushing others. They come to practice every day and make everybody work hard. Q is a great example of that, and he certainly deserves a championship ring as much as anyone."

Even if fast-talking Valvano had a hard time understanding him, others were certainly drawn to Leonard's smooth-talking drawl. Thurl Bailey might have reaped more financial rewards from the Wolfpack's fairytale run, landing a big contract with the Utah Jazz after the franchise made him the sixth pick in the 1983 draft, but no one enjoyed the off-court rewards more than Leonard.

"Let me put it this way: Quinton was the king," Lowe said of his late teammate. "God rest his soul, he always had more stories for us than anyone. And he would always have a couple of other players going along with him."

A string of fanciful companions followed Leonard throughout the season, including a member of the NC State women's basketball team, the daughter of the owner of the hotel where the Wolfpack stayed in Corvallis, Oregon, during the first two rounds of the NCAA Tournament, and even one of the University of Houston cheerleaders.

Not long after returning home from the championship, Leonard, like the rest of his teammates, was feeling pretty full of himself, strutting around town and taking advantage of his newfound celebrity. Since his eligibility was up, Leonard and fellow seniors Sidney, Bailey, and Whittenburg were flooded with opportunities to cash in by playing in barnstorming all-star games and making other public appearances. Leonard's Baptist parents called their formerly "yes, sir, no sir" son home one hot summer day, saying that some work needed to be done in the fields. He spent from dawn until dusk the next two days with a wagon and a mule, picking up rocks for no reason other than to resize the britches that had grown a couple sizes too big during the Wolfpack's national championship run. At the end of the second day, Leonard told his father, "I've learned my lesson."

Soon afterward, Leonard learned he could not live on his minor basketball celebrity forever: he broke his ankle in an all-star game in Elizabeth City, North Carolina, which ended his competitive career.

Leonard earned his long-coveted NC State degree after spending an extra year in school. He then spent two years as a high school biology teacher. But he was too much of a pushover for his students and did not last long in the classroom. With Warren's help, he turned his weekend firewood delivery service into his own tree-cutting service, called Triangle Tree Works. He spent his time shuttling between his home in Apex and his family's farm in Louisburg, making the 150-mile round trip several times a week. In his early bachelor days, he reserved plenty of free time for his former college teammates and other buddies, who were always welcome to play weekly pickup games on the dirt basketball court he had built in his backyard. They dubbed it the "Twin Creek Thunderdome." When Leonard wasn't playing, he raised himself high above the court in one of his cherry-pickers to provide play-by-play of the action.

In recent years, he gained weight, took up smoking, and endured the stress of running his own business, helping on the family farm some 70 miles away, and serving as the primary caregiver to his son while his wife, Laura, traveled as a regional sales representative for an industrial equipment company in Cary, North Carolina. "He was just a ball of nerves constantly," Warren said.

Leonard had one heart attack before he turned 40, following his family's long history of heart problems. Two of his siblings died prematurely of heart defects—one shortly after birth and the other at the age of four. His father died of a heart attack in his daughter's backyard. And just months before Quinton died, his mother underwent quadruple-bypass surgery. "Those problems ran in his family," Laura Leonard said. "But mostly, he just worked himself to death."

Leonard often said that being part of the championship team did not significantly improve his fortune in life, but it sure as hell made his college career a lot of fun. He never, ever lost his love of NC State or his pride in being part of the national championship team.

"When we were dating, I had something called the *Book of Questions*, one of those guides that asked a lot of things to see if you really knew each other before you get married," Laura Leonard said. "One of the questions was, 'What was the changing moment of your life?' I figured that was easy: winning the national championship. But it wasn't. He said it was a great moment—one that would always be with him, one that he was thrilled to be a part of—but it didn't define his life."

Yet it certainly defined who he became: a hard worker who always had time to help on the family farm, spend time with his son, or lend a hand to those who needed it. And he did it all out of the limelight, just as he had as a walk-on reserve for the Wolfpack.

In the days after her husband's death, Laura Leonard heard from several people she had never met, including a financially strapped elderly couple who had custody of their grandson. A few years earlier, the same summer he became a father, Leonard found out the couple could not afford to send their preteen grandson to basketball camp. Throughout the summer, Leonard spent 30 minutes every couple of weeks teaching their grandson a few basketball skills. He ran into the couple months later at the grocery store and gathered that they were still struggling financially. A few days later, he showed up with several bags full of groceries for the family and a few more basketball tips for their grandson.

"He never told me these things," Laura Leonard said. "I am the kind of person that if I did something like that, I would come home and say, 'I am going to Heaven.' But I am his wife and he never told me these things—or anybody else. I think that is what defined who Quinton was."

TOMMY DINARDO

Tommy DiNardo had two dreams growing up, and they both involved following in his father's footsteps: he wanted to be a mechanical engineer, and he wanted to play basketball at NC State.

"Growing up, I idolized my father," DiNardo said. "As a young kid, I wanted to be just like him."

Truth be told, as a kid, Tommy DiNardo had no clue exactly what his father, Phil, did for a living. He just knew that he was an engineer. One day, not long after his family moved from Philadelphia to rural Jamesville, North Carolina, DiNardo went to a railroad switching station near his family's home. He asked the folks there if they knew his father, the engineer. They had never heard of him. When he came home that night, DiNardo's father explained that he was a power superintendent with a mechanical engineering degree at a nearby pulp and paper mill, not the driver on a train. So Tommy decided he wanted to be a mechanical engineer, too.

Though he may not have known the difference between a train engineer and a project manager, Tommy was an astute athlete who excelled in basketball and baseball at tiny Jamesville High School. He knew all about his father's basketball career at NC State. And while he never really dreamed of being a star player or a team captain, as No. 80 had been for Hall of Fame coach Everett Case in the early days of the Atlantic Coast Conference, Tommy hoped he could follow the same path as his dad. Phil DiNardo was a forward for Case when the Wolfpack captured the first three ACC championships, winning the 1954, '55, and '56 tournaments at Reynolds Coliseum. He averaged 7.6 points and 8.2 rebounds as a forward during those three seasons, and was team captain as a junior and senior.

For the longest time, Tommy didn't think that childhood dream would ever materialize. The younger DiNardo was a 6-foot-6 center on a 1-A high school team, and he flew so far under the radar that he had to watch out for potholes. No NCAA Division I basketball program recruited him out of high school, and his options were limited to smaller schools. "I kind of put my dream of playing for State on the back burner," he said.

Somewhat dejectedly, DiNardo accepted a scholarship to Louisburg Junior College, figuring he could play two years there, transfer to NC State as a regular student, and complete his degree in mechanical engineering. At least one of his dreams could still come true.

But a funny thing happened on his way to becoming just another guy with a pocket pencil protector on the Brickyard. While DiNardo was at Louisburg, he was assigned to share a dorm room with another member of the basketball team, Quinton Leonard, a late-blooming hometown boy who had shunned offers from several smaller four-year schools with the hope that he could pursue a similar lifelong dream: to play basketball for and receive a degree from NC State. The two players formed a quick friendship.

After playing together for two years at Louisburg, DiNardo and Leonard both transferred to NC State in the fall of 1981. Since they each had an older sister at the university, their parents decided the four of them should all share an apartment—a weird yet cost-effective living arrangement for the four active college students. DiNardo's sister, Lisa, usually went home to see her boyfriend on the weekends, while Leonard's sister, Martha Lou, went home to help on the family farm. So the boys hosted frequent weekend parties at their apartment just off Avent Ferry Road, incurring the girls' wrath for the messes left behind when they returned Sunday evenings.

Leonard had performed well as a sophomore at Louisburg, averaging about 15 points a game and earning the team's most improved player award. He received a few scholarship offers from smaller schools at the time, but the lifelong Wolfpack fan jumped at NC State coach Jim Valvano's invitation to come to Raleigh as a walk-on for the 1981-82 season. Even though he had a dislocated shoulder on the October afternoon he worked out for the Wolfpack coaches, he earned the team's only available walk-on position. He spent the entire 1981-82 season as a practice player, earning brief appearances in just nine games and scoring a total of five points.

Meanwhile, DiNardo made the transition from student-athlete at Louisburg to engineering major at NC State. Louisburg hadn't offered any of the technical courses DiNardo needed for his engineering degree, so he had loaded up on basic math, calculus, and English classes. In the fall of 1981, DiNardo carried a heavy academic load, and the only chances he had to play basketball were in pickup and intramural games at Carmichael Gymnasium, across the street from Reynolds Coliseum. But that was only after he finished his schoolwork in structural properties, applied differential equations, and introduction into Fortran.

But in the fall of 1982—while taking engineering thermodynamics II, conductive radiant heat transfer, dynamics of machines, and strength of mechanical components—DiNardo heard that Valvano was going to have an open tryout. After being away from the game an entire year, DiNardo wasn't sure if he still had the skills necessary to play for a Division I basketball program. So he called his father to ask for some advice.

"To be honest, I had a little bit of a fear of failure," DiNardo said. "My dad told me, 'If you don't try, you will never know.'"

Valvano, who had picked up on a great deal of NC State basketball history in his three years as head coach, knew all about Phil DiNardo's playing career at NC State. The coach had a soft spot in his heart for Tommy, a direct link to the school's basketball heritage. But that only granted him an invitation to the walk-on tryout camp, where he competed against two dozen other students. DiNardo had no idea how he had performed until the last day of camp, when new assistant coach Ed McLean walked up and asked him what his shoe size was.

"It kind of hit me that my dream was coming true," said DiNardo (who wears a size 15). "I was as tickled as I could be."

He knew from the outset that he would not play in many games for the Wolfpack. Having attended small schools—his graduating class at Jamesville High was comprised of just 40 students—DiNardo had always played inside positions. Even at Louisburg, he was a 6-foot-4 power forward. So he didn't have the ball-handling skills necessary to play wing at a major college level, nor the size to bang around inside. He went into the season knowing his job was to show up for practice, catch a few elbows to the face from Lorenzo Charles, and help the rest of his teammates improve. "I knew playing against those guys that the caliber of my game was not the same as the caliber of their game," DiNardo said. "I was realistic about it. As the year went on, I tried to focus in on trying to help the other players as much as I could in practice."

DiNardo rarely took the floor, and he never scored a point during his two seasons with the team. Stored in the basement of Reynolds Coliseum, his player profile—which includes all pictures, feature story clips, and biographical information from his two-year career—is thinner than a Brazilian supermodel. But that never really mattered to DiNardo, who was living out dual dreams as he pursued a degree in engineering and wore the same red and white uniform as his father.

Valvano paid brief tribute to DiNardo in his book, *Too Soon To Quit*, saying, "He didn't get to play much, but he made many valuable contributions to our practices. Tommy was an important part of our team."

It wasn't easy, of course. Mechanical engineering is one of the most difficult fields of study at NC State, and DiNardo was always playing catch-up during basketball season—with the exception of one semester. "Every time we went on a road trip, I was studying or had a book in my hand," DiNardo said. "When everybody else was goofing off and just doing their thing, I was usually in the hotel room working on school. But when we got to the NCAA Tournament, I just said, 'The heck with studying; I am going to enjoy this.'"

And he did, partying with his teammates along the way and establishing the memories he still relives as a professional engineer today. But playing catch-up was a challenge.

"When we got back from Albuquerque, I was making up two or three exams a day to make up all the lost ground," he said. "Those engineering professors were really sticklers. Let's just say it wasn't my best semester academically."

DiNardo spent another year with the Wolfpack basketball team, seeing action in four games in 1983-84, and finished up his mechanical engineering degree in 1985. He now lives in Wendell, North Carolina, with his wife, Tammy, and two children, and works as the technical operations manager for drug maker Merck in nearby Wilson. Surrounded by other engineers who also received their degrees from NC State, DiNardo is asked to relive the Cardiac Pack's exploits a couple of times every week.

Whenever he's asked, he says that his goal was never to be the Wolfpack's most important player or its biggest scorer. He was just there, following in his father's footsteps athletically and professionally, hoping to live out a couple additional dreams in a season when destiny granted many wishes.

12 "PROBABLY SO, COACH"

"**D**ammit Thurl, is this for real?" Jim Valvano said. "Are you kidding me?"

The coach handed Thurl Bailey the note he had just read. The 6-foot-11 forward read the folded sheet of paper, dropped his head, grimaced in the way only an embarrassed child would, and handed it back to Valvano. "Probably so, Coach."

It was halftime of NC State's first-round game against Wake Forest in the 30th annual ACC Tournament. The Wolfpack desperately needed to win this contest to prove it deserved to be in the NCAA Tournament field for the second year in a row. Not since Sherman had anyone come to Atlanta with such a sense of purpose.

But nothing felt right about this game or this weekend. For the first time, the tournament was being played at the Omni, the now-demolished downtown Atlanta arena that looked like a rusty waffle iron. It was the ACC's first trip to Georgia for its showcase tournament and only the third time the league had held the event outside of North Carolina. Everyone was on unfamiliar ground.

What worried Valvano was that his team had just beaten the Demon Deacons by 41 points five days before in Raleigh on an emotional senior day for Bailey, Sidney Lowe, Dereck Whittenburg, and Quinton Leonard. He knew the Wolfpack could never replicate that kind of dominance against the Demon Deacons, a team that was also trying to gain entry into the newly expanded 52-team NCAA field. The Wolfpack players believed their coach when he told them this was going to be a down-to-the-wire, one-point game, which led to near disastrous consequences. At halftime, the Wolfpack was holding on to a tenuous 42-40 advantage.

With so much riding on this weekend, the last thing Valvano needed was an internal disturbance. But the note in his hand said, "Coach, if we don't get better seats, our sons are not playing in the second half." It was signed by Retha Bailey and Carrie Lowe, two moms who were upset that they were sitting high in the nosebleed section, where the Omni's legendary indoor flock of pigeons roosted. They knew that Valvano wouldn't ignore their threat to remove the team's leading scorer and field general in the most important game of the season. "Jesus Christ," Valvano thought, "I've got to deal with the game and this, too?"

Bailey didn't say it at the time, but he knew his mother wasn't joking around. Twice during domestic disputes, she pulled out a gun and shot at his father, Carl. The bullet holes remain as proof in the now-divorced couple's home in Seat Pleasant, Maryland. The senior forward had no doubt that his mom would pull him off the court in front of 16,723 people if she didn't get what she wanted. Nor did his teammates. "Thurl's still scared of his mama to this day," Whittenburg said in 2006.

Retha Bailey talked to a reporter from Raleigh's *News & Observer* the next day, which happened to be her 28th wedding anniversary. But there were no thoughts of orchids or other gifts that afternoon. "We were so high up Thurl looked like a midget," said his hopping-mad mother.

Already frustrated after watching his team let an eight-point lead slip away in the final minutes of the first half, Valvano pushed the note to team manager Gary Bryant, who took it to his father, Wolfpack Club executive secretary Charlie Bryant, the person in charge of all the school's ACC Tournament tickets. He was well acquainted with Mrs. Bailey and her seating requests. "That woman was a . . . ," Bryant trailed off, his look of disdain finishing the sentence for him. He tried to explain to her that the people with the best tickets had paid more than $20,000 for the rights to those seats, but his words had no effect on Mrs. Bailey. "Are you telling me Thurl's contributions to this school aren't worth $20,000?"

Later that weekend, Bryant was standing on the court with chancellor Bruce Poulton when they saw Retha Bailey walking toward them. As Bryant braced for the onslaught, he saw movement out of the corner of his eye. "Chancellor Poulton was literally running to get off the court," Bryant said. "He wanted no part of that woman." Bryant gave the Baileys and Lowes his four seats in the Omni's lower section, the perfect location to see the most important moment of the game: a crosscourt pass from Wake Forest's Alvis Rogers that Lowe tipped right into Bailey's hands. The play would not have happened if Retha Bailey hadn't been given better seats.

Before the Wolfpack's semifinal contest against North Carolina the next day, the Bailey, Lowe, and Whittenburg families took their seats in the seventh row of the lower section to watch what would turn out to be the most important game of the season.

One of the myths that has persisted over the course of the last 25 years is that the Wolfpack needed to win the whole thing in Atlanta in order to make the NCAA field. That's not remotely true. Late-season wins over North Carolina, Duke, and Wake Forest along with Whittenburg's return to the lineup put Valvano's team in good position as far as the NCAA selection committee was concerned, despite the squad's 10 regular-season losses.

The way Valvano figured it, both Virginia and North Carolina were locks for the national tournament even if neither won the ACC championship. That seemed unlikely to most of the fans and media who showed up for the tournament—they all assumed that the storyline for the weekend would be whether the defending national-champion Tar Heels could prevent Virginia All-American Ralph Sampson from winning the elusive ACC title he so coveted. For Valvano, the league tournament was all about putting his team in a position to earn what he thought would be a maximum of four bids to the NCAA Tournament, even though the field had just been expanded from 48 to 52 teams in the previous off-season. Valvano believed that Maryland, with 20 regular-season wins and a third-place finish in the final ACC standings, would also join the Cavaliers and Tar Heels in the big dance despite being upset by Georgia Tech in the first round of the ACC Tournament. That meant the league's final contender would likely be NC State, which had lost two of its last three games, or slumping Wake Forest, which had lost four in a row at the end of the regular season. The main difference between the two teams was the regular-season finale in Reynolds Coliseum, a 130-89 rout in which the Wolfpack set an ACC record for the most points scored in a league game.

So when Lorenzo Charles hit a free throw with three seconds to play to give the Wolfpack a 71-70 victory and its 18th win of the season, Valvano believed his team had the advantage it needed over the Demon Deacons to secure the league's fourth bid.

Beating the Tar Heels would be more difficult. North Carolina had eliminated NC State in each of Valvano's previous trips to the ACC Tournament, padding Dean Smith's winning streak over Valvano to seven games before it was broken earlier in the season at Reynolds Coliseum. Neither of those first two tournament games was close: the Tar Heels won 69-54 in a first-round game in Landover, Maryland, in Valvano's ACC Tournament debut and 58-46 in a semifinal game the year before in Greensboro, North Carolina. But neither was as important as this matchup—Valvano thought his team might need one more win to assure itself a spot in the NCAA field.

Few others did. "If we had lost [to Wake Forest] today, we wouldn't have a shot at the NCAA," Lowe said following the opening-round victory. "All we need to worry about is trying to beat Carolina. That game speaks for itself. But if we win it, I think we'll definitely be in the NCAA Tournament." Even ESPN commentator Dick Vitale, who was an ACC Tournament newbie back in 1983, said during the broadcast of the semifinal contest against the Tar Heels that the Wolfpack had secured its bid to the tournament with the quarterfinal win over Wake Forest.

Not much was known about the selection process back then since the NCAA had only been seeding teams in the tournament since 1979. No one held daily discussions concerning a team's ratings percentage index (RPI). No one spoke about strength-of-schedule formulas or how well a team had performed in its final 10 games before the NCAA Tournament. And no one talked of the concessions the selection committee made for teams whose injured players had returned to the lineup. Had this been the case, the Wolfpack would have been a shoo-in based on its brutal non-conference schedule, which included games at Louisville and Missouri, in the Meadowlands against West Virginia, and at home against Michigan State, Memphis State, and Notre Dame. "I wish we could have won more games," Valvano told the N&O's Joe Tiede the week before the ACC Tournament. "[But] we haven't lost to anybody who wasn't somebody."

Considering the larger field, Whittenburg's return, and the team's mini hot streak, there was no question that the team once ranked as high as No. 15 in the nation during the season belonged in the field after winning just one ACC Tournament game. The myth has been perpetuated over the years because some people believe it makes the Wolfpack's Cinderella story better. Frankly, the story is good enough as it is.

"I do recall that going into the tournament, NC State did have some more work to do," said Dave Gavitt in 2007. Gavitt, a founder of the Big East and a Naismith Memorial Hall of Fame member, was the selection committee chairman for the 1983 NCAA Tournament. "I don't think we ever got to the point in the deliberations that people in the room felt they had to [win the ACC] to get into the tournament," he said. "Their total body of work over the course of that season was impressive. What happened in those years was that the ACC, the Big East, and the Big Ten were so strong that even some losses didn't hurt you because of who you were losing to. So my recollection is that they did not have to win the [ACC] Tournament to be invited."

The Wolfpack also had a not-so-secret weapon in the room during the selection process: then-Metro Conference commissioner Vic Bubas, a former NC State player and assistant coach under Everett Case and the former head coach at Duke. In 1949, the Indiana native scored the first points in the history of Reynolds Coliseum. Though he left the room for the vote—anyone with close ties to a program under consideration must always excuse himself from official discussions— Bubas would have informally enlightened his fellow committee members as to the Wolfpack's trials and triumphs during the course of the season, especially since Metro champion Memphis State had played the Wolfpack earlier in the year.

Following the Wolfpack's 91-84 win over the Tar Heels—a game in which State overcame a six-point overtime deficit thanks to an offensive explosion by Dereck Whittenburg—Valvano told his team that there was an easy way to remove all doubt as to whether the Wolfpack was worthy of the NCAA Tourney. Since its inception in 1953, the ACC had used its postseason league tournament to crown a champion and determine who would receive the league's automatic bid. In the old days, when only one team per conference could go to the NCAAs, the league tournament was imbued with nail-biting tension. Anxiety reached its peak in 1974, when NC State beat Maryland 103-100 in overtime in what critics still regard as the greatest ACC game ever played. By 1980, the NCAA opened the field to an unlimited number of teams per conference, though the ACC Tournament winner still received the league's automatic invitation. Just before his team headed onto the court to play the Cavaliers for the championship game, Valvano said, "Guys, I'll tell you what—if we win this game, we are definitely in."

Making it into the big tournament wasn't something the players had thought that much about. They were just trying to stay on the roll that had begun against the Demon Deacons in the regular-season finale. "We didn't think a lot," Whittenburg said. "Coaches have a certain thought process during that time. Fans have a completely different thought process. As kids, we didn't think a whole lot about it. We just went out and played and moved on to the next game. We were awaiting our instructions, just like in the military. We knew what we had to do. We weren't all that worried about who we were playing or what the game plan was. We just went out and played."

But they also knew how important winning a championship was to their coach: in each of his first three years at NC State, Valvano made his players practice cutting down the nets and carrying him off the court on their shoulders—just in case they won a championship together.

"He's a dreamer, and he made us share his dream," Thurl Bailey said.

○ ○ ○

After Whittenburg hit a pair of free throws to secure an 81-78 victory over the Cavaliers, the Wolfpack cut down the nets for the second time that season. (The first was following the win in Reynolds over the Tar Heels.) The late Marvin "Skeeter" Francis met Valvano at midcourt with a handshake and an invitation. "I would like to officially extend to NC State as Atlantic Coast Conference champions a bid to the NCAA National Tournament." As his team hugged the championship trophy and fans back in Raleigh went crazy, Valvano accepted on the spot.

"It's almost been a Grade-B movie," Valvano said. "After one of the games, we were saying this is going to be a movie we were going to make and Whittenburg was going to come back in the ACC Tournament and he was going to knock in a jump shot against Carolina, and we were going to win the championship. And that was when the doctors were saying he wasn't even going to play. I told the team we were going to make the movie, and we'd do it as long as I could play myself. Dick Vitale wanted the part, but he doesn't have enough hair."

Raleigh was indeed wild—perhaps a little too wild for the Wolfpack baseball team. The stands at Doak Field were sparsely filled for a Sunday afternoon doubleheader against Charlotte since most NC State students were just trickling back from spring break. But just about everyone at Doak had a radio to listen to Wally Ausley and Garry Dornburg broadcast the ACC championship game, and some students in the Sullivan and Lee dorms just beyond Doak's outfield fences came back early from spring break to watch the 1 p.m. game on campus. The Wolfpack baseball team was leading 7-2 with two outs in the top of the seventh, though Charlotte had a runner on first. Future major leaguer Dan Plesac was on the mound looking for yet another victory in his phenomenal junior season and trying to impress the handful of major-league scouts at the game. He forced what should have been a game-ending ground ball to his freshman shortstop, Doug Strange.

But just as Strange was throwing the ball for the final out, the Cavaliers missed a final, desperate shot from midcourt down in Atlanta. Those lingering in the Doak Field stands and all the students

WHEN MARCH WENT MAD

in Lee and Sullivan let out a celebratory yelp, distracting Strange. "I heard this big roar and I threw the ball over the second baseman's head and up against the old press box on the first baseline," said Strange, who spent nine years in the majors after he left State in 1985. Strange's error allowed the 49ers to mount a game-tying comeback and eventually an extra-inning win, much to the disdain of irascible baseball coach Sam Esposito. "Plesac gave me a couple of dirty looks about that play, but I think once everyone realized the basketball team won, I don't think they gave a damn that I threw the ball away," said Strange, who is now an assistant general manager for the Pittsburgh Pirates. "Looking back on it now, I think it's funny as hell."

Within minutes, hundreds of students filed out of the dorms onto Hillsborough Street, the four-lane northern boundary between NC State and Raleigh. Enterprising entrepreneurs were already selling pre-printed bumper stickers that read, "Wake Forest, North Carolina, and Virginia: Breakfast of Champions." Raleigh police eventually cut off traffic as students built two bonfires in the middle of the street. It was a relatively tame party, despite the free-flowing beer, rolls of toilet paper littering the trees, and stray pieces of outdoor furniture being thrown into the bonfires. Police made only four arrests on Hillsborough that night—one for throwing bottles into the crowd, one for pouring paint on the street, and two for digging up parking meters and adding them to a bonfire.

Back in Atlanta, the basketball team returned to the Marriott Marquis downtown so the players and coaches could watch the NCAA pairings announcement on ESPN. They all shouted with joy when they saw "No. 6 seed NC State" flash on the screen, but were a little befuddled when they saw their opponent would be Pepperdine and that they would be playing in Corvallis. No one knew exactly where either was located. Team trainer Jim Rehbock, who made all travel arrangements for out-of-town trips, thought Corvallis was in California. Assistant coach Ed McLean thought it might be somewhere in Oregon. Valvano had no clue. Bailey tried the closest thing to Google back then: he called the hotel's front desk. "Can you tell me were Corvallis is?" he asked. "Is that somewhere in Atlanta?" she asked, with even less of a clue than Bailey.

Once McLean remembered that Corvallis was home to Oregon State University, Rehbock and assistant athletic director Kevin O'Connell began making arrangements with the NCAA's travel agency in New Jersey to leave for Corvallis as quickly as possible, which was not easy in those days. Valvano called someone to find out why his championship team had been shipped off to the farthest reaches of the Great Northwest. He was not happy when told that the Wolfpack would likely have been in Greensboro, less than 100 miles from Raleigh, had it lost to the Cavaliers. By winning the championship, the Wolfpack was sent to the West along with Virginia, the region's top seed. Second-seeded North Carolina got a first-round bye and a trip to nearby Greensboro. Maryland also made the field as an eighth seed, earning a trip to Houston. Bailey thought the destination put a damper on the Wolfpack's celebration. "I was disappointed we weren't somewhere close to home," Bailey said. Somewhere, Charlie Bryant was smiling, knowing none of the players' parents were likely to make the transcontinental trip.

The team quickly gathered its possessions, loaded the bus, and headed to Hartsfield International Airport for a chartered flight home. About 1,000 fans were waiting for the plane when it touched down at 10:16 p.m. at Raleigh-Durham International Airport, a raucous welcome that might have been dispersed by RDU officials had Valvano not received wind of it. Only a few dozen people and a small bonfire were waiting for the Wolfpack's bus when it pulled into Reynolds Coliseum at 11:30 p.m. Everybody else was on—or headed to—Hillsborough Street, where the celebration lasted well after midnight.

Valvano and assistant coach Tom Abatemarco nearly missed the team flight home from Atlanta. They were trying to catch up with the rest of the traveling party, but the misdirected Italians ended up at gate B-17 instead of C-17. When they looked up to see where the B-17 flight was headed, both coaches got a funny feeling. The destination was Albuquerque, New Mexico, a direct route to the "Land of Enchantment." The coaches considered it a fine omen for the team.

ACC TOURNAMENT

ATLANTA, GEORGIA

NC STATE 81, VIRGINIA 78
MARCH 12, 1983
ACC TOURNAMENT CHAMPIONSHIP GAME

What few people seemed to remember once Jim Valvano secured his first victory over North Carolina coach Dean Smith was that he was still winless against Virginia and Terry Holland. The Cavaliers were the only ACC school that Valvano had not beaten in his first three years at NC State.

Of course, losing to Virginia didn't matter nearly as much as losing to the Tar Heels. And, at that time, few teams in the country were regularly beating the Cavaliers and All-America center Ralph Sampson. Like NC State's David Thompson, whose professional career was faded by injuries and off-court problems, Sampson is no longer appreciated as the most dominant player of his generation. Those memories have been wiped out by his weak-kneed NBA career and his post-playing legal difficulties that landed him in jail in 2006 for mail fraud.

But in the early 1980s, no team in the country, not even North Carolina with James Worthy and Michael Jordan, had anyone better than Sampson, the only player other than UCLA's Bill Walton to win three consecutive national college basketball Player of the Year awards. Still, Sampson's reputation did not faze NC State's three seniors, who had heard of the giant center from Harrisonburg, Virginia, for years while growing up in Washington and had been his teammate at the Capital City Classic when they were all high school seniors. They knew first-hand that Sampson could be beaten—his first ACC loss came at Reynolds Coliseum when all four were freshmen.

Every game since then had been close, won by the Cavs by an average of 6.7 points. None of those losses stuck with Valvano more than the infamous "Mugging at Midcourt," when the Wolfpack was leading Virginia by the minimalist score of 36-35 in Reynolds. Whittenburg had the ball for a final shot, but Holland sent senior guard Jeff Jones out to foul Whittenburg in the final 30 seconds. Jones hammered Whittenburg as he dribbled down the sidelines. "What he did to Dereck would have been a felony in at least three states," Valvano said afterwards. But instead of calling a foul, the officials called a jump ball. The Wolfpack lost the ball and the game, 39-36.

Twice already in 1983, the Cavaliers beat the Wolfpack in games that changed the season. The first, of course, was in Reynolds Coliseum when Whittenburg broke his foot. The second was in Charlottesville, Virginia, Whittenburg's first game back after a 14-game absence. It was not a good outing for him or his tentative teammates. Near the end of the game, which Virginia won 86-75, Cavaliers fans taunted the Wolfpack with cheers of "N-I-T! N-I-T! N-I-T!" It was something that remained in the back of the Wolfpack players' minds over the next six weeks.

"That was ugly," Sidney Lowe said. "And God don't like ugly."

After taking come-from-behind victories over Wake Forest and North Carolina, the Wolfpack relished the opportunity to meet the Cavaliers and Sampson one more time. State was no longer a team defined by just its backcourt. Thanks to the continued improvement of sophomores Lorenzo Charles and Cozell McQueen, it was a well-rounded squad that believed it could end the Pack's seven-game losing streak to Virginia.

Besides momentum, two things were on the Wolfpack's side. NC State hadn't come to Atlanta just to get into the NCAA Tournament. They were on a mission to win the school's ninth ACC championship. Getting an automatic bid into the tournament was just a bonus. Now, only the Cavaliers stood in their way, and team confidence was at an all-time high. Secondly, even though Virginia cruised into the championship game with easy wins over Duke (109-66) and Georgia Tech (96-67), the Cavs were hurting. Starting forward Tim Mullen suffered strained knee ligaments against the Yellow Jackets, ending his season and forcing accomplished sixth-man Jim Miller into the starting lineup. Sampson was recovering from a bruised jaw he suffered in the ACC semifinals.

In the first few moments of the game, it was no contest. The Wolfpack blitzed out to a 12-1 lead, thanks to Lowe. Twice he stole the ball and turned them into layups. Then he added a three-point basket, the first of a dozen long-range bombs the Wolfpack would score in the contest. Defensively, Valvano slapped a one-three-chaser defense on the Cavaliers, directing Whittenburg to defend dangerous Virginia point guard Othell Wilson in man-to-man coverage. Valvano believed keeping Wilson in check was the key to stopping Sampson from getting the ball. The rest of the Wolfpack clogged the middle in a sagging zone defense, trying to keep Sampson in check. The Cavaliers' chemistry was obviously thrown off without Mullen in the lineup, as both Miller and Rick Carlisle struggled in the game's opening minutes. Carlisle, who had burned the Wolfpack for 23 points at University Hall earlier in the year, missed his first five shots in the game and did not score until the game's final two minutes.

The Wolfpack's lead evaporated quickly, though, as the Cavaliers scored nine unanswered points. Valvano's junk defense slowed Wilson, but it could not contain Sampson. He scored 18 points and grabbed nine rebounds before halftime and led the Cavaliers' inside game to a 25-12 rebounding advantage in the first half. The only thing that worked well for the Wolfpack was its outside scoring, especially from reserve shooting guard Terry Gannon. His third three-pointer of the half brought the Wolfpack within three points, 40-37, just before intermission. That shot was nearly negated, however, when Wilson canned a half-court basket that was eventually disallowed because it was taken after the buzzer sounded.

In the second half, the Wolfpack defense began to take root against Sampson, as Bailey stayed in front of the eventual first pick of the 1983 NBA draft and teammates Charles, McQueen, and Alvin Battle pushed him from underneath the basket to the perimeter. Almost imperceptibly, Sampson began to disappear, even though the Cavaliers continued to build on their halftime lead. With 11:51 remaining, Virginia led 59-51. Soon after, Whittenburg picked up his fourth foul of the game on a silly reach-in. An air of inevitability crept through the Omni's multicolored seats that Sampson, who was recruited to build a dynasty at Virginia, was finally going to get his long-awaited championship.

However, Holland needed to get Sampson, who was used to playing just 31 minutes a game, on the bench for a short rest. The All-America center had played all 20 minutes of the first half and needed a breather. Holland sent reserve forward Kenton Edelin, a 6-foot-7 walk-on from Alexandria, Virginia, into the game to guard Bailey. Edelin was supposed to be a defensive specialist, but Bailey knew if the Wolfpack was going to win the championship, he needed to exploit this mismatch.

Sampson was out of the game for only three minutes, but Bailey scored three quick jumpers, including his only three-pointer of the game, giving the Wolfpack its first lead of the second half. Bailey also became more aggressive defensively, gathering in four steals after intermission. With less than six minutes to play, the Wolfpack held a tenuous 69-65 lead.

Cinderella stories are made possible by the mistakes of awkward stepsisters, and the Wolfpack needed one more Virginia miscue to pull off its final upset of the weekend. With five and a half minutes to play, Wilson took a long three-pointer over Whittenburg's hands. The ball bounced off the back of the rim to the sidelines near the Virginia bench, which was brimming with tension as Holland and his excellent staff of Dave Odom and Jim Larranaga were trying to guide their team back from the late-game deficit. The ball momentarily landed in Wilson's hands, but NC State's Bailey, Lowe, and Alvin Battle all tried to take it from him in the lane. When the Cavaliers coaches heard the whistle blow, they were sure Wilson had been fouled. Imagine their surprise—like Valvano's the year before in the "Mugging at Midcourt"—when the officials signaled a jump ball. With the newly adopted alternating-possession rule, the arrow was pointing in Virginia's favor.

Holland threw open his plaid jacket and put his hands on his hips to yell at the referees. Odom plopped down in his folding chair in disbelief. And Larranaga jumped out of his seat, stormed down the sidelines, and had to be restrained by Jeff Jones, now a graduate assistant instead of a guard with felonious fouling intentions. Larranaga was immediately hit with a technical foul by game official Joe Forte. What could Holland say? He had received a similar technical the day before when he disagreed with an official's call in the game against Georgia Tech.

But Holland's technical was in the latter stages of a 29-point blowout. Larranaga's came at a crucial stage of the most important game of the season. And it could not have been more costly to the Cavaliers. Not only did Virginia lose possession of the ball, but Whittenburg made both technical shots. The Wolfpack ate up nearly 45 critical seconds, thanks to a reach-in foul on Wilson that reset the play clock. Whittenburg capped off the four-point possession—and a 13-1 overall scoring run—with a mid-range jump shot to give the Wolfpack a 75-66 advantage with 4:20 to play. So instead of being down by as little as one point, the Cavaliers trailed by nine with only seconds remaining before the 30-second shot clock was to be turned off.

For all practical purposes, the game should have been over. But the Wolfpack began to show a little fatigue from its three consecutive come-from-behind rallies. Its three-guard delay game with Lowe, Whittenburg, and sophomore Terry Gannon was a mess of bad passes and disorganized play, and its free-throw shooting was simply atrocious. Even Gannon, NC State's all-time leader in free-throw shooting percentage and the team's best shooter at the line that year, missed the front end of a one-and-one, his second in as many days.

Wilson got his team back in the game as the Cavs finally made use of the ACC's short three-point line in the last game of the league's experimental rule. The Wolfpack had built its lead with outside shooting, making 12 baskets from the three-point arc. Until the game's final minute, Virginia had made only two three-pointers. With 56 seconds remaining, Wilson followed one of Charles' missed free throws with a shot that cut the lead to just three points.

Seconds later, Charles was fouled again, and he missed yet another front end of a one-and-one chance. This time, the Cavaliers went inside for a sure basket, getting the ball past a fronting Bailey to the wide-open Sampson. It was one of the few times Sampson actually touched the ball without having one of NC State's big men at his back. Sampson, who had taken only four shots and scored just six points in the second half, knew he was open and never looked down before turning toward the basket for the easy dunk that would have cut the lead to just one point. If he had, he might have caught a glimpse of Gannon, the 6-foot, 165-pound sophomore who was surely the least intimidating player on the court.

As Sampson turned in for the dunk, Gannon stripped the ball out of the giant's hands. It was the exact same play for which Gannon was hit with a foul the day before against Braddock.

"I had no business stealing the ball from Ralph Sampson, and V let me know it," Gannon said. "Afterwards he told me, 'That was a really stupid play. What the hell did you think you were going to do, block his shot? It was a stupid, stupid thing to do. Great job, though.'"

Thirty-five seconds remained in the game, and the Wolfpack was still shaky at the free-throw line. The Cavaliers fouled Bailey, who hit one of two free throws to give his team a four-point lead. Wilson closed the gap to by hitting a wide-open three-pointer with 20 seconds to play. A couple of less-than-confident passes put the ball in Whittenburg's hands. He managed to run 14 seconds off the clock before Wilson caught him and committed his fifth foul of the game. Whittenburg, who had played more than 10 minutes without committing his fifth foul, had no intention of letting this game-winning opportunity slip away against the team that had almost ended his college career three months earlier. He easily made both shots.

Virginia still had plenty of time to get off another shot, but Wilson's replacement, Doug Newburg, took his time bringing the ball down the court, and his pass to Ricky Stokes was nearly intercepted by Gannon. Stokes got off a contested shot, but it never came close to the rim.

In the end, Sampson's 24 points and 12 rebounds were not a factor in the game. Bailey matched Sampson's scoring total, and

Charles had double-digit rebounds for the third consecutive game. Over the final seven minutes and 48 seconds—when his team needed him the most—Sampson did not score, a disappearing act that would haunt the center for years.

In the locker room, Sampson was surrounded by reporters—and his own private bodyguard. Virginia football player Jerry Glover always traveled with the basketball squad to keep the media surrounding Sampson at bay. When Sampson finally spoke, he said all the wrong things. "I think we lost," Sampson said. "I don't think they beat us."

The Wolfpack players took their victory lap around the Omni, cutting down the nets, conducting celebratory postgame interviews, and hugging the family members who worked their way from the stands down to the floor. Lowe, who followed his career-scoring high with 18 points and four assists, was named the Everett Case Award winner as the tournament's most valuable player. He reveled in the special moment of accepting the prize named after the Wolfpack's Hall of Fame coach.

When they returned to the locker room, Ernie Myers hugged the ACC championship trophy, and made the following announcement to his teammates: "Ralph's got him a house full of trophies, but he ain't got one of these!"

Charles shouted back, "Watch out what you say and don't make him mad; we might meet Ralph again."

"WHO GOES TO
13 A HOTEL
WITHOUT TVs?"

Jim Valvano knew that the high his team experienced at the ACC Tournament and in their subsequent return to Raleigh would not last. And nothing brought the skeleton traveling party of Wolfpack players, coaches, administrators, and the smattering of fans down to earth quicker than getting to Corvallis, Oregon.

Including a few dozen fans, about 50 people flew from Raleigh to Eugene, Oregon, to see the ACC champions play the first-round game against Pepperdine. They loaded two aging activity buses for the hour-long ride to Corvallis. No one was expecting limousine service and a room at the Ritz, but few were prepared for the Riverview Motel, either. It was a relatively new but decidedly lowbrow roadside inn and restaurant, hard by the north-flowing Willamette River. And there were strong suspicions that the small, family-owned hotel was taking in more than room rates, bar tabs, and restaurant bills.

"You mean the whorehouse?" asked team trainer Jim Rehbock. "There was some interesting stuff going on at that place. We finally figured it out when we realized all the waitresses in the diner lived in the rooms at the hotel."

So much for the ACC champions' spoils of victory.

"It didn't have televisions," said reserve player Mike Warren. "Who goes to a hotel room that doesn't have a television?"

Even Alvin Battle, who had seen his share of dumpy hotels while traveling up and down the West Coast during his two years at Merced Junior College in California, wasn't sure what to think. "Who booked this room?" he wondered when he and Thurl Bailey checked in.

The proprietor of the Riverview was a big guy who used the hotel bar as his office. "He was always in there with his accounting books and whatnot," said NC State board of trustees chairman Wendell Murphy, who traveled with the team throughout the 1983 postseason. "I remember most of the time his britches had fallen about halfway down his crack, and I don't think he was bothered by it at all. That's the kind of place we were in."

The Riverview had one big redeeming feature: a British-style double-decker tour bus in the parking lot. No one was sure if it was in working condition, but everyone wanted to take the party bus through the streets of Corvallis, and the owner of the Riverview promised he would let them if the Wolfpack beat Pepperdine and Nevada-Las Vegas.

At least the other students on the trip—the cheerleaders and pep-band members—were shielded from any unscrupulous activity: they arrived the day of the game and were housed across town at the Beaver Lodge, a two-story, barracks-style co-op house near the Oregon State campus, where everyone slept on bunk beds and used community showers and bathroom facilities. It was vacant for the weekend since the university was out on spring break.

The handful of North Carolina media who made the trip to the Great Northwest didn't have to worry about that. The owner of the bar attached to the Nendel's Inn where they were staying showed them where the key to the place was hidden, told them to lock the door every night before they left, and headed out to the coast for a weekend of fishing.

Valvano loved showing off his honeymoon suite at the Riverview, with its Vegas-style finery that included a heart-shaped bed with a blue velvet comforter, velour wallpaper, an in-room, two-person Jacuzzi, and mirrors on the ceilings. "The first thing he did when he saw the room," said Gary Bryant, a team manager for the Wolfpack that year, "was send me out for some wine. His wife and kids weren't with us yet. I think he enjoyed that trip more than any other we took that year." Mainly, the sleepy little town gave the master storyteller even more material. "Corvallis made Fuquay-Varina look like New York City," Valvano said after his team returned home.

It was a place of fortune for the Wolfpack players, even without taking into account the results of the Pepperdine and Nevada-Las Vegas games. One of them got lucky with a hotel maid. The Wolfpack also picked up one of its postseason good luck charms, "Cap'n" Jim Letherer, a one-legged civil rights activist and sports fan from San Diego who watched the Wolfpack win the ACC championship and decided to follow his new favorite team the rest of the tournament. So he packed up the car he had been given by football star Kellen Winslow and showed up unannounced in Corvallis, ready to latch on to Destiny's Darlings. And Valvano let him.

Valvano liked having a large entourage just in case he needed his own personal laugh track. He wanted his players to be engaged with the fans and the media. Reporters did interviews in the lobby or in hotel rooms. Fans hung out with the players and the coaches. Famously, Valvano didn't believe in bed checks or curfews, either for his players or himself.

After everyone settled in, it was time to get down to business. The Wolfpack practiced at Gill Coliseum the day before the game, and afterward, Valvano sat down to talk with CBS announcers Dick

Stockton and Steve Grote, an NCAA-required pregame ritual. When they finished, the coach saw three North Carolina newspaper reporters—John DeLong of the *High Point Enterprise*, Frank Dascenzo of the *Durham Sun* and Kevin Quirk of the *Charlotte Observer*—strolling through the hallways, and he cringed. "You guys gotta do stories?" he asked. "Please tell me you don't gotta do stories. I am all storied out. Let's just talk." Having already written their previews from the press conference back in Raleigh two days earlier, the reporters told the coach they were just checking out the surroundings. The coach started telling them about his hotel room. Before long, though, someone asked Valvano what he thought about the next day's game against Pepperdine. They knew he was concerned because Waves coach Jim Harrick had a team full of athletic, 6-foot-7 wing players who liked to run, a West Coast Wake Forest at the time.

"We can't match up with one of them, let alone all three of them," Valvano said candidly. "I don't know how we are going to guard them. They are a scary team."

Then Valvano paused before turning his eyes to Dascenzo: "But I'll tell you what, if we win this game, we're going to go all the way."

"Too bad we've already filed our previews for the next day's papers," the reporters thought to themselves. "This would have made great copy." But Valvano made them all promise to keep the conversation off the record. For the next three weeks, they all kept it under their hats, though after each successive victory, they would nudge each other and say, "Remember what V said in Corvallis?"

Valvano was right: his team didn't match up well with Pepperdine. The Wolfpack missed its first 12 shots out of the gate, and won the game only because Pepperdine's best free-throw shooter, Dane Suttle, missed two front ends of one-and-one opportunities at the free-throw line in the first overtime. The Wolfpack, down five points with 24 seconds to play, tied the game on an offensive rebound by Cozell McQueen, and won it on Dereck Whittenburg's eight free throws in the second overtime.

McQueen's rebound is the most remembered play of that game, but it might not have been the most important thing that happened that night, at least for the most superstitious members of the Wolfpack cheering party. Pam Valvano, who had arrived with the cheerleaders and pep band the day of the Pepperdine game, was a nervous spectator. During the ACC Tournament, she had walked out of The Omni with two minutes to play so she wouldn't have to watch the tension-filled final moments, just like her husband's mother Angelina Valvano used to do in the early days of her middle son's career. Pam Valvano always held in her hands a golden, wolf-shaped brooch, a good luck charm given to her by an NC State fan. A handful of other fans would keep Pam Valvano company in the musty hallways of what-ever arena the Wolfpack was playing in, with each giving the brooch a good-luck rub. But sometime during the celebration of the Pepperdine game, the brooch fell underneath the stands of Gill Coliseum. "She was frantic," said Scott Joseph, the student who had been portraying the Mr. Wuf mascot for the past three years. "She couldn't find it any-where." Without his mascot head on, Joseph was small enough to crawl under the stands, where he found the brooch charm among the paper cups and popcorn boxes, a stroke of good fortune for the band of nail-biters who had become ritualistic in the clothes they wore and their pregame routines.

Valvano called his wife's followers a cult, but he participated as much as anyone. He refused to let anyone other than team manager Gary Bryant hand him a piece of gum before or during a game. He wore three suits throughout the postseason in the same rotation: a beige three-piece, followed by a gray plaid, followed by blue pinstripes. And for nine straight games, he had to worry about his pants falling down on national television: just prior to the Wake Forest game in the ACC Tournament, Valvano's belt broke, and Pam would not let him wear one for the rest of the season. Most importantly, the coach made sure to hug Dereck Whittenburg after every postseason game, a head start on good luck for the team's next outing.

Just about everyone had a ritual, from the fans to the team to the students back in Raleigh. Pity the poor girl in Sullivan Dormitory who made the mistake of taking a shower with four minutes to play in one of the early ACC Tournament games. Over the next three weeks, she was the cleanest partier on Hillsborough Street, since everyone in the dorm made sure she showered at the same point of every game that followed. Sarah Jackson of Raleigh wore the same blouse she wore during NC State's run to the 1974 NCAA championship, nine years of fashion changes be damned. Another lady wore the same underwear that she had worn during every game of the 1974 tournament. Larry Hall of Fuquay-Varina, who went years without missing a Wolfpack home or road game, would not take his seat for a postseason game until he found a face-up penny somewhere on the ground.

"Before every game, there is so much rubbing and praying and clothing assignments, the pregame [routine] has become much tougher than the game itself," Valvano said.

Opponents had a hard time handling their end of the Wolfpack's destiny. The morning after the Pepperdine game, Waves coach Jim Harrick was still in a state of disbelief. Both DeLong and Dascenzo happened to see Harrick, his wife, and a couple of Pepperdine assistants at breakfast at the Nendel's Inn, which the Pepperdine traveling party shared with the media. He remembers that the coach was in a near-comatose state of mind and did not speak a word throughout his meal.

It was a rough morning for Harrick. He had already been pulled out of the shower by a phone call from Lee Benson, a columnist from the *Deseret News* in Salt Lake City who wanted to tell Harrick, a former assistant at Utah State, congratulations.

"Congratulations for what?" Harrick said.

"For beating NC State," Benson said. "I watched it on television. It ended around 1:30 in the morning in overtime."

"We lost," Harrick said, finally comprehending that the reporter didn't know there was a second overtime. "Our best free-throw shooter missed two chances at the end of the first overtime and they beat us at the end of two. So long season. That's life in the big leagues."

"I feel like an idiot," the reporter said.

"So do we," Harrick said.

For the Wolfpack players, the day between games was an opportunity to attend a short practice and rest from their double-overtime duty the night before. But team doctor Don Reibel took a handful of managers and non-practicing personnel to the Oregon coast to go deep-sea fishing. They brought their catch back to the Riverview, where the head cook fried it all up fish-camp style to feed the whole Wolfpack contingent late Friday evening.

Before leaving the Riverview the next day for the Nevada-Las Vegas game, Valvano reminded the hotel's owner to gas up the double-decker and be ready for a party later that evening. Not long after Thurl Bailey's game-winning shot went down, the bus was stocked with a case of champagne and two kegs of beer. It was revved up and waiting to go when the Wolfpack contingent returned from Gill Coliseum. Before leaving the parking lot, the cheerleaders presented Joseph with a cake to celebrate his 21st birthday. Dereck Whittenburg grabbed the cake before they got on the bus. "Come here, Wuf," Whittenburg said. Then he shoved Joseph's face in the cake. "That kind of set the tone for the rest of the evening," Joseph said. "It was quite a party."

The next morning, while everyone recovered from the traveling road show, the coaching staff met to figure out the team's travel plans. Since the Wolfpack originally was not due to return to North Carolina until late Sunday night and the team had to be in Ogden, Utah, no later than Tuesday afternoon for its Thursday night game against Utah, Valvano made the executive decision to keep everyone on the West Coast. Rehbock and assistant athletic director Kevin O'Connell, who was back in Raleigh, arranged a Monday morning flight from Eugene, Oregon, to Salt Lake City, via Las Vegas, and told every-one they needed to prepare to wash some clothes.

For the cheerleaders and pep-band members and a handful of other students on the trip, staying on the West Coast was completely unexpected. Most of them had only packed for three days away from campus, and no one had enough books to catch up their studies. But they had plenty of time, since they would not be joining the team on the flight to Utah. They had to take a bus. The upside was that they stayed over night in Reno, Nevada, at Carl's Supper Club, a combina-tion ranch house, restaurant, and casino.

"We had discovered earlier that you could turn in beer cans and other recyclables for money in Oregon, so we found all the empty beer cans we could and turned them in," Joseph said. "Once we got to Reno, we were glad we did that. We pretty much all took our per diem money and all the recycling money, got off the bus, and went to the nearest casino until about five o'clock in the morning."

On Monday morning, the team loaded up its rickety activity bus for the hour-long trip to the Eugene airport. Gannon and Mike Warren made a few convenience-store purchases for a week-long stay in Mormon country: they bought two cases of beer to sneak through the airport. "We were young and stupid," Gannon said. "We didn't know what to expect out there. We wanted to be prepared."

At the airport, the Wolfpack contingent bumped into CBS announcers Dick Stockton and Steve Grote. Lowe, who had seen the tape of the Pepperdine game in which Stockton declared his career over, could not resist repeating the same lines he had told Grote prior to the UNLV game: "Hey, Dick," Lowe told Stockton, "never count us out."

NCAA FIRST AND SECOND ROUNDS

CORVALLIS, OREGON

NC STATE 69, PEPPERDINE 67 (2OT)
MARCH 18, 1983
NCAA TOURNAMENT FIRST ROUND

Jim Valvano hated first-round opponents in the NCAA Tournament, especially if they had a direction or hyphen in their names. In 1982, his team lost to Tennessee-Chattanooga in a first-round game in Indianapolis, one of the most embarrassing losses the coach ever suffered. The Wolfpack, satisfied just to be in the post-season, couldn't find the basket all night long, fell behind by 20 points, and never had a chance to advance to the second round. Disgusted, Valvano threw in the towel, cleared the bench, and let the final 10 minutes of the season tick quietly off the clock.

"This year," Thurl Bailey promised after the Wolfpack won the ACC Tournament, "we are older and more experienced, and we won't let that happen."

But Valvano believed there was a good chance his team would be flatter than the leftover Asti Spumante in his refrigerator from the ACC Tournament celebration on the Brickyard when his team faced 11th-seeded Pepperdine. Why would his players take seriously a team that sounded more like a toothpaste or soft drink than a formidable opponent? The coach knew the three-time West Coast Athletic Conference champions were good. Earlier that season, Valvano happened to catch a late-night game between Pepperdine and top-ranked Houston on ESPN, a contest that went down to the wire before Houston pulled out a 93-92 victory on Pepperdine's home floor in Malibu, California.

The Waves were coached by Jim Harrick, a UCLA disciple in the mold of Louisville's Denny Crum and Memphis State's Dana Kirk, a pair of coaches who had already handed the Wolfpack two of its 10 defeats in 1983. The Wolfpack players had no idea that the Waves were going after their third first-round win in the last four years. They had no idea that senior shooting guard Dane Suttle was Pepperdine's all-time leading scorer and was ranked 13th in the nation with a 23.7 scoring average. They had no idea that the Waves had their own trio of accomplished seniors—Suttle, Orlando Phillips, and Bill Sadler—who were looking to make some final postseason noise. And, to be honest, they did not really care.

"We just beat Carolina and Virginia, two of the top five teams in the country, and now we are supposed to give a crap about Pepperdine?" Terry Gannon said years later. "We were coming off this incredible experience at the ACC Tournament, and now we go all the way to the West Coast to get a golf clap from a crowd of about 8,000 people."

Little wonder that the Wolfpack missed its first 12 shots in the game's first six minutes. The players blamed their poor shooting on the ball, which they said was not slick enough, an excuse that Valvano could not stomach. His worst fears—that his team would find a way to lose against a lesser opponent—were coming true. The Wolfpack was saved only because the Waves seemed intimidated by the ACC champions. Up 10-2 after State's opening cold streak, Pepperdine gave up eight unanswered points. Minutes later, the Wolfpack was on an 11-2 scoring run to take a six-point advantage, its biggest of the entire game.

Neither team seemed all that interested in playing in the late-night contest. No. 2 seed Nevada-Las Vegas, which had received a first-round bye in the tournament and would play the winner of this game two days later, was hardly impressed. Neither NC State nor Pepperdine shot better than 40 percent from the field in the opening 20 minutes. To make matters worse for the Waves, its three frontcourt starters had three fouls before halftime. Not that it gave NC State much of an advantage—the Wolfpack made only three of its first nine free throws.

What was supposed to be an up-and-down contest between two teams that liked to run became a low-scoring, half-court chess match in which neither team wanted to sacrifice a knight or a rook, much less its queen. No one ever expected to see such conservative—or tentative—play from the two veteran teams. Maybe a post-ACC Tournament hangover should have been expected from the Wolfpack, which attended an on-campus pep rally the day after it returned, spent a couple of days catching up on schoolwork, then bolted for the transcontinental flight to Oregon Wednesday afternoon. But who would have thought such accomplished guards like Lowe, Whittenburg, and Suttle would do more to hurt their teams than help them down the stretch?

The good thing for Valvano, it seemed, was that the slow pace and ragged nature of the game lulled most of the viewers back at home to sleep. The game was part of the new CBS late-night television package, tipping off at 11:30 p.m. in North Carolina. At halftime—long after Friday night turned into Saturday morning—

the Wolfpack held on to a shaky 27-25 lead.

The second half mirrored the first—bad basketball by two tight teams. Neither Whittenburg nor Lowe could buy a basket. Whittenburg made a critical mistake with 4:43 remaining when he was whistled for a technical foul for chirping at game official Bobby Dibbler. Suttle, Pepperdine's best free-throw shooter at 84.5 percent, stepped to the line and drained the technical free throw to tie the game.

With two minutes to play and the score tied, sophomore Lorenzo Charles fouled Pepperdine's Victor Anger, giving the Waves a chance to regain the lead. But Anger missed both shots. Charles grabbed the rebound, allowing the Wolfpack to nearly run out the clock before calling timeout with 12 seconds to play.

Valvano went to his standard play, No. 32: Lowe with the ball, Whittenburg and Gannon on the wings, and Charles and Bailey underneath the basket in rebounding position. Lowe became trapped near the sidelines by Pepperdine's Mark Wilson and Grant Gondrezick and lost control of the ball against minimal defensive pressure, an inexplicable turnover from the veteran point guard. It was the second time in three games that Lowe had the ball in his hands with a chance to win the game but failed to generate a shot in the familiar offensive set. Wilson grabbed control of the ball and quickly called timeout with two seconds on the clock. Harrick drew up a play on the sidelines, but he was mainly eager for the game to go to overtime.

Neither team had much momentum as the extra period began. Whittenburg still had not scored in the second half. Pepperdine's frontcourt players sat back on their heels, trying to avoid fouls in the lane. As a result, the Wolfpack did not go to the free-throw line between halftime and overtime. The Waves could have taken an early lead, but Anger missed an easy layup against Lowe.

After watching his team steadily grow and mature over the season, Valvano could not believe how things were falling apart. Lowe wasn't playing well. Whittenburg could not even get a shot off. And early in the first overtime, Charles made two classic underclassman mistakes: first, he was called for goal tending with 3:18 to play, and then he lost the ball on an inside post move. All the progress he had made over the last three months seemed to be going down the tubes.

The Waves, who had been manhandled on the boards all night long, went up by four after grabbing two offensive rebounds—the first on a missed one-and-one by Anger and the second by Sadler after Suttle missed a short jumper. On the other end of the court, Lowe threw a lazy pass to Bailey that was intercepted by Anger. Bailey reacted by reaching in to foul Suttle, who easily canned his two shots at the line. When Bailey lost the ball out of bounds, giving the Waves possession with a six-point lead and exactly one minute to play, the reserves on Pepperdine's bench could not contain their excitement, brandishing broad smiles as they hugged one another in front of the television cameras. "We saw them celebrating a little too early," Whittenburg said. The Wolfpack, without the three-point shot it had relied on all season long in ACC play, needed a miracle if it had any hope of pulling off its fourth consecutive come-from-behind victory.

At first, it seemed inconsequential that Lowe, who had played so raggedly in the second half, stole the inbounds pass. It hardly mattered that Gannon hit a pair of free throws to cut the lead down to four. Lowe quickly fouled Anger, who was given two shots on what was deemed an intentional foul. (Unlike today, when an intentional foul results in two shots and possession of the ball, at that time, college game officials had the option of awarding a one-and-one or two shots, depending on their perceived intent of the foul.) When Anger missed the first of his two free throws, it deepened the severity of Lowe's mistake. The Wolfpack now had to score on three possessions for any hope of making a comeback.

Lowe raced down court, feeding Charles on a baseline drive for an easy layup with 48 seconds to play as the Waves backed away to prevent a three-point play. Lowe immediately reached in on Wilson for his fifth foul of the game. As the senior point guard went to the bench, CBS announcer Dick Stockton bade him a classy farewell: "An outstanding career for Sidney Lowe . . . the smartest player Jim Valvano ever coached . . . said he wouldn't come out until he graduates. . . . Hoped it wouldn't end this way, fouling out of the game in overtime." Soon after, Wilson made one of his two shots to give his team a four-point lead.

Valvano, who had been playing three guards all night long, went to the only other point guard he had on his roster, freshman George McClain. Rusty from having played only 21 minutes in the Wolfpack's previous eight games, McClain immediately threw the ball into Wilson's hands. But instead of going down the court for an uncontested layup, Wilson tripped and fumbled the ball right back to McClain. The young guard pushed the ball over to Gannon, whose long-range shot was off target. The Waves, suddenly in control of every loose ball, grabbed the rebound. McClain tried to steal the ball from Suttle as he pushed it up the court, making the classic freshman mistake of fouling an opponent's best free-throw shooter at the end of a tight game.

Suttle had made four of his five free-throw attempts in the game, and fully expected to make these. When he stepped to the line, heads on the NC State bench sagged as they awaited Suttle's fatal blow.

"I remember standing on the free-throw line as he was getting ready to take his first shot," Gannon said, reflecting on the game 25 years later. "I looked up at the scoreboard and thought to myself, 'Gosh, this could have been something special, but I guess it isn't meant to be. Now I have to go back to history class on Monday morning. Oh well, it's been a great run.'"

On the sidelines, Stockton was telling anyone who was still awake back in North Carolina, "All the Waves have to do now is make their free throws and they can salt this one away. But they have not been very sure from the line these last couple of minutes."

Gannon and Stockton soon learned why Valvano always told his team to never give up. Suttle's first free throw bounced off the front of the rim and into Charles' hands. McClain threw a perfect cross-court pass to a streaking Bailey for a dunk with 22 seconds to play, cutting the lead to just two points. Seconds later, McClain fouled Suttle again. Pepperdine's best free-throw shooter went to the line with another opportunity to seal the victory. This time he overcompensated, and his shot spun around the rim and again fell into Charles' waiting hands. McClain slowly got the ball across midcourt, where Gannon screamed in his ear to throw the ball to Whittenburg.

Suttle capped off the worst minute of his basketball career by fouling Whittenburg with nine seconds on the clock. As Whittenburg stepped to the line, the ever-active Valvano screamed for sophomore center Cozell McQueen to replace Gannon in the lineup, a move he always made in this situation to take advantage of McQueen's height and rebounding ability. McQueen found an obstacle when he tried to take position on the left block under the basket. Charles, who had just grabbed the last two rebounds on missed free throws, thought he should be wedged between Phillips and Suttle for this attempt as well, and he held his ground until Valvano screamed for him to get the hell out of McQueen's way. The coach thought having the left-handed McQueen on the left side of the basket would give him a better opportunity to grab an offensive rebound and pass the ball back to Whittenburg, one of the few guys the coach would entrust with such an important shot on the off chance that the 80 percent free-throw shooter missed one of his foul shots.

Whittenburg, still tight, bounced the front end of the one-and-one shot off the rim. Falling backwards, McQueen grabbed the ball with his left paw. McQueen, who had not scored a single point in the game's first 44:56, was the last person Valvano wanted to see shooting the ball on the play. But the coach found a silver lining: "I know Cozell's not a great shooter," Valvano told the media the next day, "but Cozell doesn't know he's not a great shooter." Fortunately, there wasn't enough time left on the clock to tell him.

The sophomore center lofted a quick shot that bounced three times on the rim before falling through the net with three seconds remaining to tie the score.

Even now, when he's sitting around with his friends in his home-town Los Angeles, Dane Suttle gets the same question over and over again: "How'd you miss them free throws?" Everyone is still looking for the exact explanation for one of the most baffling meltdowns in NCAA Tournament history.

Suttle, who still ranks as Pepperdine's all-time leading scorer with 1,697 career points, made better than four out of every five free throws he took in college. To miss two shots in that situation still seems unfathomable to him, although he has always known the answer as to why he faltered: he had been run so ragged by Whittenburg and Gannon in a box-and-one defense that his legs were rubbery and his arms were weak when he stepped up to the line.

Harrick had Suttle running the baseline all night long, and he was used primarily as a decoy in the waning moments of the game. Wilson was still the Waves' best clutch player, the guy Harrick wanted to take any important shots.

"In defense of my free throws, I have never been more tired in a basketball game," Suttle said, reflecting on that game in 2006. "I give Valvano all the credit in the world for designing a great defense, because it made me more fatigued than I have ever been on a basketball court. When I got to the line, I just wasn't feeling normal. We still had opportunities to win that game, but we didn't box out on a missed free throw." Perhaps it was just peer pressure—both teams struggled at the line in the roughly played contest, with each missing at least 10 shots from the line during the game.

With two and a half decades of hindsight, Suttle still buys into what Valvano was telling the Wolfpack in the opposite locker room— NC State was simply destined to beat the Waves. "I think it was just meant to be for NC State," Suttle said. "It was their time. On my end, it wasn't pleasant. Some things you just can't control. Of course, a lot of people remember those free throws and don't remember the good things I did in my career, and that's a little disappointing. But I can live with it."

And he does, every day.

○ ○ ○

By the second overtime, both teams were exhausted. Pepperdine's reserves, who had celebrated heavily when the Waves were up by six with a minute to play, were now slumped over in their wooden chairs. Lowe, preparing himself for his future as the Wolfpack's coach, was calling plays from the sidelines.

Bailey blocked Pepperdine's first two shots, but the Waves took the early lead when Sadler made a short shot in the lane and was hacked by McQueen, who fouled out of the contest with only one basket the whole night. Valvano changed his lineup, keeping McClain on the bench and putting the ball in the hands of Whittenburg and

Gannon. He put junior Alvin Battle in for McQueen. Battle, though he didn't score in overtime, had the freshest legs on the floor and used them to corral a couple of important rebounds and loose balls.

Almost all of the scoring in this extra period came from the free-throw line, as tired players were caught reaching in or bumping into each other. Suttle and Anger fouled out for the Waves. Finally, the Wolfpack started hitting its free throws. Whittenburg, as he did in the overtime against North Carolina in the ACC Tournament, took over the Wolfpack's offense, making eight of 10 foul shots to help his team maintain a shaky three-point lead. With nine seconds to play, State led 69-67 as Gannon went to the line for a one-and-one opportunity. For the second game in a row, however, the 90 percent free-throw shooter missed the front end, giving Pepperdine a chance to send the game into a third overtime.

Wilson quickly brought the ball down the court and put up a 20-foot jumper with two seconds to play. Like all but one of his six shots that night, it missed the mark. The ball bounced off Battle's hands and into the arms of Charles for his game-high 14th rebound of the contest.

Something changed within the Wolfpack at that moment. They began to believe Valvano might be onto something with his talk of destiny. "We used to lose these kinds of games," Lowe said afterwards. "Tonight, we were a team. We were like a pitcher who doesn't have his best stuff, but still goes nine innings and gets the win. We played one of the worst games we've ever played and still won."

As the buzzer sounded, Wilson fell flat on the floor, spent from a miserable shooting night made worse by the miserable outcome. The Wolfpack players had just enough energy to celebrate the school's first NCAA Tournament victory since the 1974 team beat Marquette for the national championship.

"We needed a game like this," Valvano said afterwards. "Getting past that first [tournament game], especially a game like this, will make you get better."

News and Observer reporter Tom Harris suggested in his follow-up story two days later that the Wolfpack may have exhausted more than their legs in the double-overtime victory. "This odd scenario—with its missed shots and bungled opportunities—may have used up State's allotment of luck for the tourney."

He could not have been more wrong.

NC STATE 71, NEVADA-LAS VEGAS 70
MARCH 20, 1983
NCAA TOURNAMENT SECOND ROUND

Thurl Bailey has always been a gentleman about it, and he's not about to change. If he sees Sidney Green across the room at a meeting of National Basketball Association retired players, he does not bring up what happened in the second round of the NCAA Tournament between underdog NC State and second-seeded Nevada-Las Vegas.

"I just smile and go on," Bailey says.

Bailey said—and did—all he needed to on the floor of Gill Coliseum, one day after Green gave Bailey the inspiration for a career performance. "I watched the game last night, and Bailey didn't impress me that well," Green said. "I ain't worried about Bailey. The one I worry about is [Lorenzo] Charles. Me and him grew up in the same neighborhood in Brooklyn. I was two years ahead of him and he always looked up at me. We caught a look at each other last night, and I nodded to him. Charles still knows he is under me. What I am looking forward to is [third-seeded] UCLA—that tradition, prestige, and glory. That's my dream, to beat UCLA."

Admittedly, Bailey didn't play well in the Wolfpack's NCAA opener against the Waves, hitting only eight of his 18 shots and grabbing just three rebounds. And Charles, for the fourth time in a row, was a monster on the boards, getting a game-high 14 rebounds. But Bailey was not about to be ignored, especially by Green, who had played with Bailey, Sidney Lowe, and Dereck Whittenburg in the Capital Classic following their senior year of high school and was at one time thought to be coming with the trio to play for Norm Sloan and the Wolfpack. Late in the recruiting year, however, Green changed his mind and chose to play for Jerry Tarkanian at UNLV.

Bailey found newspaper clippings of Green's comments pasted all over his locker, courtesy of sports information director Ed Seaman. Bailey, who never had a technical foul in his NC State basketball career, is not someone whose buttons can be easily pushed. But Green found them.

For the first 30 minutes of the game, Green backed up what he said by outplaying Bailey, who had only 10 points midway through the second half. Bailey figured out what he was doing wrong: he was continuously trying to draw UNLV's defenders off their feet with a pump fake. They never did bite, so in the second half he went straight up with the ball, fooling them just about every time.

Lowe, who made several uncharacteristic mistakes against Pepperdine, was in spectacular form early against UNLV with five assists, five rebounds, and four points before picking up his third foul three minutes before halftime. That forced Valvano to insert freshman George McClain into the lineup. With Lowe on the sidelines, the Running Rebels built their biggest lead of the half as Green hit a turnaround jumper 31 seconds before intermission.

It was a well-played half by two teams known for aggressive defenses, which kept the shooting percentages down on both sides of the court. Lowe and UNLV point guard Danny Tarkanian were putting their teammates in good positions to score—the teams had only five combined turnovers in the first half. The biggest difference between the squads was in foul shots—the Wolfpack was again just awful, hitting only five of 11 free-throw attempts. After making three early shots, Whittenburg was completely taken out of the game by UNLV's Jeff Collins, a transfer from Arizona who joined the Runnin' Rebels team at midseason. Tarkanian's man-to-man defense forced the Wolfpack to take unwanted shots, specifically outside jumpers by sophomores Cozell McQueen and Lorenzo Charles. But the two interior players surprised everyone by making a couple of them.

Five minutes into the second half, Lowe picked up his fourth personal foul while trying to take a charge on UNLV freshman Terry Graham, forcing Valvano to sit his senior point guard down. Moments later, Green earned a double whammy of good fortune: not only was he fouled by Charles on an inside shot, but McQueen was called for goal tending well after the foul. Green converted the three-point play to give the Runnin' Rebels their biggest lead, 52-40, with just more than 11 minutes to play.

Valvano could not afford to keep Lowe on the bench any longer. In the first half, while Lowe was out of the game with three fouls, the Rebels increased their lead from one point to six. When he came out in the second half, UNLV upped its lead from seven to 12. Lowe quickly made another mistake by trying to drive in the lane, where he had the ball stripped out of his hands. Anderson slapped the ball to teammate Eldridge Hudson to start a two-on-one fast break against Bailey.

With Whittenburg struggling from the outside and Lowe in foul trouble, Bailey knew if he was ever going to impress Green, the UNLV-heavy crowd, and the Rebels' big-haired cheerleaders smiling so alluringly on the sidelines, he had to act now. So he decided to hold his ground against the Rebel onslaught. When Anderson charged at him for the layup, Bailey went straight up and altered the shot. Hudson was there to tip the ball toward the basket, but he missed a pair of put-backs over a hip-hopping Bailey, who finally pulled down the rebound to end the game-changing possession. On the other end of the court, Lowe passed the ball to Bailey in the middle of the lane for an unstoppable baby hook shot right in Green's face.

"Sidney Green made me play harder," Bailey said. "When I get upset, I play harder."

Instead of trailing by 12 again, the Wolfpack was behind by just eight points. Bailey, who made seven of his final eight shots in the game, came alive to hit three baseline jumpers. Less than five minutes later, the Wolfpack cut the Rebels' advantage to just two points following a pair of free throws by Charles. The Wolfpack got two big scares in the final five minutes, thanks to the disorganized officiating crew of Bobby Dibler, Edgar Cartotto, and Jack Hannon. Twice, they mistakenly called Lowe for his fifth foul, but eventually reversed both calls and charged the infractions to Bailey and Whittenburg, respectively. Both times, Valvano's heart stopped at the thought of playing a second consecutive contest without Lowe on the court at the most critical time of the game.

By this time, Green wasn't the only Vegas player doing a little talking on the court. Hudson and Wolfpack sophomore Terry Gannon got into a shoving match at midcourt, and Valvano and Danny Tarkanian nearly came to blows on the sidelines when the Vegas coach's son started jawing at the Wolfpack coach. "Some of the things they were saying inspired us," Whittenburg said. "They insulted us."

As in the Pepperdine game, Valvano threw his aggressive free-throw defense at the Rebels, fouling early in the possession and putting weak shooters on the line. And, for the fourth game in a row, it worked perfectly. In the final two minutes, UNLV made only two of seven shots from the line. Hudson, a freshman, could have given his team a three-point lead with 32 seconds to play, but he missed the front end of a one-and-one. Charles claimed the ball for his fifth consecutive double-digit rebounding effort. Valvano waved off any possibility of calling a timeout that might have given the Rebels a chance to settle down. "It was kind of wild out there and I wanted to keep it that way," Valvano said.

With eight seconds to play, Whittenburg put up a 16-foot jumper and watched helplessly as it bounced twice on the rim. Bailey, who was left free in the lane as UNLV's defense rushed out to cover Whittenburg, out-jumped Hudson and tipped the ball toward the basket. He had little control of where the ball went, and it bounced off the side. Bailey grabbed the rebound out of Green's hands. As the clocked ticked down, Bailey put the ball up for a basket that gave the Wolfpack its first lead since the 8:48 mark of the first half. It was Bailey's 17th point of the second half and his 25th point of the game. Even Green had to be impressed.

"It was poetic justice for me," Bailey said.

The Rebels called timeout to stop the clock, then advanced the ball with a pass to just above the free-throw line, where they called another timeout with two seconds to play to set up their final shot. Tarkanian wanted to get the ball to Anderson, who had already made six long jumpers in the game, but Whittenburg had him completely covered. Hudson had no choice but to throw the ball to reserve Eric Booker, who had taken only one shot the entire game. Booker had some experience in this situation: he had made a three-pointer in overtime of the Pacific Coast Athletics Association Tournament championship game against Fresno State to give the Runnin' Rebels the title and an automatic berth into the NCAA Tournament. This time, however, Booker's 40-footer sailed far over the top of the backboard and into the deep end zone between the basket and the bleachers.

Wendell Murphy, who sat right behind the Wolfpack bench the whole game, still has an indelible image of Valvano's reaction when he saw the ball come down as the buzzer sounded.

"What a horseshit shot!" the coach screamed. "What a horseshit shot!"

Finally, Jimmy Valvano—the kid from Queens, New York, the guy who liked to call himself "The King of Corona," a Southern transplant who said he got the runs so badly from eating barbecue 42 times in 35 days during his first Wolfpack Club tour that he had to go to the bathroom every time he saw a pig—had learned to talk like a farmer.

14 "DERECK DISTRACTED ME"

Not only did the Wolfpack have a difficult time adjusting to the caffeine-, nicotine-, and alcohol-free world of Latter Day Saints they found nestled at the base of the Wasatch Mountains, they also had trouble adjusting to the freezing weather. Ogden, Utah, was a cold and snowy place in late March 1983 as Mother Nature dumped some six feet of snow on the surrounding mountains. No one in the Wolfpack traveling party had any trouble believing that "wasatch," as some non-Mormon historians claim, is a derivation of the Paiute Indian word for "frozen penis."

Jim Valvano was clearly the smartest person of the bunch: when the team landed in Las Vegas for its connecting flight to Salt Lake City, the coach and his wife took off in the opposite direction for a one-day getaway to San Francisco. There, they hooked up with Valvano's college roommate and backcourt partner at Rutgers, Bob Lloyd, so the two families could have a quick dinner and catch up on old times. The Valvanos arrived in Ogden a day later, leaving the coaching and caretaking responsibilities to the Wolfpack's three assistants. Of course, by this time, the players didn't particularly need—or expect—Valvano to attend practice.

"[Assistant coach] Eddie McLean would run practice for the most part, along with the seniors," Gannon said. "Half the time, V would be there for the start of practice, but he wouldn't say a word until halfway through. The seniors would take us all the way through stretching and drills and stuff and Eddie was there, also. When it was time to work on a game plan, V would step out and take it from there. Most of the time, he was looking for an audience, and we were busy, so he had to go find someone else."

Dozens of congratulatory telegrams from fans back East were stacked at the front desk of the Ogden Hilton, including one from Washington Redskins quarterback Joe Theismann, who had just led his team to a surprise win in the 1983 Super Bowl over Miami. "I believe in teams of destiny," he said. "I'm pulling for NC State all the way." Raleigh newspapers, television shows, and radio stations urged fans to write the team by repeatedly giving out the hotel's address. "We are like a traveling army," Valvano quipped. "We've had mail call the last two mornings at 11:00." Many of the letters in the two mailbags that arrived in Ogden contained newspaper accounts of the now-legendary parties that were breaking out on Hillsborough Street and the Brickyard.

At least the accommodations were better, if not a little weird. Three of the region's four teams—NC State, Virginia, Boston College— stayed at the 292-room Hilton, along with the media and NCAA administrative staff. By midweek, the coaches at Utah, located just 40 minutes south in Salt Lake City, moved their players there, too, when a developing storm threatened heavy snow prior to the Thursday night game against the Wolfpack. None of the opponents could avoid each other in a cowboy town that virtually shut down after 10 p.m. as they crisscrossed the hotel lobby, ate in the restaurant, or played games in the video lounge.

After practice at a high school gymnasium Tuesday evening, Ernie Myers was in the video lounge playing his favorite game, PacMan. Virginia center Ralph Sampson walked in and challenged the Wolfpack freshman to a ghost-eating duel on the popular computer game. "Ralph thought he was better than me," said Myers, who walked around with a pocketful of quarters on every road trip. "Ralph thought he was outstanding at everything."

Myers, as he had been all season long, was ready for the challenge. When the competition started, Whittenburg walked into the lounge and began cheering on Myers and berating Sampson, the 7-foot-4 giant who nearly had to double over to reach the joystick. "Whitt spent the entire time cracking on every thing Ralph did," Myers said. "I ended up beating him, and Ralph was like, 'Dereck distracted me!' 'Whatever, Ralph.' I think that's the moment we got into his head out there."

Not everything was fun and video games. Academic support personnel arrived with the team Monday afternoon to conduct classes and tutor the players on homework. It wasn't the most structured learning environment, of course. "We were having the time of our lives," said team trainer Jim Rehbock, who joined Dr. Don Reibel, Francis Combs, and some other members of the traveling party on a one-day skiing excursion. "The players were stuck in the hotel room studying, though exactly how much school work that was done out there is highly questionable."

The weather turned colder as the week continued, and Ogden's side-hill elevation, which runs from 4,300 feet to 5,400 feet above sea level, made for quick climate changes. "We practiced at a high school that was at the bottom of town, and when we left, it was raining," said reserve Mike Warren. "By the time we arrived at the Dee Events Center for our public practice at the top of town, it was snowing. I took that as a good sign since it snowed in Greensboro on the day that NC

State won the 1974 [NCAA] title."

Whittenburg made a showman's entrance at the Wolfpack's first practice in the 11,592-seat arena, a circular mini-dome that sat at the base of the snow-covered mountains. Several students from host Weber State College were in the stands when the Wolfpack players walked in, and they were certain that Whittenburg's reputation as a three-point marksman was overstated. They had heard that the ACC's 19-foot three-point line was the shortest of any of the 14 conferences using experimental rules. They were sure that the Big Sky Conference's 21-foot, three-inch line, the longest bonus shot in college basketball, would be too much for him.

"Is that all?" Whittenburg said, looking at the line. "Put your money where your three-point line is."

The students threw down a couple of fives while Whittenburg went to find a ball. Still wearing his heavy overcoat, Whittenburg shot from behind the line, hitting nothing but the bottom of the net. Someone threw the ball back to him, and he did it again. Smiling, Whittenburg picked up the cash lying on the floor, gave the awestruck students a wink, and went to the locker room to dress for practice.

"Easiest money I made in a long time," said Whittenburg, who went on to score 51 points in the Wolfpack's two wins in Ogden.

Later that evening, the Wolfpack coaching staff gathered in a meeting room back at the hotel to put together a scouting report on Utah. They had borrowed an early-round UCLA-Utah game tape from Virginia coach Terry Holland, but a VCR malfunction had taped over the game with a *Saturday Night Live* rerun. It was the perfect mistake for Valvano's traveling comedy show. "We can guard Eddie Murphy down low now," Valvano said. At 2 a.m. on the morning of the game, assistant coach Ed McLean had to borrow an intact version of the UCLA-Utah game tape from Boston College coach Gary Williams.

The scouting tape obviously helped—Valvano's team scored its only double-digit victory of the postseason over the Running Utes, a

75-56 decision that earned the Wolfpack a spot in the regional championship game. Virginia set up an ACC championship game rematch by beating Boston College in an unconventional manner—the Wahoos played more than half the game without superstar Ralph Sampson, who spent most of the contest on the bench in foul trouble.

"Yeah, we want them," Sampson told Caulton Tudor of the *Raleigh Times*. "At this point, we want anybody. Getting another shot at them is something extra."

Valvano suggested moving the game between the two old rivals to Greensboro Coliseum instead of playing 2,000 miles from home, but the NCAA was not keen on the idea. Clearly, life on the road was turning weary for the Wolfpack players and coaches, who had spent only two days at home since leaving for a spring break trip to the ACC Tournament in Atlanta. Having then traveled to both Oregon and Utah, Valvano had grown weary of living out of hotels. And despite the excitement on the court, life on the road was becoming a bore.

"All we do is eat," the coach said. "We eat 17 meals a day. We eat when we get up; we eat at 11 a.m. At 5 p.m., we watch films of us eating at 11 p.m.. Utah is doing what it normally does out here—ski and watch the snow."

The team was conducting daily practices, attending class in hotel meeting rooms, and receiving treatment for various aches and pains. Due to the snowy weather outside, the players had to turn to practical jokes to while away the time. Warren still remembers the look of sheer terror on one cheerleader's face as Whittenburg, who had covered his face in green skin lubricant, chased her down the hall. "I don't know what she thought he was going to do, but she was very scared," Warren said. "Whit was a funny guy, but he scared people." Or got into their heads.

After Friday's practice, the players climbed on a bus for a scenic tour of the snow-covered mountains. "We looked down on Salt Lake City at night," said reserve Tommy DiNardo. "It was an awe-inspiring sight."

On Saturday afternoon, Whittenburg played one of the great games in NC State basketball history. He answered his 27-point performance against Utah with a 24-point performance against the Cavaliers, hitting the game-tying shot and passing the ball to a wide-open Lorenzo Charles to set up a pair of winning free throws. He was named the region's Most Outstanding Player after leading the Wolfpack to a 63-62 victory over Virginia, its ACC brother.

After the game, Whittenburg and Lowe rolled around on the floor, screaming, "We're going to Albuquerque! We're going to Albuquerque!"

"We always said that before we left NC State, we'd go to the Final Four," Lowe said in the postgame press conference. "There at the end, I just told Dereck, 'We're going to Albuquerque. We'll crawl there if we have to.'"

The players cut down the nets for the third time that season, but it was much easier this time around. The moveable baskets were lowered to chest height, allowing the players to stand on the court as they snipped the strands of nylon. This change also made it easier for McQueen and Charles, who sat on top of the backboard during the celebration—a test run for the following week in Albuquerque, New Mexico.

Frank Weedon, NC State's emotional senior associate athletic director, paced from one end of the Dee Events Center to the other, marching in front of some 500 Wolfpack fans who stayed in their seats to savor the victory. "This is bigger than 1974!" Weedon said, according to *Greensboro Daily News* columnist Wilt Browning. "In '74, we were supposed to win. We weren't this year!"

There were plenty of yuks in the postgame press conference as Valvano, Whittenburg, Lowe, and Bailey absorbed the fact that they were headed to the Final Four. "We have to give a lot of credit to our coaching staff," Whittenburg said on the podium. "Coach tells us to go out and play and he means it. He makes you feel like you are out there to have fun, like you are out on a playground or something."

Finally, after the longest road trip of the season, it was time to go home. The Wolfpack loaded its chartered airplane for Raleigh-Durham Airport, where hundreds of fans were gathered outside the gates just to see if the DC-8 would turn into a pumpkin when it landed. Valvano stepped off the plane, threw up his arms, and waved to the masses. "We came home," he said, "because we ran out of clean underwear." Meanwhile, thousands more people were still partying on Hillsborough Street.

The next day, several Wolfpack players gathered to watch the North Carolina-Georgia game to find out their NCAA semifinal opponent. Opinions vary as to whether the Wolfpack was actually rooting for the Tar Heels to win or for the Bulldogs to pull off another upset as they did over the East Region's top seed, St. John's. "We definitely wanted North Carolina to win," Terry Gannon said. "They were the devil we knew. We had played them three times and had beaten them twice in a row." But that's not the way Whittenburg recalls it. "I think I would remember a bunch of State guys sitting in a room cheering for North Carolina to win," he said. "I don't believe it. You have to be careful with stories. That's why they call them 'stories.'"

The Tar Heels clearly took lightly a team that had never been to the NCAA Tournament in its history. Before the game, UNC center Sam Perkins said, "I don't even know what conference [Georgia] is in." The reigning national champions quickly learned that the Bulldogs were in the Southeastern Conference, which happened to be the direction the Tar Heels flew on their way home after Georgia's 82-77 upset.

SWEET SIXTEEN

OGDEN, UTAH

NC STATE 75, UTAH 56
MARCH 24, 1983
NCAA TOURNAMENT SWEET SIXTEEN

Utah, with the worst regular-season record of any team in the 52-team NCAA Tournament field, considered itself the biggest surprise of the 1983 NCAA Tournament. Coach Jerry Pimm's team was coming off an 11-17 season in 1981-82 and was 7-10 midway through the 1982-83 season, including a 23-point loss to Virginia and a 25-point loss to Houston in a pair of games in Tokyo.

Relying on guards Pace Mannion and Peter Williams, the Utes turned their season around enough to finish in a three-way tie for the Western Athletic Conference championship, earning the league's automatic berth into the NCAAs thanks to a complicated tie-breaker procedure.

The badly misnamed Running Utes—Pimm liked to slow the

tempo and play half-court offense—seemed to be the classic one-and-done conference champion. But they surprised Illinois in their NCAA opener and stunned perennial national power UCLA in the second round in a pair of games in Boise, Idaho. The Utes returned home brimful of confidence.

"We'll give NC State trouble," Mannion said before the contest. "I think all the people who are predicting that NC State will blow us out are wrong. Right now, we are a good team. We haven't been all year long, but we are right now."

Valvano, who had correctly anticipated that the games against Wake Forest, Pepperdine, and UNLV would all be close, said the game would be "another one-pointer at the buzzer." He was particularly worried that his team, on the road now for most of the last three weeks, would be playing a decent team in its own backyard: Utah's campus in Salt Lake City is less than 40 miles from Weber State's Dee Events Center, host site of the West Regionals. Ute fans had caught the fever of their Cinderella team. Thanks to local sales and a midweek snowstorm that made travel difficult for the other three teams, Utah packed some 9,000 of its fans into the 11,800-seat arena.

After five last-second escapes by a total of just 14 points, the Wolfpack players were eager to prove they could survive and advance without so much drama. The game was close throughout the entire first half, even though the Wolfpack seemed on the verge of breaking it open on several occasions thanks to Dereck Whittenburg's unconscious shooting and sophomore Lorenzo Charles' 10 points in the game's first seven minutes. Pimm was impressed enough by Bailey that he put all of his team's defensive efforts into stopping the senior forward, surrounding him with double-teams on every possession. With Bailey held scoreless, the biggest lead NC State could muster in the first half was six points.

The turning point of the game came early in the second half, after Utah scored three straight baskets to take a two-point lead, stirring the heavily partisan crowd into a tizzy. Whittenburg misfired on a jumper against Utah's Angelo Robinson, but was fouled on the shot, a call Pimm vehemently protested. The coach was primarily upset because his team had gotten the rebound on Whittenburg's rare miss that day and thought one more basket might pull the Wolfpack out of its zone defense. Whittenburg drained his two free throws to tie the game at 32, then gave his team the lead for good with an outside jumper on his team's next possession.

Stealing a strategy he remembered North Carolina's Dean Smith using the year before against the Utes, Valvano put his quickest line-up in to chase the plodding Utes all over the floor, alternating fleet-footed George McClain and outside shooter Terry Gannon in the third guard spot. That kept center Cozell McQueen, who played a season-low 13 minutes, on the bench, a defensive shift that caught the Utes off-guard.

Whittenburg, who had not been in pre-injury form in the Wolfpack's first five postseason games, put on an unparalleled shooting exhibition that afternoon, hitting 10 of his 13 shots from the field for a game-high 27 points. He made a few driving layups, but most of his shots came from well behind the 20-foot arc painted on the floor. "I was just happy to be playing on a court with a three-point line," Whittenburg said. "It didn't matter how far it was."

Valvano made some cursory comments about the game being closer than it appeared, but it was pretty obvious that the Wolfpack players wanted to win big just to prove they didn't have to wait until the last minute. The Pack's 19-point margin of victory was five more than the combined difference of its last five games.

Just about every shot NC State threw toward the basket that Thursday evening seemed to go in. Amazingly, the Wolfpack missed only four shots in the second half, going 15 of 19 from the field for a

78.9 shooting percentage. The defense was just as hot—during a 10-point scoring burst, the Wolfpack forced the Utes to miss six consecutive shots and commit two turnovers. And, unlike a couple of the previous games, the Wolfpack was confident at the free-throw line, missing just three of its 22 foul shots.

"We thought they were a good ball club, but we didn't think they were this good," Pimm said. "The shots they made, they earned. A lot of those shots would have been three-point goals in the pros. . . . I don't know what we could have done differently."

NC STATE 63, VIRGINIA 62
MARCH 26, 1983
NCAA TOURNAMENT ELITE EIGHT

So confident was Virginia as it headed into its fourth game of the year against NC State that Cavaliers coach Terry Holland and his team loosened their collars for a few minutes on the day before the NCAA West Region final. They actually made jokes, a wholly uncharacteristic development for a team that had played the entire season piano-wire tight.

They were at least trying to emulate the loose atmosphere that had garnered so much attention for the comedian Jim Valvano and his traveling troupe of warm-up acts, who were eager to face the Wahoos one more time.

"They feel like they are a team of destiny or something," said Virginia All-American Ralph Sampson. "But we will be ready to play, too."

Under their jolly façade, the Cavaliers were unhappy to see the Wolfpack, with a healthy Dereck Whittenburg back in the lineup, yet again. "We did not think that it was fair to have to play an ACC team a fourth time in the regional finals," Holland said in 2007. "The men's basketball committee did not think so either and later made it a policy to protect a No. 1 seed from playing a member of its own conference until at least the Final Four. Plus, by that time in the 1983 season, State was one of the best teams in the country."

So were the Cavaliers. They had seemingly answered their biggest question while beating Boston College—coached by an extremely young Gary Williams, who would later win a national championship at Maryland—just two nights before. Sampson played in less than half of the 95-92 victory because of foul trouble. The Cavs actually trailed when Sampson committed his fourth foul on the first play of the second half. By the time he came back in the game, Holland's team had outscored the Eagles 15-1 to grab an 11-point lead. Proving to the outside world that they were good enough to play without Sampson—as they had when they beat Houston earlier in the season in Tokyo, Japan—was the last real hurdle the Cavaliers faced that season. "Ralph Sampson gets all the attention," Williams said after the contest. "Nobody knows just how good their other players are."

The Wolfpack players were delighted to face the Cavaliers again so they could prove two things. First, after the ACC Tournament, Sampson said that the Wolfpack was the benefactor of a Virginia gift—that it had done little to actually win the game except take advantage of Virginia's mistakes. Secondly, Valvano's team wanted to show that it could beat the Cavaliers without the ACC's experimental three-point and shot-clock rules, which had given the Wolfpack an offensive advantage all year long.

The Wolfpack had attempted and made more three-pointers than any team in the ACC. Early in the season, Holland made a conscious decision to avoid the three-point shot, mainly because he knew it would not be used in the NCAA Tournament. And there was nothing the Cavaliers were more focused on than winning a national title in Sampson's final year.

For the season, NC State made more three-pointers (172) than the Cavaliers even attempted (124). In three previous games between the two teams, the Wolfpack had a 29-6 advantage in three-point baskets, and in the ACC title game, the Wolfpack made four times as many three-point shots as Virginia did (12-4). "If we play that game under NCAA rules, we win this game," Holland said bluntly after the title contest in Atlanta.

It is never that simple, of course. Fans and opposing coaches alike seemed to forget about the importance of the 30-second shot clock. With it, the Wolfpack could push the tempo with a faster-paced, fast-break offense. Without it, senior point guard Sidney Lowe was masterful at controlling the pace of play. And even for a perimeter-oriented offense like the Wolfpack, learning to play different styles with and without the shot clock was one of the most important lessons of the regular season.

"I think the tempo will be a bit more conservative," Valvano said. "I think the score will be in the 20s. We're going to go work out for an hour and practice not taking shots."

Early in the contest, the Cavaliers were comfortably in control. Sampson was not only scoring points, he was keeping Thurl Bailey in check, both in the Cavaliers' man-to-man and zone defenses. Bailey made only two of his nine field-goal attempts in the first half. Whittenburg was on fire just as he had been in Raleigh more than two months before, but his multiple shots around the Big Sky three-point line at the Dee Events Center counted for only two points. The Cavaliers were content with letting him take those shots, figuring he could not possibly keep up his torrid shooting pace.

Virginia's only struggles seemed to come from inside—with five minutes to play in the first half, Othell Wilson charged into Terry Gannon and was called for a foul. He stared down game official Gary Muncy, something he frequently did when he disagreed with a call. In a game of such importance, the Virginia coaches told Wilson to cease and desist. "If you don't like it, take me out," Wilson snapped at the Cavaliers' bench. And they did, inserting Ricky Stokes to play the point guard until intermission.

In the second half, Virginia gradually built its lead to as many as 10 points, with Sampson showing the kind of fire that he had lacked in the ACC championship game. With 7:24 to play, the Cavaliers had a comfortable seven-point lead—just as Pepperdine had a comfortable five-point lead with 24 seconds remaining in the first overtime; just as UNLV had a comfortable 11-point lead with 11:34 remaining.

The Wolfpack needed less than two minutes to come back. Whittenburg hit a pair of free throws, Bailey hit a pair of baseline jumpers over Craig Robinson, Sampson traveled against Cozell McQueen's defense, and Lowe, after missing six of his first seven shots, drained a 22-foot jumper. With just under four minutes to play, Charles scored over Sampson for the fifth tie of the game.

The performances by both teams that day were amazing. The Cavaliers made 10 of their first 13 field goals in the second half, a 77 percent shooting clip. The Wolfpack made only seven turnovers in the game. In a perfect sequence with less than three minutes to play, Sampson threw down a thunderous alley-oop dunk, an exclamation point that said he had no intention of ending his career without a championship. Whittenburg answered immediately, pulling up for a top-of-the-key jumper in Wilson's face, making sure not to land on the Virginia guard's foot when he landed. As the clock wound down to the one-minute mark, the teams were tied at 61.

Virginia tried to run out the clock, but Valvano wanted to try his free-throw strategy yet again. He had watched as the Cavaliers made only 11 of 26 from the line against Boston College. With 54 seconds to play, in a nice twist of poetic justice, Whittenburg chased Wilson to the sideline and knocked him down near midcourt for a two-shot foul. After an NC State timeout, Wilson, a 74 percent free-throw shooter, made the first of two shots to give his team a one-point lead. But the Wolfpack's free-throw defense worked on the second as Wilson's shot hit the front of the rim and fell into Bailey's waiting hands. It was the Cavaliers' ninth missed free throw of the game.

After State called a timeout, Whittenburg wanted the ball. He had made five straight shots, all from outside. He was 11 of 16 from the field, almost all of which would have counted for three points in the ACC. After everything that had happened to him against the Cavaliers—the injury, the return, and a sub-par shooting performance in the ACC title game—Whittenburg wanted to be the one to end Sampson's career. The 6-foot-1 guard had been overshadowed by the giants of the game long enough.

After Lowe and Terry Gannon ran 20 seconds off the clock in the Wolfpack's stall offense, Whittenburg received the ball off a pick. He dribbled by Rick Carlisle and made the unlikeliest play of the game, if not his entire career: he passed the ball.

Lorenzo Charles was wide open underneath the basket, and Whittenburg could not resist setting up a high-percentage shot, quite an unlikely tribute to Charles' growth and maturity over the final two months of the season. In January, Whittenburg would never have dreamed of passing the ball away to an unproven sophomore. But after hitting the winning free throw against Wake Forest and becoming a dominant inside player in seven postseason games, Charles had earned the pass from the senior guard.

"Lorenzo had a better shot than I did," said Whittenburg, almost apologetically.

Sampson immediately fouled Charles, and the Cavaliers called timeout to ice the sophomore. On the sidelines, Valvano was offering all the positive reinforcement he could. He only talked about what the team would do after Charles made the free throws. He never mentioned the possibility of Charles missing. Then, as the team broke the huddle, Valvano whispered to Lowe, "Here is what we do if Lorenzo misses."

Walking to the free-throw line, Charles nodded to Whittenburg in appreciation for the pass. "I'm gonna made deese," Charles said in his Brooklyn accent.

"You *better* make deese," Whittenburg said as he walked by the sophomore forward.

Charles took six dribbles on each shot, and drained them both, giving the Wolfpack a one-point lead with 23 seconds to play.

Virginia had plenty of time and one last timeout to set up a game-tying play. Holland's first option was to get the ball to Sampson, a no-brainer. The second was to feed it to Wilson to create some sort of a drive. His final option was to throw it to a shooter on the wing and hope for an uncontested shot.

Just like in the ACC title game, when Sampson did not take a shot in the final eight minutes, the All-America center did not get his hands on the ball when it counted most. With Whittenburg chasing Wilson and Bailey and McQueen surrounding Sampson, the Cavs' only real option was to throw it to sophomore Tim Mullen, a one-time starter who had missed most of the Cavaliers' last four games with strained knee ligaments. He had played only six minutes of the regional final before taking his only shot of the contest.

"We were not going to let Wilson or Sampson beat us," Valvano said. "Now, if somebody else does, then you can put your head on your pillow and not worry about it. If Mullen hits that shot, it's his only two points of the game, and you can live with that. But if Sampson beat us, I was going to go put a bullet in my brain."

Not surprisingly, Mullen's shot bounced off the rim. Wilson caught it, but his hurried attempt at a follow-up basket did not even touch the rim. Sampson, who had been blocked out of the lane completely by McQueen, got his hands on the ball and threw it through the basket well after the buzzer had sounded.

The Ralph Era had ended; the Wolfpack, a team that had needed miracles to win six of its last seven games, was headed to New Mexico, "The Land of Enchantment."

15 "THE GREATEST MOMENT OF MY LIFE"

After nearly three weeks on the road, NC State coach Jim Valvano figured that his team needed some time at home before going to Albuquerque. He was wrong. The atmosphere in Raleigh was so electric that no one could actually get anything done.

The team participated in yet another pep rally on the Brickyard early Monday afternoon and threw the doors open to practice at Reynolds Coliseum. More than 5,000 people showed up, turning the basic shootaround into a 45-minute exhibition of dunking and scrimmaging that wasn't exactly beneficial to putting together a championship game plan.

"Coach, what the hell are all these people doing here?" team captain Dereck Whittenburg asked. "Where were they when we were 9-7?"

"Dereck, just enjoy it," Valvano said.

On Tuesday, the team held a luncheon with the press and another public practice. "A wise philosopher once said, 'Anticipation is greater than realization,'" Valvano told the media. "He never coached college basketball. Going to the Final Four has been even greater than I had anticipated. It is the greatest thing I have accomplished in my career in athletics. I don't care if we win or lose—I am going to sit back and enjoy this entire experience."

Of course, that was before a starter and two reserves completely missed Tuesday's practice when a quick errand to nearby Clinton turned into a town-wide celebration with a ribbon cutting, a perform-ance by the local high school band, and an autograph session. Even Valvano, who never met an adoring crowd he didn't like, knew it was time to head west.

On the bus ride to the airport Wednesday afternoon, about 500 students from Meredith College, the private all-girls school on the other side of Hillsborough Street, crowded onto an overpass on the Raleigh Beltline just to wave goodbye to the Wolfpack.

When the chartered plane landed in Albuquerque, a handful of tel-evision cameras were waiting for the arrival. The coach hopped off the plane, skipped over to the cameras, and shouted, "Welcome to the Jim Valvano Show!"

Albuquerque was not really big enough to host the increasing Final Four spectacle. The University of New Mexico Arena—commonly known as The Pit—was a small on-campus arena, exactly the kind of place that the NCAA Tournament was rapidly outgrowing. The year before, few people complained when the Final Four was held in the cav-ernous SuperDome in New Orleans, where 61,612 fans enjoyed both the semifinal and finals—even if it had all the intimacy of a mannequin's kiss. So the NCAA knew this would be its final visit to a small-time arena.

The Duke City won the Final Four when New Mexico athletic direc-tor Lavon McDonald, an unapologetic schmoozer, wined and dined—

and in some cases, as a member of the NCAA extra events committee, appointed—the group of fellow athletics directors who selected the Final Four sites. One of the members of that committee was NC State athletic director Willis Casey. Because McDonald knew the NCAA was about to increase the minimum-seating requirement for hosting a Final Four, he approved popping the top on The Pit, putting in a new upper-level mezzanine that increased the seating capacity to 17,121, which was just above the NCAA's minimum for hosting the Final Four. (Today, The Pit is not even big enough to host a first-round sub-regional under NCAA Tournament capacity guidelines.) He also made plans to build a $500,000 building adjacent to The Pit to be solely used by the media, if McDonald's schmoozing ever won Albuquerque the rights to host the men's basketball championship. That day came on June 13, 1978, in Park City, Utah, when the University of New Mexico was chosen as host of the 1983 Final Four.

Not long after, the New Mexico basketball program got into serious trouble with the NCAA because of a grade-fixing scandal known locally as "Lobogate." At one time, five different investigations were probing the program, including one by the FBI. Both McDonald and Lobos basketball coach Norm Ellenburger were fired less than a year after Albuquerque was chosen as the host city. When the NCAA Infractions Committee began considering sanctions, local officials feared that New Mexico might be forced to give up the Final Four.

NCAA Executive Vice President Tom Jernstedt, who has run the men's basketball tournament for more than four decades, said no one seriously considered taking the Final Four away, but that was not the feeling in the town around Albuquerque.

"To be honest, it was more of an accomplishment to keep it than to get it in the first place," said Dennis Latta, the director of the New Mexico Sports Authority and the former sports editor of the *Albuquerque Journal*.

"THE GREATEST MOMENT OF MY LIFE"

O O O

As a host city, however, the Old West desert town was a lovely place. Albuquerque is located just west of the Sandia Mountains, a range with a 10,000-foot peak and a distinct red glow at sunset that gave the range its name. "Sandia" is the Spanish word for watermelon, a vastly better translation than the Wasatch Mountains the Wolfpack left behind in Utah. It was the perfect setting for this Final Four since NC State, Louisville, Houston, and Georgia all used red as their primary school color.

The town of less than half a million, located at a lung-burning altitude of 5,200 feet, embraced the Final Four, even if its 8,000 hotel rooms could not quite accommodate the 16,000 coaches, media, fans, and support personnel who flocked to town for the event and for the National Association of Basketball Coaches convention. The hotel situation was so dire that Barron Hilton—the co-chairman of the board of the famous hotel empire—could not get a room at the Albuquerque Hilton, according to newspaper reports at the time.

Before the teams arrived, scalpers were having a field day, selling tickets for the two Final Four sessions for as much as $1,500. However, the bottom soon fell in that market. As much as people wanted to see the games, it became virtually impossible to attain a flight into Albuquerque. For one, it was Easter weekend and the commercial airlines cut their service to the city. And by Friday afternoon, an April blizzard had forced the cancellation of all connecting flights from the West. After three bright days in which the sun burned several Wolfpack players by the pool, the Albuquerque area was hit by an early-spring gale accompanied by snow and thick dust kicked up by 60-mile-an-hour winds.

NC State relied on three planes from Raleigh and one from Charlotte chartered by the Wolfpack Club to transport most of its 1,600 fans to Albuquerque. Dozens more, including a handful of supportive Wolfpack football players, made the 30-hour drive from North Carolina. Georgia, Louisville, and Houston also chartered three planes apiece to bring in fans. Mostly, however, the Old West town was over-run by boot-scooting Texans who had made the 900-mile road trip from Houston across the dusty plain. By game time Saturday, the depressed scalpers' market had knocked tickets prices down to about $100 each.

The Wolfpack set its headquarters at the sprawling Ramada Inn North, a three-story motor lodge with outdoor hallways that backed up to an I-40 exit ramp and overlooked a field of tumbleweed and low-lying pinon trees. It was much closer to the Riverview in Corvallis than the Hilton in Ogden.

"To us, it was the Ritz," said Sidney Lowe.

Near-disaster struck soon after NC State's team arrived in Albuquerque—Whittenburg started having chills. By Thursday morning, he had a 102-degree temperature and a raging case of the same flu that had kept teammate Walt Densmore in his room during the entire trip to Corvalis. On the advice of team doctors who had not yet arrived in Albuquerque, trainer Jim Rehbock began an aggressive treatment with medication for Type-A flu, hoping that Whittenburg would be ready for the Saturday afternoon semifinal against Georgia. As a precaution, Whittenburg's roommate, Alvin Battle, moved out of the room.

Whittenburg missed the team's Thursday practice, Friday morn-ing's closed practice at an Albuquerque high school, and the Friday afternoon public practice at The Pit, where 10,000 eager college bas-ketball fans showed up just to watch the four teams go through some rudimentary drills.

"This is more people than we get for most of our games," said Houston coach Guy V. Lewis. And he was right—only twice that season did the No. 1 ranked Cougars, who were on a 25-game winning streak, draw more than 10,000 spectators.

The Cougars saw it as a chance to show off the dunking skills that had earned Houston the nickname "Phi Slama Jama," a term coined by *Houston Post* columnist Tommy Bonk in a throwaway line after he saw Lewis' team dismantle Pacific 112-58. College basketball's first dunking fraternity officially adopted the nickname and wore warm-up suits with the phrase stitched across the front.

"This was a team that was pre-Michael Jordan," said Bonk, now a columnist for the *Los Angeles Times*. "They were way ahead of their time because they were so unbelievably athletic. They were my idea of what basketball should be all about. They were maybe a little bit out of control, but they were so good, they made it look easy."

Valvano was not worried about Houston, or even Georgia, at that time. He was simply worried that Whittenburg would lose the edge that enabled him to score a combined 51 points against Utah and Virginia. But just as Whittenburg never doubted that he would return from his broken foot in January, he was sure he would be in the lineup for Saturday's semifinal, thanks to a motivational pep talk in his hotel room.

"My father, the late Don Whittenburg, walked into the room, looked at me for just a moment, and said, 'I'm sure you are going to be ready for the biggest basketball game of your life, right?'" Whittenburg recalled. "Then he just walked out. It was almost like, 'If you don't hurry up and get out of that bed, I am going to take this belt off and whup your butt.' All of a sudden, I started feeling a little better."

In the national semifinal against Georgia the next day, Whittenburg drilled in two long-range jumpers in the first minute of the game en route to a 20-point performance. The Wolfpack never trailed in the game and cruised to a 67-60 win, one of only two comfortable victories it had in the postseason.

Even though the hard-partying Valvano did not actually need to paint this watermelon-colored town red, he did anyway. Thursday night, on the recommendation of the manager of the Ramada Inn, Valvano and his staff went to a little place called The Hungry Bear, a combination restaurant and dance club that served as Valvano's own personal hospitality suite for the rest of his stay in Albuquerque.

"Jimmy was just so loose," said then-Wolfpack assistant Tom Abatemarco. "Usually, coaches in the Final Four just lock themselves in their hotel rooms and work. We intended to go there and spend about a half-hour or so, then go back and watch tape. But all our friends were there, and Jimmy danced all night long."

Valvano spread the story in the media that he won a dance contest on his first night in town, but that was basically an embellishment. A patron who had watched Valvano whoop it up with his staff and a cadre of Italian basketball coaches handed him a napkin that read, "Runner-up, Hungry Bear Dance Contest, amateur division." (Sadly, the Hungry Bear no longer exists. It was torn down years ago and replaced by a Phillips 66 gas station and convenience store—just across the street from another Phillips 66 gas station and convenience store.)

Valvano, a self-proclaimed first-team All-Lobby selection in 12 straight Final Fours, was not so worried about Whittenburg's illness that he was going to let it derail his good times.

"I would sit in the lobby and say, 'There goes so-and-so,'" Valvano said. "Then I would throw down a few beers into the wee hours. I love the NCAA Tournament and the Final Four. There's a lot of kid in me. Now there's the realization that I'm going to have one of the better seats in the house—down at the bottom."

Most mornings, Valvano would meet with a handful of reporters from the North Carolina media, allowing them to finish their stories before practice, beat their East Coast deadlines, and, as one of them put it, "start drinking earlier." The North Carolina media corps was also a lively bunch, some of whom had had been chased out of Utah by the husbands of their week-long hot-tub partners at the Salt Lake City hotel that served as media headquarters.

On the Thursday night of the Final Four, a group of younger reporters went to see a new band at an Albuquerque nightclub. The next morning, as they were talking to Valvano in the lobby of the Ramada, they saw the band checking out of the same hotel.

As several of them wandered over to speak to the band, Valvano wanted to know what all the fuss was about. "This is the greatest Cinderella story in the history of college basketball and you guys want to go talk to Huey Lewis and the News?" the coach said in mock indignation.

Nobody upstaged Valvano.

Saturday evening's second semifinal took some of the life out of the entire NC State contingent as they watched top-ranked Houston and second-ranked Louisville play one of the most talked-about games in NCAA Tournament history. The two teams were mirror images of one another: high-flying, athletic, cocky, and on a roll. Houston had won 25 games in a row and Louisville 15, the two longest winning streaks in the country. The Cardinals, who had beaten the Wolfpack in a game at Louisville earlier in the season, advanced to the Final Four by cutting out the heart of its biggest rival, Kentucky, outscoring the Wildcats 18-6 in overtime in the Mideast Region final in Knoxville, Tennessee, for a 80-66 victory.

Houston, which won a first-round bye in the tournament, cruised through its first three NCAA games, winning 60-50 against a Maryland team that had twice beaten NC State; capturing a 70-63 victory over a Memphis State team that had also defeated the Wolfpack, and whipping Villanova 89-71 in the Midwest Regional final.

Louisville led the free-spirited game by eight points at the half.

By the time intermission was almost over, NC State players Terry Gannon and Mike Warren were walking down the ramp that leads from The Pit's upstairs locker rooms to the court, only to find that Houston's team was blocking the entrance. The Cougars, wearing their Phi Slama Jama warm-up suits, were huddled together, preparing for the start of the second half. They broke apart not with a traditional "1-2-3 Houston," "Defense," or any of those other corny motivational catchwords. The players simply shouted, in unison, "They dunk; we dunk better!"

"If that's not a game plan, I don't know what is," Warren said.

And it worked. The Cougars scored the first eight points of the second half, six of them on dunks. Louisville finally scored a free throw, but Houston answered with 13 more in a row. "The Houston-Louisville game was one of the most exciting basketball games any of us had ever seen," said Latta. "It seemed like Monday's championship game was a mere formality. The Georgia-NC State game might have been a good game, but compared to Houston-Louisville, it was yesterday's garbage."

The Cougars won 94-81, and wondered what all the fuss was about. They simply played the way they had all year long.

"It was the first time all year long that we played against a team that could match us," said Houston point guard Reid Gettys. "I think that is what made the game such an eye-popping, futuristic kind of game. We just jammed down the accelerator and kept it jammed down. What I remember about the game was that during timeouts, Coach Lewis said, 'They are tired. We got 'em. Faster, faster. Push harder.'"

Houston had one thing the Cardinals could not compete with: Akeem "The Dream" Olajuwon, as he was then known. The 19-year-old native of Lagos, Nigeria, had only been playing basketball for four years, but was well on his way to becoming a Hall of Fame-caliber player. Against Louisville, he had 21 points and 22 rebounds. Fifteen of his boards came in the second half, when the Cougars went on a 21-1 scoring run to secure its 26th consecutive victory.

"Louisville matched up at four positions, but they didn't have anyone who could stop Olajuwon," Latta said.

Afterwards, Houston coach Guy Lewis said, "We didn't have enough dunks." He was only half joking.

It was an awe-inspiring sight, especially for the Wolfpack players and fans. "We watched that game, and we just kept looking at each other, saying, 'Jesus . . .'" remembered Sidney Lowe.

Gannon and Warren noticed that during every timeout, several players would grab masks and start sucking oxygen, a common remedy when playing in the high-desert altitude. The Wolfpack players, however, were under strict orders from team trainer Jim Rehbock not to touch the stuff, which caused a crack-like addiction for the rubbery legs that often accompanied altitude sickness: once you tried it, the body just craved more.

"You will go up and come right back down," Warren said. "I think Thurl might have hit it once on our team, but Houston, in the semifinal and in the championship game, was sucking on it like it was Gatorade."

Maybe there *was* a flaw in the fraternity.

After the games ended Saturday, there was still plenty of time to hit Albuquerque's nightlife. Four of NC State's reserves were at a bar in Old Town, the original city center of Albuquerque that has now been redeveloped into a roaming hub for tourist traffic. They happened to run into several members of the Houston cheerleading squad. The two groups spent the rest of the evening together before heading back to the players' rooms at the Ramada, where a bathtub was full of iced-down beer.

The cheerleaders were smitten.

"It's kind of funny," said reserve forward Tommy DiNardo, who ended up dating one of the cheerleaders for more than a year. "They were sitting catty-corner from our bench during the championship game, and every time they would come on the floor, they would wink at us and say, 'We're all cheering for you guys.'"

The Wolfpack cheerleaders had different intents in their postgame celebrations.

"We spent most of our time with camera guys from CBS," said Barbara Day, one of the eight NC State cheerleaders who made the trip. "We wanted to make sure we got on television."

The next morning was Easter, but Valvano found that he could not rise again from his bed. Another victim of Densmore's flu, he woke up with his own 103-degree temperature. He attended the Wolfpack's mandatory open practice session, but the physical demands of the season had long since worn him down. He suffered most of the season with a painful hernia that forced him to wear a truss at all times. Long ago, he had scheduled surgery for the Wednesday after the Final Four to fix the problem.

This angry case of the flu turned his raspy voice into a gravel pit, but he still managed to growl out one of the more famous lines in Final Four history when asked during a Sunday afternoon press conference what his strategy would be against Houston. "If we get the opening tap, we are going to hold the ball until Tuesday morning," Valvano said.

In the press building adjacent to The Pit, just about every member of the media was trying to come up with the most unique way to express how badly Houston would destroy NC State. *Washington Post* columnist Dave Kindred began his column, "Trees will tap dance, elephants will ride in the Indianapolis 500, and Orson Wells will skip breakfast, lunch, and dinner before State finds a way to beat

Houston."

Wrote Joe Henderson of the *Tampa Tribune*: "Rain would make it perfect. It always rains at an execution."

Dozens of writers from the Southeast tried to give the Wolfpack a chance. Two non-North Carolina writers—Rich Bozich of the *Louisville Courier Journal* and Bob Lipper of the *Richmond Times*—even went so far to say that the Wolfpack's guards were good enough to complete the Cinderella tale. But they were thought to be loons.

David Casstevens of the *Dallas Morning News* wrote, "Anyone who watched Houston dunk Louisville either is blindly partisan or only kidding himself to think the Cougars can be beaten. Once upon a time they could. But not now. No way."

But as Valvano always liked to remind doubters, fairytales always begin with "once upon at time."

Some 70 miles northwest of Albuquerque, one-quarter of the NC State fans were stranded in a little place called Grants, a depressed mining town that once billed itself the "Uranium Capital of the World."

Fans from other schools snapped up overflow hotel rooms in Santa Fe and other more attractive outlying locations. Grants, on the other hand, was a dying little town with a hospitable heart that needed a dose of Cardiac Pack hope. It had two relatively new motels, the Grants Inn and the Holiday Inn, between Interstate 40 and the remnants of Route 66 that served as the town's main street. The 450 howling Wolfpack fans gave the town, with its 33 percent unemployment rate, a three-day economic boost that to this day has not been forgotten. Not even now that the town has been reborn as the prison capital of New Mexico, with a state penitentiary, a women's prison, a county jail, and less than six percent unemployment.

But in 1983, Grants had exactly what the Wolfpack faithful were looking for on the Sunday between Final Four games: plenty of Easter sunrise services. The 10 buses that had brought the Wolfpack fans from the airport lined up outside the two hotels to take the fans to the denomination of their choice, including a feast day celebration at "Sky City," the ancient Navajo Indian pueblos between Albuquerque and Grants.

By Monday morning, however, there were fears that the spring blizzard that had swept across the western Plains might prevent the Wolfpack faithful from making it to the championship game later that day. The fans hurriedly loaded their buses early Monday morning and made their way down icy I-40, just a few hours before two-foot snow-drifts closed the road. They quickly checked into the hotel rooms that had been vacated by departing Georgia and Louisville fans.

Sunday afternoon was miserable in Albuquerque. Swirling snow and dust covered the city. It was freezing cold. And a number of the NC State fans who had watched the Houston-Louisville game were afraid that the come-from-the-back Pack was about to receive its comeuppance.

"The day between games in Albuquerque was the most miserable day of my life," said Wendell Murphy, one of the school's largest athletic boosters who later became the chairman of the NC State board of trustees. "My room was cold; there was no heat. It was snowing sideways outside. All I can think about is how we are going to be humbled by Houston the next day. I envisioned the most lopsided final in NCAA history. I think that day I would have paid a thousand dollars not to have to go to that game."

Now, Murphy smiles when remembering what happened on that Monday night in Albuquerque, especially when he learns that the two biggest blowout losses of the first 69 NCAA championship games belong elsewhere in the Triangle: Duke lost 103-73 to Nevada-Las Vegas in 1990 and North Carolina lost 78-55 to UCLA in 1968.

Over at The Pit, the Wolfpack players got an up-close glimpse of the Phi Slama Jama fraternity, and they did not care for what they saw.

"They came in with their Walkmans, their shades, and their slippers, and they were be-bopping around," Lowe said. "We pretty much went from 'Wow, these guys are good' to 'We don't like these guys' to 'We are going to beat these guys.'"

Uncharacteristically, Houston actually spent some time discussing the Wolfpack's strengths and weaknesses during its Sunday practice. "Throughout the whole season, we spent 90 percent of our time talking about what we were going to do and how we were going to do it," Gettys said. "We actually spent more time talking about NC State than any other team we played that year, with the exception of Texas Christian, who we played three times. The one thing I have continued to hear through the years is that we thought the semifinals were the championship game, and nothing could be further from the truth. What the coaches kept telling us was that we were playing a team that won the ACC Tournament and was playing in the national championship game. We went into that Sunday practice thinking they were a really, really good team. The only thing I adamantly disagree with that has been written over the years is that we were overlooking them."

It snowed again Monday morning, just as it had on the Monday nine years earlier in Greensboro, when NC State beat Marquette to claim the 1974 NCAA championship. Everyone went through their pregame checklist of superstitions one last time, finding lucky pennies, pressing gameday attire, and making sure their lucky underwear was dry.

Valvano, who still had a raging fever, was too sick to participate much. He cancelled the team's gameday shootaround. Mostly, everyone sat around the hotel. Mike Warren swears that football tight end Bobby Longmire and a couple other Wolfpack players joined him and Terry Gannon when they tried out some Coors beer, which was still banned back east for its higher alcohol content.

The players made the rounds in the hotel, talking to the fans who had been part of the incredible journey. One of those fans was Wolfpack Club president Ronnie Shavlik, an All-America center who had helped establish the Wolfpack's basketball tradition in the mid-1950s under Everett Case.

One of the first national recruits ever to play in the ACC, the Denver native knew he was dying of pancreatic cancer. But Shavlik went to Albuquerque to see the high-desert mountains one last time—and to see NC State win one more game.

○ ○ ○

Valvano always wanted to be the guy who represented the "Thrill of Victory" on the opening credits of the *Wide World of Sports*. As soon as Lorenzo Charles' dunk ended the 1983 championship game with a 54-52 NC State victory, Valvano began a sprint across the floor of The Pit that has been immortalized as the pinnacle of joy in college basketball for the last quarter-century. The coach was hoping to jump into the arms of Whittenburg, as he did after nearly all of the Wolfpack's come-from-behind, postseason victories. But on the greatest night of his life, Valvano found his star player already in Lowe's arms. Valvano had no one to hug.

He jumped on a pile of other celebrants, one of whom may have been NC State athletic director Willis Casey. As Valvano told the story time after time over the next 10 years, his crusty old boss leaned over and kissed him right on the mouth. Like most of Valvano's stories, that's probably a wild exaggeration. Still, it started the most compelling postgame celebration in NCAA Tournament history.

In the first seconds after the dunk, Charles stood frozen on the court, doubt furrowing his brow. Valvano later told the team that the burly forward was too busy looking for yellow flags to celebrate. But no penalty had occurred on the play, and bedlam quickly overtook the court.

Alvin Battle and Mike Warren hopped off the bench, took two steps, and mauled Charles, expressing three weeks of emotion that had captivated the country and attracted the largest audience ever for a NCAA title game broadcast—some 50 million people worldwide. For seconds they clutched him until he uttered his first post-dunk words. "Yo, man, let go of me," he said. "I can't breathe." Eventually, Charles walked over and embraced his father, who was standing by press row.

A Houston player dropped to his knees and began slamming his hands on the court. Akeem Olajuwon rolled onto his back and stayed sprawled there until Scott Joseph, NC State's Mr. Wuf mascot, implored him to stand up before he was trampled. Olajuwon refused to speak to anyone, telling two reporters, "I got nothing to say, dammit" as he trudged up the ramp to the locker room. He came back down to accept his Most Valuable Player award, but spent the rest of his NCAA-required time in the postgame locker room, camped in a shower stall.

Lowe did not stick around for the on-court celebration, either. He took off for the stands to look for his mother, Carrie, the woman who worked hundreds of hours of overtime so her youngest son could attend a private Catholic high school. She was sitting in some of the best seats in the house midway up the stands right beside Thurl Bailey's parents, just as she had in the final two games of the ACC Tournament. "I just wanted to hug her," Lowe said.

Bailey stood on the court with his arms outstretched, wrapped in the glory of the moment. Whittenburg was at the bottom of a pile of players on the court.

One of the few visual images that can compete with Valvano's jubilant sprint is Cozell McQueen climbing on the backboard and standing on the rim with a red "Pack Power" sign in his hands. Moments later, freshman Ernie Myers took a seat beside him.

Reserve George McClain went looking for the ball that Charles had stuffed through the basket. But it was already in the arms of Houston forward Larry "Mr. Mean" Michaeux, who had a vacant stare in his icy eyes. "I ain't messing with that guy," McClain said, as he joined his teammates' celebration on the court. Moments later, Houston's Bryan Williams plopped down on the court and shielded his face from the cameras that intruded on his misery.

Like Lowe, Terry Gannon bolted for the stands as soon as the game was over. He went to find his father, Jim, a former high school basketball coach who had helped mold his undersized son into a talented scorer. Even now, if he slows down the replay of the postgame celebration, Gannon can actually follow his trek from the court to the stands and back to the floor. The cameras captured everything except the argument they had with a security guard who did not want to let them back onto the court.

"I can pick out the two of us together dancing across the floor," Gannon said. "Everything that I had worked for in my life came together in that moment: all those shots I had taken in the snow in Joliet, Illinois; all that time I spent working with my dad. To be able to share that with him on the floor—the guy who had taken me every step of the way—was just an incredible moment. They say getting married and having kids are wonderful things, and they are. But this was something so different. For a dad and his kid to share that, it was the greatest moment of my life."

That evening, another former high school coach proudly watched as his son completed a transformation into something more than just a happy-go-lucky quipster. Rocco Valvano celebrated with his wife, Angelina, long after the nets were cut down and his son had been whisked next door for the postgame press conference.

"You've got to remember that for years he was known as my son,"

FINAL FOUR

ALBUQUERQUE, NEW MEXICO

NC STATE 67, GEORGIA 60
APRIL 2, 1983
NCAA TOURNAMENT QUARTERFINALS

I t was an undercard of underdogs, a meeting between two teams, Georgia and NC State, that had crashed the party in Albuquerque and were vying only for the opportunity to be crushed in the national championship game two days later. Welcome to "Cinderella" versus "A Team of Destiny."

The afternoon warm-up at The Pit reminded many of those not-too-far-gone days of the early 1970s, when freshman games were played immediately before the varsity took the court. Later that afternoon, the two best teams remaining in the NCAA Tournament, top-ranked Houston and second-ranked Louisville, would square off in the game that would *really* decide the national championship.

NC State fans should have been familiar with this scenario: It happened for the Wolfpack in 1974, when the trio of David Thompson, Tommy Burleson, and Monte Towe faced UCLA's Bill Walton in the semifinals in Greensboro. Who even remembers who Marquette played in the first semifinal, besides a few people in Kansas? The national championship was truly decided when Thompson and crew finally ended UCLA's grip on the national championship with an 80-77 double-overtime victory. Marquette was dispatched rather quickly two nights later.

If anything, Georgia was the more surprising of the two teams to end up in Albuquerque, despite being the fourth seed in the East Region and the recipient of a first-round bye. Picked to finish seventh in the Southeastern Conference, the Bulldogs had never been to the NCAA Tournament before and had suffered four straight losses during one stretch of the season. This was a year after the best player in school history, Washington, North Carolina, native Dominique Wilkins, had left early for the NBA. Coach Hugh Durham's team was extremely athletic, but undersized, with no starter taller than 6-foot-7. The Bulldogs managed to finish in a four-way tie for fourth place in the SEC regular-season standings, but like the Wolfpack, they went on a roll in the conference tournament to gain an automatic berth into the NCAA field.

Their reward, however, was to be placed in the tough NCAA East Region, along with top-seeded St. John's, which had just been declared the "The Beast From the East" by *Sports Illustrated*, and defending national champions North Carolina, which had Michael Jordan, Sam Perkins, and Brad Daugherty. Playing in Greensboro, North Carolina, the Bulldogs scraped into the East Regional semifinals thanks to a buzzer-beating shot by James Banks in their opening contest against Virginia Commonwealth.

Moving on to Syracuse, New York, to play in the massive Carrier Dome, the Bulldogs stunned top-seeded St. John's in a Friday night contest thanks to a career night by forward Terry Fair. He doubled his scoring average with 27 points and added nine rebounds, three blocks, and six steals. On Sunday, Durham's team eliminated defending national champion North Carolina in the East Region finals, just as Durham's Florida State team had eliminated the Dean Smith-coached Tar Heels in the 1972 Final Four to earn the coach his first bid to the Final Four.

The undersized Bulldogs eliminated the Tar Heels in an unlikely fashion, hitting outside jumpers and forcing UNC coach Dean Smith to switch from a tightly packed zone to a man-to-man defense in which his taller team could not handle the quicker, more aggressive Bulldogs. "We were not that good a shooting team that year," said Eddie Biedenbach, a former NC State player and Norm Sloan assistant who was in his first season as an assistant for Durham at Georgia. "Lamar Heard was probably the worst shooter we had, but he made three long jumpers in a row and they came out of the zone and played us in a man-to-man the rest of the night. They really weren't mobile enough to keep up with us."

The Bulldogs, despite the lack of expectations, had a bona fide star in Vern Fleming, and excellent complementary players like Fair, Banks, and Heard. They were an experienced team, with Banks and Fleming starting every Bulldog game for three consecutive seasons. By tournament time of their senior season, the trio had made the Bulldogs one of the best teams in the country. They became the first team to reach the Final Four in their initial appearance in the NCAA Tournament since Kentucky and Stanford both made the national semifinals in 1942, when the event had only eight teams total.

By the time the Bulldogs tipped off against the Wolfpack in the first semifinal game, both teams had heard ad nauseum that they were playing for little more than the consolation prize of being sacrificed high atop a mesa two nights later. Somewhat prophetically, Georgia coach Hugh Durham had the right perspective.

"[Having two underdogs in the Final Four] might be the best

thing to happen to college basketball," he said. "Now everyone will think they have a chance to get here."

When the game started, however, the two teams actually did seem to be the jayvee undercard. NC State's Thurl Bailey was looking down when the ball was thrown up for the opening tip, and the Bulldogs gained possession uncontested. But Georgia missed its first shot of the game, and scads more later on. Wolfpack senior Dereck Whittenburg, who had been sick in bed with the flu the previous two days, showed no effects of his illness or the change in altitude. He drained his first shot of the day from 22 feet, then followed with another jumper from essentially the same spot.

The Wolfpack never trailed in the contest, the closest thing the Wolfpack had to a breather since the regular-season finale against Wake Forest. Unlike the game against North Carolina, the Bulldogs couldn't hit the broad side of a pueblo, making only 28 percent of their first-half shots and just 35.1 percent of their shots in the game. NC State's Cozell McQueen, who towered over Georgia's diminutive frontcourt, amassed a career-high 13 rebounds in the contest and blocked four shots, mostly because the Bulldogs' shooters weren't convinced they were having an off night. At one point in the first half, the Bulldogs went five minutes without putting a point on the scoreboard. With six minutes remaining in the game, Thurl Bailey tapped in a missed shot, giving the Wolfpack a 59-41 advantage—its largest lead of the game.

Georgia, which had relied on its athleticism and good shooting to pull off earlier upsets, decided to put pressure on Wolfpack guards Whittenburg and Lowe. Georgia made a significant run and narrowed the Wolfpack's lead down to just four points with a little over a minute to play. But the outcome was never really in doubt with an experienced backcourt in charge.

"We should be able to milk a lead like that," Wolfpack coach Jim

Valvano said after the game. "We are, after all, an agricultural school."

NC STATE 54, HOUSTON 52
APRIL 4, 1983
ALBUQUERQUE, NEW MEXICO

When Sidney Lowe and Dereck Whittenburg were seniors at DeMatha High School, they traveled to Shreveport, Louisiana, to play a pre-Christmas game against Houston's Phyllis Wheatley High School. The game was dramatic enough: a five-overtime contest in which Lowe carried the team after Whittenburg suffered a broken foot, a precursor to the same injury that had kept him on the sidelines for the Wolfpack earlier in the 1982-83 season. But what Wheatley coach Jackie Carr said afterwards was downright disrespectful: "There are 10 teams in Houston that are better than DeMatha."

Apparently, something inherent about teams led by this undersized backcourt duo was easy for coaches from Houston to underestimate. Because on the night of April 4, 1983, University of Houston coach Guy V. Lewis messed up. He thought his team—composed of lithe forwards, a dominant, shot-swatting center, and a couple of somewhat green guards—could sweep away Lowe, Whittenburg, and the rest of NC State's underdog basketball team with its superior athletic ability.

The Cougars were on the nation's longest winning streak, 26 consecutive wins since losing to back-to-back games at Syracuse and against Virginia in Tokyo. After returning to the mainland, the Cougars were all but unstoppable. They beat every member of the old Southwest Conference at least twice by an average victory margin of 19.7 points. Two days before the championship game, the Cougars stepped on the gas after halftime against Louisville and cruised to the title game, thanks to a 21-1 outburst. That semifinal game was college basketball's first post-modern spectacle: a run-and-dunk free-for-all some eight years after the NCAA lifted its ban on stuffing the basketball.

While the Wolfpack was impressed by the Cougars, they were also a little annoyed by their arrogance. NC State coach Jim Valvano feigned fright when talking about Lewis' team, memorably saying he planned to hold the ball until Tuesday morning if the Wolfpack won the opening tip. Houston had heard it all before.

"Everybody we played slowed the game down, with the exception of Louisville," said Reid Gettys, who was a sophomore point guard for the Cougars that season. "Nobody came out and said, 'We are going to run against them.' So for us to go into a game where an opponent said they were going to slow it down was like, 'Duh, you think?' That is the way everybody played us."

And that was Valvano's style: thanks to Lowe's dribbling efforts and the lack of a shot clock in college basketball the year before, the Wolfpack had been the lowest-scoring team in the ACC, recording but 57 ½ points per game. Throughout the 1982-83 season, the Wolfpack was able to run-and-gun with the best teams in the nation when using the ACC's experimental shot clock and three-point line. But Lowe was still capable of turning the tempo of a game to a crawl, which is exactly what everyone expected for the championship game.

Houston's plan was the same as it had been all year: to out-run, out-rebound and out-dunk its opposition. With a smile, Lewis told CBS before the tip-off, "Usually the team that wins the rebounding war wins the game. We have one other slogan, though, that we add to that: the team with the most dunks wins the game."

The Cougars did not scare the Wolfpack. Valvano's team had already played nine games that season against teams that were at some point ranked at the top of the Associated Press writers' poll:

four against Virginia, three against North Carolina, and one each against Memphis State and Nevada-Las Vegas. Houston, ranked No. 1 in the final AP poll, was the Wolfpack's 10th game against a team that had been ranked No. 1, a total that no team before or since has ever matched.

"A lot of people looked at us as the underdog in that game, but we never felt that way," said Lorenzo Charles. "Playing in the ACC, our mentality was that anybody else from any other conference just wasn't really that good. If you take that same Houston team and put them in the ACC in the 1980s, they would have taken four or five losses. When you play against Ralph Sampson at Virginia and James Worthy, Sam Perkins, and Michael Jordan at Carolina in January and February, you are ready for whoever might come at you in the NCAA Tournament. There was no intimidation on our part in that game."

But the Wolfpack still needed some motivational brilliance from Valvano to beat the Cougars. As the clock slowly ran down toward tip-off of the national title game, Valvano gathered his team in the University of New Mexico's home locker room. For 20 minutes, assistant coach Ed McLean went over the scouting report, telling the team how to slow the tempo, keep the score in the 50s, and find every opportunity to deflate the ball. After McLean finished, Valvano slowly walked up to the whiteboard where his assistant had carefully listed every component of the game plan. He picked up an eraser, wiped the board clean, and flung the eraser across the room, which nearly hit three of his players as it whizzed by.

Valvano, seemingly brain-addled by his 102-degree fever and in severe pain because of the hernia he had suffered in January, had a different look in his eyes, as intense and serious as his players had ever seen. "If you think," he said, "we have come all this way, won all these close games, and made it to the national championship game just to hold the ball in front of 50 million people, you are out of your fucking minds. We are going to shove it up their ass. This is what we

FINAL FOUR

265

have been fighting for!"

As Valvano related in his book, *They Gave Me a Lifetime Contract, and Then They Declared Me Dead*, he went around the room, pointing his finger in the face of every starter on the team and gave them a reason to play the game of their lives: "You, Sidney Lowe! This is your last game ever. You're the finest point guard I have ever coached and tonight you are going to play flawlessly. You, Dereck Whittenburg! You've come back from the dead. They said you'd never play again. You are going to get those passes [from Lowe] and hit those downtown Js from all over the gym. You, Cozell McQueen. You're getting every rebound there is tonight. You're going against Akeem the Dream and you're going to do a job on him. And Lorenzo Charles! You're going to get inside position and power for points and rebounds. And Thurl Bailey! You're going to hit jumpers. And grab rebounds. And block shots. And dunk the dunkers. You're going to jump and bang and control the glass."

He punctuated every sentence with "and lead us to the national championship." His words were a relief and a blessing to the Wolfpack's wide-eyed players. Lowe remembers being settled by the idea that he would not have to hold the ball. He wanted to run, just as Squid and Tweetie Bird did the first time they played together on the outdoor courts at St. John's High School seven years before.

"That was so perfect," said Terry Gannon. "You think back on it now, 25 years later, and it might seem a little contrived or something. But V was able to pull that off. That was exactly what we needed to hear at that moment. We didn't need to hear that Olajuwon goes to his left better than his right or that Drexler follows his shot. We needed to hear, somehow, some way, that he believed we could win the game doing what we had done all year long. It created the perfect atmosphere for us."

For the first three minutes of the game, the Wolfpack ran right at the Cougars. Whittenburg took the opening tip from Olajuwon right out of freshman Alvin Franklin's hands. Thurl Bailey scored the game's first basket, dunking on a rebound off a Whittenburg miss. CBS analyst Billy Packer was amazed. Fifty million people were caught off-guard. For a few moments, Houston did not know what to think.

That locker-room emotion ran out pretty quickly, of course. The Wolfpack misfired on 15 shots in the first six minutes, including a string of 10 consecutive misses after it scored the game's first six points. What little production the team had during those lean 10 minutes came from unexpected sources: Alvin Battle, a 52 percent shooter from the foul line, made two free throws, and Cozell McQueen, who shot two airballs after making strong inside moves against Olajuwon, hit an 18-foot jump shot from the top of the key. Houston took the Wolfpack guards completely out of the offense, forcing them to miss nine of their 11 shots in the first half.

As in the Pepperdine game, NC State kept the score close even though its players were taking bad shots and making precious few. The Cougars, meanwhile, were a little out of control. Senior Larry Micheaux, who had scored a career-high 30 points and grabbed 12 rebounds in the Midwest Region final against Villanova, was not performing well: he shot an airball over McQueen the first time he touched the ball and was called for traveling the second time. He fouled Bailey in the backcourt after Bailey beat him for a rebound, then stepped into the free-throw lane too early on the second of Olajuwon's two free throws. And he gave up 15 first-half points to Bailey. By halftime, Lewis had seen enough of his only senior starter, and "Mr. Mean" sat on the bench for all but two minutes of the second half.

Clyde Drexler, too, seemed over-anxious, especially on defense. He held Charles on one possession, reached in on Battle minutes later, then slammed into Lowe while going for a loose ball—all within the first seven minutes of the game. Before anyone on the

Houston bench knew it, Drexler had three fouls, mainly because he had knocked the ball out of bounds when he collided with Lowe. The coaching staff thought it was just a change of possession instead of a foul. The four adults on the Houston bench had had trouble all weekend counting to five: against Louisville, Micheaux fouled out with 14 minutes to play because no one told Lewis to get him off the court. "I've got all kinds of assistants on the bench, and not one of them knew he had four fouls at the time," Lewis said. The same thing happened after Drexler picked up his third foul of the first half.

Valvano never told his team to take the ball at Drexler: he did not want to call timeout and give Lewis opportunity to take him out of the game. The future Hall of Fame player was clearly more cautious afterward as the Wolfpack began to build another lead. Whittenburg finally scored his first basket of the game with less than 10 minutes to play in the first half, but Bailey continued to carry the Wolfpack, hitting outside jumpers that Micheaux could not defend. Terry Gannon came into the game to hit a quick jumper, and with six minutes left in the half, the Wolfpack was ahead by a surprisingly comfortable seven-point margin.

Then, on one of the most humiliating shots of Lowe's career, something incredible happened. Lowe drove into the lane and tried to put up a running jumper over Olajuwon. The 7-foot center swatted Lowe's shot all the way into the backcourt, where Gannon outraced Houston freshman Alvin Franklin to grab it. Gannon passed the ball to the opposite side of the court to Lowe, who threw it down the floor to a wide-open Whittenburg. But the senior guard's 20-foot jumper bounced off Bailey's arms and into Micheaux's hands. Drexler took off for the other end of the court, outracing everyone to midcourt, where Micheaux threw a perfect lead pass. Gannon had never returned to the Wolfpack's end of the court after retrieving Lowe's blocked shot and found himself one-on-one with one of the top 50 players in basketball history.

Earlier in the tournament, Memphis State guard Andre Turner had been in a similar situation, defending Drexler all alone on a fast break. As Turner set his feet in the lane, Drexler cupped the ball in one hand, twisted his body to avoid Turner, and jammed the ball through the hoop without ever making contact with the defender, an awesome display of athletic power and control that defined the legend of Phi Slama Jama. Images of that dunk were replaying in the mind of Gannon, the smallest player on the court, as he saw Drexler charging at him with no help in sight.

"This son of a bitch is not going to jump over me in front of 50 million people," Gannon thought as Drexler built up a head of steam. "I am going to just tackle him. I am not going to be the guy on the poster for Phi Slama Jama for the rest of eternity."

So Gannon shuffled into Drexler's path, set his feet, and locked his arms around Drexler's body as the Houston forward laid the ball into the basket. But when ACC official Joe Forte blew his whistle, he called a charging foul on Drexler, not a holding penalty on Gannon. Forte also waved off the layup, which would have pulled the Cougars within three points.

"Until recently," Gannon said in 2006, "no one at NC State—in football, basketball, soccer, any sport—ever made a better tackle."

Amazingly, Drexler stayed in the game for another 90 seconds before Lewis was able to pull him out. Bailey continued to carry the Wolfpack offense. He made five consecutive baskets at the end of the first half. Not even reserve Benny Anders' two baskets in the final 30 seconds gave the Cougars much of an emotional lift. Valvano's take-it-to-them plan had the Wolfpack ahead 33-25 at intermission, 20 minutes away from the national championship.

At halftime, Valvano continued with his motivational madness. "He was convinced they were going to win the game," said Michael Danoff, an Albuquerque lawyer who served as the Wolfpack's host for the Final Four and followed the team from hotel to locker room to courtside. "He went to every player and asked, 'Are you going to outplay your man?' And he ended every question with, 'Because I am going to outcoach their coach.'"

The Cougars charged out of the locker room after halftime almost as hard as the Wolfpack did at the beginning of the game, scoring the first 10 points of the second half. Lewis changed his line-up, putting junior Bryan Williams in the lineup for Drexler and replacing Micheaux with Anders. Even without two starters on the floor, Lewis threw a full-court press at Lowe and Whittenburg, and in the process ran his own players a little ragged in the opening minutes of the half.

For the first six and a half minutes of the second half, Phi Slama Jama made all the pregame prognosticators look brilliant, outscoring the Wolfpack 17-2 to take a seven-point lead. Olajuwon ruled the paint on offense and the Cougars owned the boards. They grabbed every loose ball and nearly every missed shot. The Wolfpack's only basket during that blitz was an outside jumper by Whittenburg, a perversely good sign considering how little outside production the Wolfpack had in the first half. Williams completely shut Bailey down, pushing him out too far on the perimeter to get a good look at the basket.

The Wolfpack missed 10 of its first 11 shots after intermission. But by giving up the lead, Valvano's team entered familiar territory: this marked the eighth time in nine postseason games that the Wolfpack had trailed at some point in the second half. Valvano called two timeouts to settle his team down, but nothing seemed to work as the Cougars built as much as a seven-point lead.

Something of a turning point happened midway through the second half when Olajuwon went up for another inside shot against McQueen. The 7-foot Nigerian had already scored 16 points and grabbed 17 rebounds in the game, but McQueen blocked this particular shot and saved it from going out of bounds. Olajuwon, already showing signs of exhaustion, expended more energy when he repaid McQueen's rejection with his seventh block of the game.

As the Cougars raced down the court one more time, Olajuwon looked like an overridden pony. He was bent over at the foul line, pulling on the bottom of his shorts and gasping for air, clearly affected by Albuquerque's thin air. So was Williams, who had chased Bailey all over the court for more than 10 minutes. On the CBS telecast, Billy Packer said, "Guy Lewis is pulling the ball out so Olajuwon can rest. This is a really smart move."

History does not remember it that way. Lewis' decision to go to the Locomotion offense, his name for his half-court delay game, is considered one of the 10 worst coaching blunders in the history of modern sports. "We couldn't believe they did that," said NC State coach Ed McLean. "They had the lead. It was not a bad strategy, but it helped us."

With 10 minutes to play, Olajuwon had to come out of the game, practically forcing Lewis to put Micheaux back in the game and go to his spread offense. Some thought this spelled trouble for the Wolfpack, since Olajuwon went to the sideline to rest up for the stretch run.

"I thought we were in a lot of trouble, because I didn't think we could catch them the way we were playing offensively," said Tom Abatemarco, Valvano's other assistant at the time. "But Jimmy was excited when they spread the court because we were on the verge of getting blown out."

That was certainly the feeling on press row, where deadline-pushing writers immediately began their excoriation of Lewis for turning to the Locomotion. *Houston Post* columnist Tommy Bonk, who came up with the Cougars' Phi Slama Jama nickname, said, "It was just plain loco." "He's the right-handed Lefty Driesell," said another. *Washington Post* columnist Dave Kindred wrote that Lewis slept for the first 30 minutes of the game, then woke up and thought he was Dean Smith, the North Carolina Hall of Fame coach famous for his "Four Corners" stall offense.

"I couldn't believe he slowed it down," Kindred said, with 25 years of hindsight. "It was as if Valvano somehow hypnotized Guy Lewis. The only thing that could have allowed NC State to win that game was what Guy Lewis ordered his team to do in the second half."

But there was a legitimate reason behind it—the Cougars simply could not keep up with the pace they had set in the first six minutes of the second half.

"It was probably a smart coaching move on paper, because they had done it all year long," Gannon said. "You could see that the altitude was getting to them. Olajuwon was on the bench with the oxygen mask on. They were exhausted. But it ended up being a horrible move. If they would have kept playing, they would have beaten us by 13 or 14 points."

Gettys has always believed that Lewis made the right call and has spent nearly 25 years defending the move.

"We ran that offense a lot because Coach Lewis practically invented it," said Gettys, who is now a Houston lawyer and a part-time basketball analyst for Fox Sports. "It wasn't some random, radical new thing. We worked on it everyday in practice. We didn't use it much in games because we didn't need to—we were usually so far ahead of everybody. It was absolutely a hundred times out of a hundred the right decision to make. We were playing our absolute worst game of the year. Clyde was in foul trouble and Larry was playing just awful. If I am a coach in that situation and I get the lead, I make exactly the same decision every single time."

However, even Gettys' teammates second-guessed the call when the game was over, upset that Lewis deflated the ball and allowed the Wolfpack to get back in the game. "We should have been taking it to them instead of slowing it down," Anders said. "I wish we'd kept running the ball." A frustrated Michael Young, hiding out in the shower stalls from the media after the game was over, screamed for all to hear, "Guy blew it!"

But those same players bore some of the responsibility for what happened in the last 10 minutes of the game, mainly because all season long the Cougars could not figure out a way to dunk foul shots. Houston came into the national championship game making just 61 percent of its free throws, the perfect opponent to succumb to Valvano's foul-and-hope strategy that the Wolfpack had come to depend on in the postseason.

The Wolfpack began its comeback from seven points down as Olajuwon sat on the bench sucking on an oxygen mask. With Micheaux standing in the middle court, Lowe snuck up behind him and stripped the ball out of his hands, took off down the court, and threw the ball to Whittenburg on the wing for the Wolfpack's second field goal of the second half. Whittenburg quickly scored another jumper after McQueen grabbed an offensive rebound. Lowe stole a lazy inbounds pass in the backcourt and Gettys fouled Gannon on a layup. He made one of his two free throws, cutting Houston's lead to four points with seven and a half minutes to play.

Gannon, whose quick hands had helped the Wolfpack win three postseason games already, made another important play when he slapped the ball off Anders' knee as the Houston forward was driving in for a back-door layup at the tail end of a 90-second possession. The Wolfpack tried to go back inside to Bailey—who had not scored in the second half—but Olajuwon blocked Bailey's baby hook shot in the lane.

Lowe pulled the Wolfpack offense back out to look for a good shot against the Cougars' two-three zone and discovered that no one was guarding him at all. He quickly made back-to-back jumpers, cutting Houston's lead to just two points.

"The scouting report we had on Sidney was to stay off of him the entire game," Gettys said. "We thought we could sag off him and double-team Bailey. We thought Lowe might make one or two shots, but not enough to beat us. After he hit his fourth shot in a row . . . Coach told me, 'Hey, you better get out on him.'"

Valvano directed his team to start fouling the Cougars—not to get back in the game, as he had so often over the last three weeks, but to bring Houston closer to the one-and-one. The Wolfpack had committed just three fouls in the first 15 minutes of the second half, so Gannon fouled Franklin on back-to-back possessions, inching the second-half foul total to five. But the Cougars were still in control, particularly after Young, Houston's leading scorer, hit a jumper and was fouled by McQueen. Young went to the line with the opportunity to give his team a seven-point lead with four minutes to play, but he could not convert the free throw.

Bailey put Houston in the one-and-one by fouling Drexler at the top of the key with 3:19 to play. Drexler, Houston's best free-throw shooter, foiled the fouling strategy by making both shots to give his team another six-point lead. But those were the last two points scored that season by Phi Slama Jama.

Lowe made another long jumper, and Charles immediately fouled Young, who had missed three in a row at the line. He made it four straight by bouncing his one-and-one chance off the back of the rim. Whittenburg grabbed the rebound.

On Whittenburg's first attempt to cut Houston's lead to two points, he drove in the lane against Olajuwon and couldn't even hit the backboard on a layup attempt. Olajuwon tried to throw a long outlet pass to Franklin, but Lowe intercepted it in the backcourt and immediately gave it back to Whittenburg, who was standing open in the corner. The senior guard knew better than to go back in against Olajuwon, so he easily drained a jumper to pulled his team within two points.

When Olajuwon missed Houston's final field-goal attempt of the game, McQueen started a fast break by tapping the ball out to Lowe. He dribbled to the lane, but saw Whittenburg open again on the wing just as the clock ticked inside two minutes. It was an easy shot to tie the game at 52, even though Whittenburg was well behind the Pit's 21-foot three-point line.

Houston had the ball and planned to play for a final shot. There was no way Valvano would let that happen. The Cougars would have to make free throws to win the national championship. Valvano told his players to wait until the one-minute mark, then foul either Young or Franklin. Whittenburg missed on his first attempt to foul Franklin as he, Gettys, and Young played three-man keep-away from the Wolfpack. But with 65 seconds to play, Whittenburg reached in for an unintentional foul near midcourt.

The only person in the entire arena who looked more uncomfortable than Franklin as he headed toward the line for his only free-throw attempt of the game was Lewis, the Cougars' coach. He nervously buried his head in his famous red-and-white tea towel, unable to watch as Franklin, a 63 percent free-throw shooter, stepped to the line. As soon as Franklin let go of the ball, the young freshman's face twisted into a grimace. He knew it had no chance of going in. It was the Cougars' ninth miss in 19 tries at the free-throw line.

"The thing that everybody said all year long would kill us was our free-throw shooting," Lewis said. "It finally happened in the championship game."

The Cougars were almost saved when neither Bailey nor McQueen could get a firm hold on the rebound, which was headed out of bounds before McQueen snagged it and made an off-balance throw to a waiting Lowe.

The Wolfpack had possession of the ball in a tie ball game. "All we ever wanted, all year long," Valvano said after the game, "was to be in a position to win."

Unlike the Vegas game earlier in the tournament, Valvano wanted Lowe to bring the ball to midcourt and call timeout. When the clock stopped, only 44 seconds remained. For the superstitious Wolfpack fans, seeing the two fours on the clock was an appropriate omen—it meant the spirit of David Thompson, the All-America forward who led the school to its first NCAA basketball championship in 1974, was hovering over the arena.

No one in the Wolfpack huddle had time to think about that, however. Valvano was too busy instructing his players what to do—too busy, in fact, to tell Gannon to go into the game for McQueen. Gannon did it anyway out of habit.

There was no doubt about what play Valvano would call: No. 32. It was the same one he had run in crunch situations throughout his three years as the Wolfpack's head coach, putting the ball in Lowe's hands, sending two guards out on the wings, and posting his forwards under the basket. In this case, Whittenburg and Gannon were on opposite sides and Bailey and Charles were down low. It was the same play the Wolfpack ran in the regular season against Notre Dame, when Gannon missed the game-winning shot at the buzzer. It was the same play he had called against Wake Forest and North Carolina in the ACC Tournament. And it was the same play he had used against Pepperdine on the final possession of regulation. The only time the play actually worked, however, was against the Demon Deacons, when Lowe got the ball to a wide-open Charles under the basket. Charles was fouled on the play and hit one of his two free throws to give the Wolfpack a one-point win, the first in the Wolfpack's transcontinental Cinderella journey. Charles hit another pair of free throws to beat Virginia in the West Region finals, but he had been largely absent from the championship game, wheezing up and down the court from its outset. The last thing Valvano said as his team set up for the inbounds pass was directed at Charles: "Lorenzo, you haven't done anything all night long. I wish you would wake up." It was true: in the game's first 39 minutes, Charles had exactly one basket and three rebounds.

In the other huddle, Lewis was designing a curve ball: assuming Valvano would expect straight-up man-to-man defense, he called for his team to run its 50-VA defense, a one-three-one half-court trap. For all of the grief Lewis caught for the Locomotion, no one ever gave him credit for calling the perfect defense to flummox the Wolfpack on that final possession. It worked perfectly.

The Wolfpack made 19 passes on the final possession, four of which were nearly thrown away or intercepted. Lowe tossed the ball all the way across the court to Whittenburg early on. Bailey was trapped in the corner and made a weak bounce pass to Gannon in the middle. Whittenburg, with a hard-charging Anders coming at him, nearly threw the ball right into Drexler's hands. Instead, Gannon put his hands on the ball and turned just in time for Drexler, who was third in the nation in steals that season, to miss the ball.

"The final play was nothing like we diagrammed," Whittenburg told Michael Wilbon of the *Washington Post* in 1984. "It was like studying economics and having it come out chemistry."

Gannon threw the ball to Lowe, who never started his move to the basket. Instead, he threw it to Bailey in the corner as the clock ticked down to seven seconds. Bailey saw Young coming toward him and he quickly got rid of the ball with a 25-foot pass to Whittenburg, who was standing halfway between the top of the key and the mid-court line. Anders anticipated the pass perfectly and got his finger-tips on the ball, anxious to take off for an uncontested dunk. Whittenburg managed to gain control of the ball, but it seemed to be a perfectly wasted possession. As Whittenburg wheeled around to take a desperation shot from 28 feet out, Valvano was already thinking about his overtime strategy. Clearly, he needed something different, because nothing in the final 42 seconds of regulation had gone right.

"That's where you are absolutely wrong," Gettys said.

"Everything went perfect. We took them completely out of their offense. We created a total chaos situation on the court, exactly what that defense is designed to do. That wasn't chaos on our part—we forced them to throw all of those dangerous passes and had someone running through the passing lanes on every one of them. Benny was supposed to steal that last pass, and he missed it by fingertips. It was an absolutely great coaching move, because there is no way NC State was prepared for a half-court, all-hell-break-loose zone trap."

For more than three weeks, NC State believed it was destined to do something special—to win the ACC championship, advance in the NCAA Tournament, and continue to slay college basketball's biggest giants. The Wolfpack players believed a magical hand had made them the darlings of the media and the world of college basketball. That's why they all took such special care to follow their rituals and to shine, as Whittenburg called his high-tops, their "Cinderella boots."

What other explanation could there be for Charles, an out-of-position sophomore, to come up with the biggest offensive rebound in NCAA Tournament history? It was magical because Charles was nowhere near where he was supposed to be to make a great play. But neither was Olajuwon, who briefly broke for the other end of the court when he saw Anders tip the ball out of Whittenburg's hands on the game's final pass. By the time Whittenburg lofted college basketball's most famous airball, it was too late for Olajuwon to recover.

"Most people say I was the guy who was in the right place at the right time," Charles said in 2004. "Actually, I was in the wrong place at the right time. I was under the cylinder, which is exactly where you don't want to be if you are going to be a decent offensive rebounder."

No one criticized the results after Charles slammed the ball through the basket as the final seconds ticked off the clock: the

Wolfpack beat Phi Slama Jama 54 points to 52 and two dunks to one.

JIM VALVANO

When Jim Valvano said goodbye to his 1983 NCAA championship team, he did not have to run around in search of someone to hug. Most of his players were standing right in front of him on the afternoon of February 21, 1993, in Reynolds Coliseum, at the Wolfpack's 10th anniversary reunion. It was a difficult, exhilarating day for the dying coach, who was losing his public battle with bone cancer. Just three years earlier, he and the school had gone through a bitter divorce, the result of a trumped-up NCAA investigation and a media witch hunt that put his basketball program on probation for minor violations and forced Valvano to resign his position as coach and athletic director.

Despite the palpable acrimony that still existed between the school's administration and the coach, Valvano could not refuse the opportunity to celebrate the anniversary of his greatest achievement with the guys who had helped him win the school's second NCAA title. So prior to a nationally televised game between Duke and NC State—the last game the coach-turned-award-winning-television-analyst ever worked—Valvano struggled onto the court of Reynolds, the site of so many wonderful moments, to bid farewell to his players and to the Wolfpack nation. In the winter of 1993, the Wolfpack nation needed a heavy dose of inspiration as a trying 8-19 season was drawing to a painful close. NC State graduate and future athletic director Les Robinson was suffering through his worst season as a head coach and the school's worst men's basketball record in 26 years.

A sellout crowd cheered uproariously—while Duke coach Mike Krzyzewski pitched a fit in the locker room over the game's delay—as Valvano hummed the fight song, acknowledged the friends and fans gathered in his honor, and, most of all, reunited with his players. The hurt of the previous five years, in which the media raked Valvano over the coals for losing control of his basketball program, was a distant, though still painful, memory—yet the crowds had never really stopped adoring the coach.

Not everyone from the '83 championship team was in attendance. Sidney Lowe, then the head coach of the NBA's Minnesota Timberwolves, had to attend mandatory league coaches meetings. Lorenzo Charles and Cozell McQueen were still playing professional basketball overseas. Walter "Dinky" Proctor chose not to participate, working his usual day shift at a Triangle convenience store. Thurl Bailey arrived a little bit late because a snowstorm had delayed his flight from Utah.

Everyone else, however, lined up on the court of Reynolds, waiting to give the stiffly moving ex-coach the hug he was denied in Albuquerque a decade before. Valvano bowed in front of Dereck Whittenburg. When he got to the end of the line, he climbed onto a folding chair to hug the 6-foot-11 Bailey. Valvano was not yet sick enough to pass up a comedic moment. What he whispered in Bailey's ear, though, was heartfelt and simple, "I love you, Thurl."

As he addressed the crowd, Valvano managed to put together words that placed the 1983 championship into the perfect context: It was more than just a string of basketball wins. It was more than just a collection of guys doing what their coach told them to do. It was more than just a bunch of college kids winning a few close games. It was then—and remains today—a team that inspired others to do unimaginable things.

"They are special not because they put that banner up there," Valvano said. "They're special because they taught me and the world so many important lessons. Number one: hope. What does hope mean? Hope that things can get better in spite of adversity. The '83 team taught us that. When Dereck Whittenburg went down and everybody said . . . there was no way we could win, and a kid named Ernie Myers stepped in and we lost a few, then we won a few, and then Dereck came back and every sportswriter in America said that—I remember my favorite quote—that 'trees would tap dance, elephants would drive in the Indianapolis 500, and Orson Welles would skip breakfast, lunch, and dinner before NC State figured out a way to win the NCAA [championship].' This team taught me that elephants would drive in the Indianapolis 500 one day.

"The '83 team taught me about dreaming and the importance of dreams, because nothing can happen if not first a dream. . . . Don't ever give up; don't ever stop fighting! The '83 team gave you hope, gave you pride, told you what hard work was about. It gave you the meaning of believing in a cause. And lastly, what they taught me is to love each other. . . . They taught me what love means. When you have a goal, when you have a dream, and when you have belief, and you throw in that concept of never stop believing in and loving each other, you can accomplish miracles."

Valvano grew up under the elevated train in Queens, New York, the middle of three sons born to Rocco and Angelina Valvano. The biggest talker in a loud, Italian family—his mom declared that her middle son was immunized by a phonograph's needle—Valvano was more than a dinner-table comedian. He was also the best athlete in the family. When his family moved to Long Island, Valvano played football, basketball, and baseball at Seaford High School, earning 10 varsity letters. He also won the election for student body president.

"Jimmy was a hell of a baseball player and a pretty good quarterback," Nick Valvano said. "He broke his leg as a high school junior and didn't get to play football, but he was back for basketball. He was a tough kid and he loved football. But he threw kickoffs: all of his passes were end-over-end. In baseball, the Kansas City A's and the San Francisco Giants wanted to draft him, but our dad wanted him to go to college. So he played basketball, which was probably the sport where he achieved the least in high school."

Not many recruiters beat a path to the 6-foot, 155-pound athlete's home in Long Island. So he chose to attend Rutgers and walk on to Bill Foster's basketball team. By the time he was a senior, he had become both the team's starting point guard and co-captain. Along with roommate Bob Lloyd, he helped lead the Scarlet Knights to the National Invitation Tournament finals. He finished his career with 1,122 points, which was among the top 10 totals in school history at the time.

Valvano earned more than just a degree in English while Rutgers. He also established a relationship with one of college basketball's biggest legends, UCLA coach John Wooden. While working legendary Temple coach Harry Litwack's Catskills basketball camps after his freshman year of college, the ever-bold Valvano struck up a conversation with Wooden, another English major who believed there was more to being a basketball coach than just Xs and Os.

"I have often said that the one player I ever had that was born to be a coach was Denny Crum," Wooden said of his former pupil, who won the 1980 and '86 NCAA titles as Louisville's coach. "He was the most inquisitive player I ever had, wanting to know not just why we were doing something, but the reason behind why we were doing everything. The only other person I have known like that was Jim Valvano. He wanted to know about everything. He and Denny Crum are the only two people I know who were born to be coaches."

Following the Wolfpack's 1983 championship, Wooden sat down to write his young friend a letter of congratulations, as he did to every coach who won the NCAA title. But this one meant a little more than the others because of a relationship that went back to those long-ago basketball camps in the Catskills.

"As one English major, albeit quite older and non-Italian, 'Yuh dun good!' Seriously, Jimmy, congratulations on an outstanding coaching job and best wishes for continued success in all ways. I have said a number of times and sincerely feel that your effort in the tournament this year and that of Don Haskins in 1966 are the two finest NCAA Tournament coaching jobs I have ever seen. You are great for the profession, Jimmy. Please do not change. Sincerely, John."

Valvano reaped most of the glory and practically all of the financial rewards in the aftermath of the 1983 championship, using it to promote himself and NC State University on a national stage. In the weeks following the championship, he made two trips to the White House to meet with President Ronald Reagan. The players were not allowed to go with him on the first trip due to a never-before-invoked NCAA rule that prevented teams from traveling more than 100 miles away from campus for a championship celebration. While Valvano sat in the Oval Office with Reagan and North Carolina senators Jesse Helms and John East, the players were connected to the White House by a satellite hook-up from Raleigh television station WRAL, just across Western Boulevard from campus. On the second trip, Valvano took Lowe and Whittenburg with him.

In the months following the season, Valvano entertained writers from the *Washington Post*, the *New York Times*, *Sports Illustrated*, *Sport Magazine*, *Scholastic Coach Magazine*, and just about any other national or local outlet that wanted to bottle Valvano's lightning into a couple thousand words. No one captured it completely, but almost all of them decided that Valvano, as he showed during his team's title run months before, was a breath of fresh air in the staid world of college basketball.

The hyperactive Valvano, who always spent his summers running his own basketball camps, making public appearances, recruiting, and handling the other off-season responsibilities of a modern college basketball coach, wrote a book chronicling the team's championship and introduced his own "Jimmy V" clothing line. He accepted a handful of additional endorsements, one for the soft drink Mountain Dew and another for the fast-food chain Hardees. He was completely unapologetic for taking part in the same activities he had always participated in, but on a grander scale.

"It was different from every other summer only in the amount of publicity I received," Valvano said in a November 1983 interview with *Technician* reporter Devin Steele. "I would like to think that this is what my grandfather had in mind when he landed at Ellis Island from Naples, Italy. I am what this country is supposed to be about: hard work creating success. The last time I looked, I have been working pretty hard. I don't have a lot of hobbies. I don't play a lot of golf. I don't take weekends off. I work.

"But I have also had a lot of fun doing these things. I love speaking to groups. I love traveling the country and gathering the pulse of American business. I loved working for Hardees and having clinics in parking lots for little kids around the state. I shook more hands, tousled more hair, signed more autographs, and talked more about NC State than a lot of other people who are in this profession. I enjoyed that. As for the commercials, I had never done one and I wanted to see what it was like. I have a very inquisitive mind. All these things help me promote my program and NC State University and help me do my job, which is to recruit the best student-athletes I can so I can have the best basketball program."

"What happened was a whole new world opened up to Jim," said older brother Nick Valvano. "It didn't open up to him as an outsider looking in. It was like everything came to him. Jim always said, 'I can do this, I can do this.'"

And he wanted to do everything. He set up his own production company, JTV Enterprises. He became a fixture on the motivational speech circuit. He developed a clothing line, which included a terry-cloth wrap that basketball players could wear in postgame locker rooms that were being increasingly infiltrated by female reporters. He commissioned an artist to create a signed print every year for the team that won the national championship. Everything he touched, it seemed, was born into success.

"He was really too smart to be a coach," said Whittenburg, who eventually became a graduate assistant and assistant coach on Valvano's staff. "He shouldn't have been coaching. He should have been on Wall Street."

At one point, the coach was even offered his own television talk show, with Vanna White as his sidekick. But what Valvano never saw as he increased his personal-appearance load to as many as 150 per year, raised his fee for corporate motivational speeches to $50,000 a pop, and began making weekly appearances on the *CBS Morning Show* with Phyllis George was that he had begun to take his eye off the Wolfpack program.

When *USA Today* revealed in 1985 that Valvano was the nation's highest paid college coach, making nearly $500,000 a year in salary and endorsements, the same media that had adored him immediately after the championship decided that the air around Valvano was not so fresh anymore.

The coach made two critical mistakes in the aftermath of the '83 championship: he brought in a slew of talented players with questionable academic and behavioral backgrounds that created off-court headaches for Valvano and his staff, and he replaced Willis Casey as NC State's athletic director in January 1986.

"Part of Jim, ever since he was a kid, was that there was not a thing he couldn't do," Nick Valvano said. "There also wasn't a thing he didn't want to do. He felt he could juggle as many balls in the air as he threw up. Later in his life, the only thing he said he would change would be to only have 10 balls in the air instead of 20. He was never going to have just one. He never lost his passion to be a basketball coach. But he never lost his passion to do other things, either."

His overtaxing schedule changed the connection he had with and the control he had over the talented players he brought to NC State in his quest to win another championship. As he juggled more responsibilities, he no longer had such close relationships with his players, many of whom were perfectly willing to take advantage of their coach's scarcity. "The guys who came later didn't know the same Coach V we knew," said former player and graduate assistant Max Perry.

Valvano had always been a players' coach and was always available for a heart-to-heart talk or an occasional beer and pizza with kids who weren't much older than he acted. In the early days, the doors to his golf-course home in the small suburb of Cary were open to his players 24 hours a day. Usually unable to sleep, Valvano whiled away most nights in front of the television, watching game tapes or Lenny Bruce movies on a new-fangled machine called a

VCR.

"I'm an insomniac," Valvano once told Gerald Martin of the *Raleigh News & Observer*. "I just don't believe in sleep as an activity. My mind doesn't allow for sleep."

He was always a kid at heart and unafraid to show it. Shortly after he was hired to replace Norm Sloan, Valvano pulled his red Mazda 300ZX into the parking lot at the College Inn, a converted hotel on Western Boulevard where most of his players lived. Many of them were out back on a grassy field playing drunken touch football—one of the many physical activities that are generally forbidden by coaches who worry about the fragile knees of their players.

"We were all thinking we were in deep shit," Perry said. "He comes walking out, right past the keg, and looks at us: 'OK, I'm the quarterback. Whose team am I on?' We all looked at each other and said, 'This is going to be good.'"

For several years, it was. From the day he arrived on campus, Valvano told his players that he would win a national championship. *N & O* reporter Chip Alexander remembers a brief conversation with the coach during a quiet moment in Reynolds Coliseum shortly after Valvano was hired. Valvano was looking around the arena, and Alexander pointed at the 1974 championship banner hanging in the rafters. "It might be nice to put another one of those up there," Alexander said. "Oh, we will," Valvano said. "We will." There was never any doubt in his mind.

But after it happened, Valvano wanted another one. To get it, he recruited players who needed more hands-on attention from their coach than he could give them. They were supremely talented but unable to fit into a university setting during the early days of the NCAA's academic reforms. Valvano always had trouble keeping his attention focused on his team, leaving a good bit of the grunt work— like practice—to his assistant coaches.

As talented a juggler as he was, Valvano could not keep up with everything and eventually lost control of his program. On January 27, 1983, the coach met two writers, Barry Jacobs and Ron Morris, at Amedeo's Italian Restaurant on Western Boulevard for a long lunch. Valvano had just signed a 10-year contract with NC State and received a huge raise. Jacobs was working on a piece that appeared in the *New York Times*, while Morris was writing a profile for North Carolina's *Durham Morning Herald*. The quick lunch turned into a three-hour feast of anecdotes, basketball insights, and off-the-record tales. By three o'clock, the coach was still going strong and invited the two writers to come with him to practice. They headed over to Reynolds Coliseum just in time for stretching exercises. But no players stood on the synthetic rubber surface, just a bunch of Coliseum workers setting up a stage and chairs for a concert performed by the Vienna Boys Choir two days later. The coach had no idea that his team was practicing across the street at Carmichael Gymnasium.

After having nearly every detail of his program poked and prodded by the NCAA and the *Raleigh News & Observer*, Valvano was deemed to be a liability to the university and forced to resign in the spring of 1990. He reached a settlement with the school in excess of $600,000. Not long afterwards, he wrote a book with *Sports Illustrated*'s Curry Kirkpatrick entitled, *They Gave Me a Lifetime Contract, and Then They Declared Me Dead*. Hardly any bitterness existed at all.

"What hurt Jim the most was not being able to leave coaching the way he wanted to," said Nick Valvano.

In the spring of 1992, while playing golf at a Spanish course overlooking the Mediterranean Ocean, Valvano did not feel like himself. He lacked energy. He went to bed at night and actually slept. He had a tight feeling in his testicles that would not go away.

After an MRI test at Duke University, a doctor told Valvano that the black mess that was supposed to be the lower vertebrae of his spine was most likely cancer. Soon after, Valvano heard the doctors tell him that the official diagnosis was metastatic adenocarcinoma, an aggressive form of cancer that is almost always fatal when detected, as Valvano's was, in its later stages. The tightness in his testicles was nothing compared to that kick in the balls.

The last 12 months of Valvano's life were a blur of chemotherapy, hospital visits, empty afternoons at home in his bathrobe, and a few basketball games as a color commentator for ESPN and ABC. He was so sick that his former gunning guard, Terry Gannon, was on 24-hour call to replace Valvano in the broadcast booth. The former coach was bitterly disappointed that all the other things he wanted to do would not get done and that his eternal dreams would be packed into less than half a century of life.

"I remember sitting upstairs in his room when he was sick and he had thrown everybody out of the room but me," Nick Valvano said. "He would say, 'I have so much more I want to do. I am so pissed off about this.' But the thing is, and I told him this, if it was 20 years later and he was not sick, we would still be having this same conversation, that he still had so much more that he wanted to do. We actually laughed about it, and he said, 'Yeah, you're right.'"

Pam Valvano, Jim's wife of 25 years, was used to finding 3x5 index cards listing simply stated life goals in her husband's clothes. For years, those cards contained his dreams. One said, "Become Division I head coach," another said, "Get an NCAA bid," and another said, "Win the national championship." The last one she ever found simply read, "Find a cure for cancer." Valvano's dreams were always bigger than the cards he used.

On March 4, 1993, at the inaugural ESPY Awards, Valvano announced that ESPN was establishing a charity that would bear his name, the V Foundation for Cancer Research. His speech that night—when he implored the audience, "Don't give up. Don't ever give up"—has defined Valvano's legacy.

A year later, the V Foundation gave away its first grant, a modest $100,000, to Dr. Gerold Bepler, a young investigator at Duke who was looking into the causes of lung cancer. Bepler is now the leader of the Thoracic Oncology Program at the H. Lee Moffitt Cancer Center and Research Institute in Tampa, Florida. In the years since receiving the V Foundation's first grant, he has raised more than $13 million in additional grants to fund his research lab, which has recently defined several proteins that are actual causes of some forms of lung cancer. "I would expect to see Gerold and his lab produce some sort of therapeutic drug very soon," Nick Valvano said in 2007.

Through the fundraising efforts of Nick Valvano, who serves as the charity's executive director, the V Foundation has raised more than $60 million for cancer research. Rated a four-star charity for four years in a row, it is one of the few nonprofit organizations with an endowment large enough to fully cover all of its operating expenses, which means it can give away 100 percent of all the money it raises. In 2006, the V Foundation gave away more than $8 million in grants ranging from $100,000 to $2 million.

The foundation has completely changed the way Valvano—once vilified for his lack of institutional control and raked over the coals for the way he ran his program—is remembered.

"What I think is ironic is that Jimmy's legacy isn't basketball anymore," said Bobby Cremins, a longtime friend and competitor of Valvano's. "It's not the '83 championship anymore. It's fighting cancer and the V Foundation. Jimmy had incredible foresight. He was always ahead of his time. His mind operated always in the future. That was one of his problems, too. He wasn't in the present too much. He was rarely in the past. But he was always in the future."

That foresight ended at 10:30 a.m. April 28, 1993, barely 10 years after Valvano reached the pinnacle of his coaching career and only seven weeks after he struggled to the stage to make his legendary ESPY appearance. He slipped into a coma and died peacefully at Duke University Hospital. He was just 47 years old.

"You know what Jimmy'd say about the V Foundation?" Nick Valvano said. "He would say, 'Jesus Christ, Nick, can't you do a little better? What the hell is taking you so long? I got you started. I gave you the speech. And this is all you have done?'"

Jim Valvano was more than just a dreamer. He forced others to work just as hard as he did to make his dreams come true.

EPILOGUE

For years, the members of NC State's second national championship team have listened to people tell them exactly where they were and what they were doing on the night of April 4, 1983. They could have been running through an airport to catch a plane, trying to sell a used car, or talking to the president of the United States.

No matter what they have done since, nothing outshines those magical days 25 years ago, especially for Lorenzo Charles, whose game-winning dunk against Houston will be replayed as long as the NCAA has a championship basketball tournament.

"It's still kind of amazing to me that here it is more than 20 years later and people are still talking about it," Charles said in a 2004 interview. "I remember when it first happened I figured I would have my 15 minutes of fame and that would be it. But it is still a conversation piece. I don't think that was the only great Final Four that has been played since then. But for some reason people just single out that game, maybe because it was such a David-and-Goliath-type deal."

Thurl Bailey played professional basketball for 16 years—longer than anybody else in that celebrated 1979 recruiting class, including Ralph Sampson, Dominique Wilkins, James Worthy, Isiah Thomas, and John Paxson. He became captain of the Jazz and is the second-leading scorer in franchise history. Since settling in Salt Lake City, the 6-foot-11 Bailey has released several inspirational music compact discs, become an in-demand speaker for the Church of Latter Day Saints, and developed his own clothing line. Yet he still answers more questions about the 1983 championship than anything else he has ever accomplished.

"Especially in March, when they replay some of the classic games, that championship will always be included," Bailey said. "People know all about it. They have seen it. People talk to their sons and grandsons about it and tell them about one of the greatest finishes in NCAA history. People love that underdog story. It lives on. People are always asking me about it, and it never, ever, ever gets old."

"How could it?" asked Dereck Whittenburg.

In his first year as NC State's head basketball coach, Sidney Lowe found himself answering almost as many questions about his senior year of college as he did about upcoming opponents. Just about everything he and his team did—from beating second-ranked North Carolina in his first meeting with NC State's biggest rival to advancing to the ACC Tournament championship game—was compared to the events of 1983.

"Every time someone mentioned it, it just reminded me of the impact that we had on so many people," Lowe said. "The big thing is that they always tell you where they were. To me, it's amazing that they even remember that. People always ask me, 'Don't you get tired of talking about it?' Never ever."

In the summer of 2006, Terry Gannon was at his five-year-old son's tee-ball game in California when his wife, Lisa, happened to mention to the team's coach that Gannon played on the '83 national championship team. "Holy shit," the coach said. "I was on a business trip from New York to Raleigh and stayed through the weekend just so I could party on the Brickyard after that Houston game. I helped throw a couch on the fire."

"Even today, no matter where I travel or whatever sport I may be covering, if someone in the group says, 'Oh, yeah, Terry played on a national championship basketball team,' other people might not care," said Gannon, an ABC network commentator for basketball, golf, and figure skating. "But if someone says, 'Terry played on the team that won with a dunk at the buzzer to beat Phi Slama Jama . . . ,' I have never encountered a person who didn't know what that was. It has somehow become a sports version of the Kennedy assassination, the man walking on the moon, or 9/11. People remember where they were. They are always willing to convey what they were doing. Most of the stories start with 'I was in a bar . . .'"

In 2004, Mike Warren donated $25,000 to George W. Bush's reelection campaign just so he and his wife could have their picture taken with the president. As they waited in line, they were given specific instructions not to strike up a personal conversation with the leader of the free world.

Channeling the spirit of Jimmy V—who yukked it up with President Ronald Reagan during two trips to the White House in the month after the '83 championship—Warren ignored that directive.

"You guys owe me a trip to the White House," Warren said to President Bush, explaining that he was a member of the 1983 national championship team, which never got its chance to meet and greet the president.

"You have ruined my day," said Bush, the former governor of Texas. "That was one of my three worst days as a sports fan. I remember I was at . . . "

And then, as he has heard countless times since that night in Albuquerque, New Mexico, Warren listened to another college basketball fan tell him exactly where he was and what he was doing the night the Cardiac Pack slammed Phi Slama Jama.

MG

√12/07